Bloom's Modern Critical Interpretations

Bloom's Modern Critical Interpretations

F. Scott Fitzgerald's
The Great Gatsby
New Edition

Edited and with an introduction by
Harold Bloom
Sterling Professor of the Humanities
Yale University

BLOOM'S
LITERARY CRITICISM
An imprint of Infobase Publishing

Bloom's Modern Critical Interpretations: The Great Gatsby—New Edition
Copyright © 2010 by Infobase Publishing
Introduction © 2010 by Harold Bloom

Bloom's Literary Criticism
An imprint of Infobase Publishing
132 West 31st Street
New York NY 10001

Library of Congress Cataloging-in-Publication Data
F. Scott Fitzgerald's The great Gatsby / edited and with an introduction by Harold Bloom. — New ed.
    p. cm. — (Bloom's modern critical interpretations)
    Includes bibliographical references and index.
    ISBN 978-1-60413-820-7
    1. Fitzgerald, F. Scott (Francis Scott), 1896–1940. Great Gatsby.   I. Bloom, Harold.
    PS3511.I9G83733 2010
    813'.52—dc22
                                    2009050922

Bloom's Literary Criticism books are available at special discounts when purchased in bulk quantities for businesses, associations, institutions, or sales promotions. Please call our Special Sales Department in New York at (212)967-8800 or (800)322-8755.

You can find Chelsea House on the World Wide Web at
http://www.chelseahouse.com

Contributing editor: Pamela Loos
Cover design by Alicia Post
Composition by IBT Global, Troy NY
Cover printed by IBT Global, Troy NY
Book printed and bound by IBT Global, Troy NY
Date printed: March 2010
Printed in the United States of America

10 9 8 7 6 5 4 3 2 1

This book is printed on acid-free paper.

All links and Web addresses were checked and verified to be correct at the time of publication. Because of the dynamic nature of the Web, some addresses and links may have changed since publication and may no longer be valid.

Contents

Editor's Note

My introduction centers on the book's relation to the poetry of John Keats and so, in a sense, to Fitzgerald's own "negative capability."

Barbara Hochman examines the ways reading and writing informed Fitzgerald's composition of the novel, and Alberto Lena sees the decadent Tom Buchanan as the book's embodiment of moral and cultural decline.

Richard Lehan traces a few of the limitless meanings he detects within the work, while John Hilgart explores indeterminacy in the uncertainty and contradictions Fitzgerald introduces throughout.

Janet Giltrow and David Stouck enter the pastoral mode, followed by Winifred Farrant Bevilacqua, who explores the novel's bacchanalian sensibilities.

For Barbara Will, language in *Gatsby* works against the demands of veracity, while Philip McGowan is the volume's second author to take up the novel's carnivalesque qualities.

In the final essay, Scott Donaldson turns his attention to the slippery snob Nick Carraway.

HAROLD BLOOM

Introduction

1

Lionel Trilling justly observed of *The Great Gatsby* that "if the book grows in weight of significance with the years, we can be sure that this could not have happened had its form and style not been as right as they are." Trilling, critically accurate, was also prophetic in regard to the novel's augmenting importance. Indeed, that importance transcends *The Great Gatsby*'s formal achievement, its aesthetic dignity of shape and style. The book has become part of what must be called that American mythology, just as Fitzgerald himself now possesses mythological status, like Hemingway, or, in a different sense, Norman Mailer. Myth is gossip grown old, according to the modern Polish aphorist Stanislaw Lec. Fitzgerald's social aspirations, his mode of living, his marriage to Zelda, his "crack-up" and death at the age of forty-four: these now have aged into myth. But that is popular myth; *The Great Gatsby* is myth of another mode also, the mode of John Keats, whose spirit never departs from Fitzgerald's best writing.

The Great Gatsby is a lyrical novel, a triumph of sensibility, worthy of the poet who wrote *Lamia*, *The Fall of Hyperion*, the great Odes, and "La Belle Dame Sans Merci." Consider a single scene in Gatsby, toward the end of chapter 5. Gatsby is showing Daisy (and Nick Carraway, the Conradian narrator) his house. They enter his bedroom, where Daisy takes up a hairbrush of "pure dull gold" and smooths her hair, causing Gatsby, too happy in her happiness, to laugh too boisterously:

> "It's the funniest thing, old sport," he said hilariously. "I can't—
> When I try to—"

He had passed visibly through two states and was entering upon a third. After his embarrassment and his unreasoning joy he was consumed with wonder at her presence. He had been full of the idea so long, dreamed it right through to the end, waited with his teeth set, so to speak, at the inconceivable pitch of intensity. Now, in the reaction, he was running down like an overwound clock.

Recovering himself in a minute he opened for us two hulking patent cabinets which held his massed suits and dressing-gowns and ties, and his shirts, piled like bricks in stacks a dozen high.

"I've got a man in England who buys me clothes. He sends over a selection of things at the beginning of each season, spring and fall."

He took out a pile of shirts and began throwing them, one by one, before us, shirts of sheer linen and thick silk and fine flannel, which lost their folds as they fell and covered the table in many-colored disarray. While we admired he brought more and the soft rich heap mounted higher—shirts with stripes and scrolls and plaids in coral and apple-green and lavender and faint orange, with monograms of Indian blue. Suddenly with a strained sound, Daisy bent her head into the shirts and began to cry stormily.

"They're such beautiful shirts," she sobbed, her voice muffled in the thick folds. "It makes me sad because I've never seen such—such beautiful shirts before."

This grand passage is an epitome of the novel and an apotheosis of Fitzgerald's Keatsian art. Gatsby, piling up the soft rich heap in its many-colored disarray of "stripes and scrolls and plaids in coral and apple-green and lavender and faint orange, with monograms of Indian blue," is surely a version of another passionate lover: Porphyro in *The Eve of St. Agnes*:

Then by the bed-side, where the faded moon
Made a dim, silver twilight, soft he set
A table, and, half anguished, threw thereon
A cloth of woven crimson, gold, and jet:—
O for some drowsy Morphean amulet!
The boisterous, midnight, festive clarion,
The kettle-drum, and far-heard clarinet,
Affray his ears, though but in dying tone:—
The hall door shuts again, and all the noise is gone.

And still she slept an azure-lidded sleep,
In blanchèd linen, smooth, and lavendered,

While he from forth the closet brought a heap
Of candied apple, quince, and plum, and gourd,
With jellies smoother than the creamy curd,
And lucent syrups, tinct with cinnamon;
Manna and dates, in argosy transferred
From Fez; and spiced dainties, every one,
From silken Samarcand to cedared Lebanon.

These delicates he heaped with glowing hand
On golden dishes and in baskets bright
Of wreathed silver: sumptuous they stand
In the retired quiet of the night,
Filling the chilly room with perfume light.—
'And now, my love, my seraph fair, awake!
Thou art my heaven, and I thine eremite:
Open thine eyes, for meek St. Agnes' sake,
Or I shall drowse beside thee, so my soul doth ache.'

The heap of edible dainties and delicates has been replaced by the soft rich heap of multicolored shirts, and Madeline is asleep while Daisy is awake, yet Fitzgerald's exquisitely displaced allusion is clear enough. The masterful revision that makes Fitzgerald's scene into high art is Daisy's sudden storm of tears as she so erotically bends her head into the shirts. A further revision is even more in the Keatsian spirit, when it becomes clear to Gatsby how doom-eager and idealized his passion truly has become, profoundly in excess of the object:

After the house, we were to see the grounds and the swimming pool, and the hydroplane and the mid-summer flowers—but outside Gatsby's window it began to rain again, so we stood in a row looking at the corrugated surface of the Sound.

"If it wasn't for the mist we could see your home across the bay," said Gatsby. "You always have a green light that burns all night at the end of your dock."

Daisy put her arm through his abruptly, but he seemed absorbed in what he had just said. Possibly it had occurred to him that the colossal significance of that light had now vanished forever. Compared to the great distance that had separated him from Daisy it had seemed very near to her, almost touching her.

It had seemed as close as a star to the moon. Now it was again a green light on a dock. His count of enchanted objects had diminished by one.

Working as Keats told Shelley a poet must work—"*an artist* must serve Mammon—and 'load every rift' of your subject with ore"—Fitzgerald too follows a Spenserian loading of every rift, and ends his novel with a return of that green light of the ideal:

> And as I sat there brooding on the old, unknown world, I thought of Gatsby's wonder when he first picked out the green light at the end of Daisy's dock. He had come a long way to this blue lawn, and his dream must have seemed so close that he could hardly fail to grasp it. He did not know that it was already behind him, somewhere back in that vast obscurity beyond the city, where the dark fields of the republic rolled on under the night.
>
> Gatsby believed in the green light, the orgastic future that year by year recedes before us. It eluded us then, but that's no matter—tomorrow we will run faster, stretch out our arms farther. And one fine morning—
>
> So we beat on, boats against the current, borne back ceaselessly into the past.

In so concluding, Fitzgerald consciously culminated a Keatsian version of the quest. The man of imagination, however comprised, quests perpetually for an immortal female, more daemonic than human. Poor Daisy may seem an inadequate version of a Lamia, but she is precisely a possible American Belle Dame Sans Merci of 1925, and Gatsby is her inevitable victim, who does not want to know better and so is not deceived. His marvelous dismissal of Daisy's love for her dreadful husband—"In any case, it was just personal"—is his clear self-recognition. It cannot matter that Daisy is an absurd object, because Gatsby's drive is transcendental. What matters is what the Yeatsian quester of *A Full Moon in March* calls "the image in my head." In love with that image, Gatsby truly is self-engendered and dies more than adequately.

If there is an American sublime, going beyond irony, in modern American fiction, then it is located most centrally in *The Great Gatsby*. Fitzgerald fittingly could have chosen for an epigraph to his novel the final stanza of the "Ode on Melancholy" by Keats:

> She dwells with Beauty—Beauty that must die;
> And Joy, whose hand is ever at his lips
>
> Bidding adieu, and aching Pleasure nigh,
> Turning to poison while the bee-mouth sips:

Ay, in the very temple of Delight
Veiled Melancholy has her sovereign shrine,
Though seen of none save him whose strenuous tongue

Can burst Joy's grape against his palate fine;

His soul shall taste the sadness of her might,
And be among her cloudy trophies hung.

Gatsby, whatever his limitations, had been that quester and is always to
be remembered as one of those trophies, and not the least among them.

2

It is reasonable to assert that Jay Gatsby was *the* major literary character
of the United States in the twentieth century. No single figure created by
Faulkner or Hemingway, or by our principal dramatists, was as central a
presence in our national mythology as Gatsby. There are few living Americans, of whatever gender, race, ethnic origin, or social class, who do not have
at least a little touch of Gatsby in them. Whatever the American Dream
has become, its truest contemporary representative remains Jay Gatsby, at
once a gangster and a romantic idealist, and above all a victim of his own
High Romantic, Keatsian dream of love. Like his creator, Scott Fitzgerald,
Gatsby is the American hero of romance, a vulnerable quester whose fate has
the aesthetic dignity of the romance mode at its strongest. Gatsby is neither
pathetic nor tragic, because as a quester he meets his appropriate fate, which
is to die still lacking in the knowledge that would destroy the spell of his
enchantment. His death preserves his greatness and justifies the title of his
story, a title that is anything but ironic.

Gatsby, doom-eager yet desiring a perfect love, or perhaps doom-eager
out of that desire, is a wholly American personality, as tender as he is tough.
Indeed, Gatsby's Americanism is so central to him that any other national
origin would be impossible for him. Fitzgerald memorably remarked of his
protagonist that "Jay Gatsby . . . sprang from his Platonic conception of himself," and for "Platonic" we could substitute "Emersonian," the proper name
for any American Platonism. As a son of God, Gatsby pragmatically seems
to have fathered himself. And that may be why Fitzgerald had to portray
his hero in the Conradian mode, with Carraway mediating Gatsby for us as
Marlow mediates Jim in *Lord Jim*. Gatsby does not reveal himself to us but
to Carraway, who plays Horatio to Gatsby's Hamlet. Perhaps a character who
lives in a consuming and destructive hope always has to be mediated for us,

lest we be confronted directly by the madness of a Wordsworthian solitary or a Blakean emanation. It is Gatsby's glory that he is not a "realistic" character. How could he be, since his essence is his aspiration, which again is at once sordid and transcendental?

Since Gatsby is a character in a romance and not a realistic fiction, we cannot apply the criteria of moral realism to his love for the absurdly vacuous Daisy. She is to Gatsby as his enchanted Dulcinea is to Don Quixote: a vision of the ideal. Just as Daisy's love for her brutal husband can be sublimely dismissed by Gatsby as "merely personal," so her defects of character and taste cannot affect Gatsby's attitude toward her, as Carraway teaches us:

> There must have been moments even that afternoon when Daisy tumbled short of his dreams—not through her own fault, but because of the colossal vitality of his illusion. It had gone beyond her, beyond everything. He had thrown himself into it with a creative passion, adding to it all the time, decking it out with every bright feather that drifted his way. No amount of fire or freshness can challenge what a man can store up in his ghostly heart.

It must seem odd to argue for Gatsby's religious significance, since his mindless idealism has no relevance to Christian terms. But it takes on a peculiarly intense meaning if the context is the American religion, which is oddly both Protestant and post-Christian. Gatsby's mythic projection is one of a more than Adamic innocence, in which his perpetual optimism, amoral goodness, and visionary hope all are centered in an escape from history, in a sense of being self-begotten. Daisy Buchanan, according to the late Malcolm Cowley, is named for Henry James's Daisy Miller, and *The Great Gatsby*, for all its debt to Conrad, partakes more in the Americanism of Henry James, though the Jamesian dream of innocence is marked by a more pervasive irony. But then Gatsby's Daisy is a snow queen, ice cold, while Daisy Miller has more of Gatsby's own warmth. A heroine of American romance, she shares Gatsby's deprecation of time and history and his exaltation of the questing self.

Is Gatsby, as Marius Bewley once wrote, a criticism of America? I hardly think so, since his effect on Nick Carraway, and so on the reader, is so wonderful and so affectionate. Nick, like Fitzgerald, declines to culminate in the irony of irony; Gatsby saves Nick from that abyss of nihilism, as well as from the pomposities of mere moralizing. More subtly, he seems to give Nick an image of the male side of heterosexual love that can be placed against the sadistic masculinity of Tom Buchanan. We do not know what life Carraway will return to when he goes west, but evidently it will be a life somewhat illuminated by Gatsby's dream of an ideal, heterosexual romantic love, though the illumination may not prove to be pragmatic.

What would it mean if we interpreted Gatsby the dreamer as an ignorant and failed American lyric poet, whose value somehow survives both ignorance and failure? Gatsby cannot tell his dreams; every attempt he makes to describe his love for Daisy collapses into banality, and yet we no more doubt the reality of Gatsby's passion for Daisy than we doubt the terrible authenticity of the dying Keats's intense desire for Fanny Brawne. It seems absurd to compare the vulgar grandiosity of poor Gatsby's diction to the supreme eloquence of John Keats, but Gatsby is profoundly Keatsian, a direct descendant of the poet-quester in *The Fall of Hyperion*. I take it that a repressed echo of Keats is behind Carraway's sense of a lost, High Romantic music even as he listens to Gatsby's turgid discourses:

> Through all he said, even through his appalling sentimentality, I was reminded of something—an elusive rhythm, a fragment of lost words that I had heard somewhere a long time ago. For a moment a phrase tried to take shape in my mouth and my lips parted like a dumb man's, as though there was more struggling upon them than a wisp of startled air. But they made no sound, and what I had almost remembered was incommunicable forever.

What Carraway (and Fitzgerald) almost remembered may be a crucial passage in *The Fall of Hyperion*, where the poet-quester is nearly destroyed by his silence and his inability to move:

> I heard, I looked: two senses both at once,
> So fine, so subtle, felt the tyranny
> Of that fierce threat and the hard task proposed.
> Prodigious seemed the toil; the leaves were yet
> Burning—when suddenly a palsied chill
> Struck from the paved level up my limbs,
> And was ascending quick to put cold grasp
> Upon those streams that pulse beside the throat:
> I shrieked, and the sharp anguish of my shriek
> Stung my own ears—I strove hard to escape
> The numbness; strove to gain the lowest step.
> Slow, heavy, deadly was my pace: the cold
> Grew stifling, suffocating, at the heart;

And when I clasped my hands I felt them not.
One minute before death, my iced foot touched
The lowest stair; and as it touched, life seemed
To pour in at the toes . . .

Carraway remains mute; the anguish of Keats's shriek reawakens the
poet to life and to poetry. Part of Carraway's function surely is to contrast his
own recalcitrances with Gatsby's continual vitality and sense of wonder. But
Carraway anticipates his own narrative of Gatsby's destruction. Gatsby's foot
never touches the lowest stair; there is for him no purgatorial redemption.
But how could there have been "something commensurate to his capacity for
wonder"? The greatness of Gatsby is that there was no authentic object for
his desire, as Daisy's inadequacies render so clear. Like every true quester in
romantic tradition, Gatsby is both subject and object of his own quest, though
he never could hope to have learned this bewildering contingency.

Many readers sense that there is a "drowned god" aspect to Gatsby's
fate, doubtless suggested to Fitzgerald by Eliot's *The Waste Land*. Yet it is difficult to fit such a figure into American myth, as we can see by contrasting
the powerful but enigmatic figure of Whitman's drowned swimmer in "The
Sleepers" to the more evocative and contextualized image of President Lin-
coln in "When Lilacs Last in the Dooryard Bloom'd." The American visionary can die as a father or as a son, but not as a ritual sacrifice to rekindle the
dead land, because even now our land is far from dead. Gatsby, a son of God,
dies with a curiously religious significance but one that is beyond Carraway's
understanding. What is best and oldest in Gatsby cannot die but returns to
the living fullness of the American Dream, itself undying despite all of its
cancellations and farewells, which prove never to have been final.

What Carraway does come to understand is that Gatsby's freedom was
invested in solitude and not even in the possibility of Daisy, since marriage
to the actual Daisy could not have sufficed for very long. If your belief is in
"the orgiastic future that year by year recedes," then your belief is in what
Freud called repression, a process that implies that everything significant is
already in your past. Gatsby's deepest need was to reverse time, to see his late-
ness as an ever-early origin. To fulfill that need, you have to be Emerson or
Whitman, or if you are a fictive self, then Huck Finn will serve as example.
Loving a dream of freedom will work only if you can detach that dream from
other individuals, and Gatsby was too open and generous to exercise such
detachment.

It does seem, after all, that Fitzgerald placed much of the best of himself
in Gatsby. His relation to Gatsby is quite parallel to Flaubert's rueful identi-
fication with Emma Bovary. Even Flaubert could not protect himself by his

own formidable irony; he suffered with Emma, and so do we. Fitzgerald did not protect himself at all, and he contaminated us with his vulnerability. Perhaps Gatsby does not suffer, being so lost in his dream. We suffer for Gatsby, as Carraway does, but what mitigates that suffering is the extent to which we too, as Americans, are lost in the same dream of love and wealth.

3

The Great Gatsby has only a few rivals as the great American novel of the twentieth century; doubtless they would include works by Faulkner, Hemingway, Cather, and Dreiser. Formal shaping is one of the many aesthetic virtues of F. Scott Fitzgerald's masterwork: style, characterization, and plot are all superbly balanced to achieve a highly unified end. Rereading the book, yet once more, my initial and prime reaction is pleasure renewed; it is as though *The Great Gatsby*'s freshness never can wear off. Though it is regarded as the classic of what Fitzgerald himself permanently named the Jazz Age, the novel is anything but a "period piece." Even after many decades, the relevance of *The Great Gatsby* increases, because it is the definitive romance of the American Dream, a concept or vision that haunts our society. Critics differ as to whether the theme of the novel is "the withering of the American dream," as Marius Bewley argued, or else a celebration of a romantic hope in America despite all the ugly realities. Fitzgerald himself, as much a High Romantic as his favorite poet, John Keats, was too great an artist not to entertain both possibilities. In one register, *The Great Gatsby* is a companion work to T.S. Eliot's *The Waste Land*, a desolate vision of a world without faith or order. And yet, in a finer tone, the novel keeps faith with Jay Gatsby's dream of a perfect love, of a fulfillment that transcends the absurdity of Daisy, who in herself is hardly a fit representative of Gatsby's idealized yearnings.

Bewley shrewdly sees Fitzgerald's involvement in Gatsby's aspirations, but again Bewley argues that Gatsby's death is also a spiritual failure. A reader can be legitimately uncertain as to exactly how Gatsby ought to be apprehended. Much depends on how much the reader places himself under the control of the novel's narrator, Nick Carraway. By mediating Gatsby for us, precisely in the way that Joseph Conrad's Marlow mediates Jim in *Lord Jim* or Kurtz in *Heart of Darkness*, Carraway's consciousness dominates the novel, and Carraway is no more Fitzgerald than Marlow is Conrad. Marlow's romanticism is echoed by Carraway's, though Marlow rarely gets in the way of the story's progress, while Carraway frequently does. It is not clear how Fitzgerald wished us to regard Carraway's sometimes less than subtle ironies, but I suspect that they are devices for distancing the novelist from his fictive narrator. Carraway is a very decent fellow, but he does not transcend the

the fashions of his time and place, as Fitzgerald does. This limitation is one of Carraway's ultimate strengths, because it allows him his own dream of Jay Gatsby as the romantic hero of the American experience. Fitzgerald, like Conrad before him, regards the deep self as unknowable; Carraway in contrast finds in Gatsby "some heightened sensitivity to the promises of life." The English critic Malcolm Bradbury memorably termed Gatsby "a coarse Platonist" yet any Platonist ultimately is not a materialist. Since Gatsby's dream of love depends on an alchemy that metamorphoses wealth into eros, we can be reminded of Emerson's wonderful irony: "Money, in some of its effects, is as beautiful as roses."

Gatsby's greatest strength is a "Platonic conception of himself," which gives him the hope that he can roll back time, that he and the unlikely Daisy can somehow be as Adam and Eve early in the morning. Despite the absurd distance of this dream from reality, Gatsby never yields up his hope. That refusal to surrender to reality kills him, yet it also gives him his peculiar greatness, justifying the book's title as being more than an irony. Gatsby's refusal of history is profoundly Emersonian, though doubtless Gatsby had never heard of Emerson. Edith Wharton told Fitzgerald in a letter that "to make Gatsby really great, you ought to have given us his early career." Perhaps, but that is to forget that we know only Carraway's Gatsby, the finished product of an American quest and a figure curiously beyond judgment. Actually Fitzgerald had written what we now know as the short story "Absolution" to serve as a picture of Gatsby's early life, but he decided to omit it from the novel so as to preserve some sense of mystery about his hero. Mystery certainly remains: Gatsby's death, though squalid, transfigures him in the reader's imagination. The dreamer dies so that an image, however grotesque, of the American Dream can continue to live. It is not possible that Gatsby dies as a vicarious atonement for the reader, and yet that may be Gatsby's function in regard to Carraway. Nick goes west at the book's conclusion still sustained by the idealism of Gatsby's effect on him.

It is one of Fitzgerald's oddest triumphs that we accept his vision of Gatsby's permanent innocence; the gross reality of Daisy's love for her brutal husband, Tom Buchanan, is dismissed by Gatsby as merely "personal" and as something that can be canceled by a simple denial. We come to understand that Gatsby is in love neither with Daisy nor with love itself, but rather with a moment out of time that he persuades himself he shared with Daisy. Gangster and dreamer, Gatsby is more of an inarticulate American poet than he is an episode in the later history of American transcendentalism. Since Fitzgerald is so superbly articulate a writer, Carraway again is necessary as a mediator between the author and his tragic hero. Gatsby's vitalism, his wonderful capacity for hope, is enhanced when Fitzgerald compares him to the endlessly recalcitrant

Carraway, whose non-relationship with Jordan Baker heightens our sense of the sexual ambiguity of both characters. What moves Carraway about Gatsby is the image of generosity, of having given oneself away to a dream. Fitzgerald makes us suspect that Gatsby, unlike Carraway, is not deceived altogether by his own dreaming. However inarticulate his own poetic vision is, Gatsby seems to grasp that Daisy indeed is *his* fiction. To believe in your own fiction, while knowing it to be a fiction, is the nicer knowledge of belief, according to Wallace Stevens, who was not being ironic. Gatsby also transcends the ironies of his own story and so earns his greatness.

BARBARA HOCHMAN

Disembodied Voices and Narrating
Bodies in The Great Gatsby

[I]nk . . . the ineffable destroyer of thought that fades an emotion
into that slatternly thing, a written-down mental excretion.

(Fitzgerald, Letters 148)

In "The Storyteller" (1936), Walter Benjamin juxtaposes the plight of the
modern novelist, his text produced in isolation and consumed in private,
with the idyllic situation of the oral storyteller: physically present to an audience, engaging his responsive "community of listeners" in the process of narration, and leaving traces of his presence in his story like "the handprints of
the potter" on his pot (91–92). *The Great Gatsby* (1925) reflects Fitzgerald's
concern with a series of analogous oppositions: with stories written and told,
absent and present authors and listeners, voices converted into inky "excre-
tions," and voices emanating from physically present bodies in a network of
ongoing relationships.

These oppositions are implicit, to begin with, in the contrast between
Nick's story itself (written, like Fitzgerald's, for anonymous readers) and
stories exchanged by individual characters in the course of the novel. Every
imagined relationship between writer and reader is shaped by the silence,
the distance, and the elliptical sequences of narrative. *The Great Gatsby* highlights the disjunctures of the writer-reader interaction through a recurrent
focus on the direct contact and personal exchange of face-to-face narration.

From *Style* 28, no. 1 (Spring 1994): 95–118. © 1994 by *Style*.

13

Throughout *Gatsby*, characters in close proximity to one another swap stories in person rather than in print. Such stories are seen to derive at least part of their meaning from the interaction of teller and listener as visible, physical presences, temporarily bound to one another as well as to the tale being told.

In *This Side of Paradise*, the act of reading—particularly reading aloud—becomes the basis of emotionally satisfying, intensely binding human contact. Amory Blaine and his roommate virtually dispel the devil one night by reading aloud to one another till the dawn (119). Fitzgerald's rendering of Amory's last love affair, moreover, becomes a kind of meditation on certain particularly intense, if somewhat uncanny, rewards of the reading experience.

> There was something most passionate in Eleanor's reading aloud. [She and Amory] seemed nearer, not only mentally, but physically, when they read, than when she was in his arms. . . . (231)

This passage provides one of the earliest and starkest examples of a recurrent motif in Fitzgerald's work. From the start of his career Fitzgerald associates the "scene of reading" with the notion of physical proximity, even intimacy. In *Paradise*, the figure of Eleanor, a kind of "double" for Amory from the outset, is naturally his most receptive reader. (Years later, Amory and Eleanor still send each other their poems.) As a figure for Fitzgerald's own reader, however, Eleanor projects only part of the story, a young author's idealized image.

The Great Gatsby is written by a more cautious and skeptical Fitzgerald; the later novel reflects a more complex and oblique (if no less intense) imagination of the pleasures and pitfalls of writing, reading, and being read. Like other authors in the heyday of the best-seller and writer celebrity, Fitzgerald conceived of his readers as distant and alien on the one hand: as particularly close, indeed too close for comfort, on the other. In late nineteenth-century America, the rapidly changing conditions of professional authorship had multiplied the novelist's opportunities for publicity and profit even while increasing the writer's sense of isolation, anonymity, and exposure.[1] By the 1880s the discomfort created by the growing distance between the "celebrated" author and the anonymous public was inscribed within texts of the period. Numerous motifs within realist fiction reflect a profound yearning for and fear of contact with the reader (Hochman, "Rewards" and "Portrait"). After the turn of the century as the reading public continued to expand (and to grow more heterogeneous), it came to seem ever more distant, unknowable, invisible. Fitzgerald himself was acutely conscious of these changes[2] but uncertain as to their implications for himself either with regard to the marketing and advertising of his fiction or with regard to his own narrative posture within it.

The Great Gatsby reflects Fitzgerald's mixed feelings about an author's public visibility, but it reflects a still deeper uncertainty about the status of a writer's voice both in relation to a written text and in relation to "the stranger reading it" (*Letters* 308), that "stranger" in whose "mouth" Fitzgerald sought to "leave the taste of the whole book" (*Letters* 152).[3] As I will show, Fitzgerald shared Benjamin's concern with the isolating properties of the novel and repeatedly groped, like Benjamin, for a way to elicit the feel of human interaction from the activity of reading. Thus Gatsby itself can be read as Peter Brooks has read Benjamin's "Storyteller": as an expression of discomfort with "the decontextualization of discourse" and an attempt "to rediscover certain contextual coordinates of narrative in narrative voice . . . in the transaction . . . that takes place every time that one recounts something to someone" ("The Tale" 289–90). Throughout *Gatsby*, Fitzgerald's uncertainty about his position not only vis à vis the reader, but also within his own text is reflected in a recurrent focus on what Brooks calls "the communicative situation" ("The Tale" 290). For Fitzgerald, as for Benjamin, there is nostalgia attached to "the spirit of storytelling" and the "companionship" implied not only by oral narration but also by "the gift of listening" that it fosters (Benjamin 89, 100, 91). Yet Fitzgerald is ultimately as skeptical about spoken as about written discourse, alive to the dangers and disjunctures that inform face-to-face interactions no less than written exchanges.

Fitzgerald knew that the process of conveying meaning is far from instantaneous or automatic, whether on paper or in person. On the one hand, *Gatsby* dramatizes the distinction between speech and writing as if Fitzgerald, anticipating Benjamin, privileges the "lived exchange" of spoken discourse (Brooks, "The Tale" 290). On the other hand, Fitzgerald knew as well as Bakhtin or Derrida that the spoken word itself cannot guarantee simple, direct, univalent exchanges of meaning. Indeed, throughout *Gatsby*, spoken voices are seen to generate considerable complications of their own. *The Great Gatsby* thus dramatizes the intricacies of all narrative transactions. By repeatedly underscoring the illusion-destroying, disenchanting effects of bodily presence, the novel demonstrates the strategic advantages of written over spoken language; yet there is no gainsaying the text's recurrent celebration of the spellbinding, "inexhaustible charm" of Daisy's speaking voice, that "cymbal's song" (120), the "deathless song" of a voice "that could not be over-dreamed" (97).

Nick's recurrent emphasis on the ethereal and mesmerizing qualities of Daisy's voice at once deflects and betrays his implicit awareness that this voice is inseparable from a mortal, sexual human being. While Nick himself attempts to deny the interdependence of voices and bodies, *Gatsby* repeatedly dramatizes the fact that voices tend to be inextricably bound to the bodies from which they emerge. The most spellbinding voices—spoken or written—always have an admixture of the earthbound and material. Thus Fitzgerald's own sense of himself as "a sort of magician with words" becomes merely "an odd delusion" when he recalls how "desperately hard" he has "worked . . . to develop a hard, colorful prose style" (*Letters* 16).

Is Fitzgerald a magician or a hardworking craftsman? Does he produce illusions by virtue of effortless magic[4] or through painstaking labor? How does fiction manage to transcend its own physical status as a book, "one of those things that look like a brick but open on one side" (*Letters* 115). Such questions are clearly inscribed in the imagery and structure of Fitzgerald's most self-consciously crafted work. I will be suggesting that *Gatsby* is pervaded by Fitzgerald's sense of analogy between Gatsby's (or Daisy's) illusion-making effects and his own. While the text is surely informed by Fitzgerald's enduring commitment to certain kinds of magic (dreams, voices, fictions), it is also informed by his preoccupation with the difficult and delicate process that brings illusion into being to begin with, that sometimes sustains it against considerable odds, and that is always in danger of calling attention to its own dynamic and its own constituent parts, thereby subverting the effect of enchantment.

In an early draft of *Gatsby*, Nick is said to "read" Gatsby himself as if he were a character in a magazine within which Nick is "reading the climaxes only" (qtd. in Eble 90). The logical impossibility of a story made only of "climaxes" reflects Fitzgerald's sense of narrative as precisely the opposite: a structure that depends for its effect upon a finely differentiated process of modulation and pacing. Fitzgerald repeatedly renders the "communicative situation" as a complex, dynamic interaction unfolding in time. His keen sense of both telling and listening as time-bound transactions pervades the narration of *Gatsby*.

Like Benjamin's "Storyteller," *The Great Gatsby* reflects a concern with the nature of reading; but the idea of reading that emerges from Fitzgerald's text is more ambivalent, less nostalgic, than Benjamin's. Brooks suggests that Benjamin's figure of the oral tale "challenges the novel to reclaim something that it has largely lost from its heritage: the situation of live communication, the presence of voice" ("The Tale" 291).[5] It would be difficult to find a text more responsive to this challenge than *Gatsby*. Yet, as I have begun to suggest, for Fitzgerald the presence of voice always ends up implying the whole range of mortal, physical being.[6] By the same token, the act of writing becomes an act of separation, of distancing, with considerable advantages of its own. Thus as I will show, Nick's wish to separate voice from body can be related both to his motivation for telling his story in writing and to the functions, for Fitzgerald, of employing the figure of Nick as his own voice, his primary narrating presence in this book.

Storytelling Voices

From the start of the novel Nick is highly responsive to the sound of speaking voices. Particularly intrigued by Daisy's voice, he repeatedly renders it in writings. Gatsby's notorious statement about Daisy—"her voice is full of money" (120)—has long overshadowed Nick's descriptions of that voice.[7] But Gatsby's famous definition is framed by Nick Carraway's comments:

> "She's got an indiscreet voice," I remarked. "It's full of—" I hesitated.
> "Her voice is full of money," [Gatsby] said suddenly. That was it. I'd never understood before. It was full of money—that was the inexhaustible charm that rose and fell in it, the jingle of it, the cymbals' song of it. . . . High in a white palace the king's daughter, the golden girl. . . . (120)

If Gatsby says tersely that Daisy's "voice is full of money," Nick, for his part, elaborates the magical, musical, fairy-tale potential implicit in Gatsby's words. Here as elsewhere, the juxtaposition of Gatsby's language with Nick's exposes the discrepancy between material object and metaphoric resonance, the incommensurability between an object and the "capacity for wonder" (182) it elicits. That discrepancy or incommensurability is thematically central throughout the text. Daisy Buchanan of Louisville and East Egg cannot justify the devotion her image inspires in Gatsby, as the twentieth-century America of the novel fails to sustain the promise implicit in Fitzgerald's well-known image of the awestruck Dutch sailors who contemplate the "green breast of the new world" (182) for one "transitory, enchanted moment" (182).

The disjuncture between vehicle and tenor gains further resonance when considered in relation to the act of reading (and writing) itself. Fried characterizes "the ontological status of writing for the writer (and on somewhat different grounds the reader)" as a "hovering between animateness and inanimateness" (123). The reading process confronts every reader of fiction with the need to negotiate a movement from the concrete or visible material of the printed page to the imagined or invisible "represented space" of the fictional text. This movement may have seemed particularly treacherous in late nineteenth-, early twentieth-century America.[8] Fitzgerald's preoccupation with the hazards of the inky passage to and from imagined worlds is inscribed throughout his work.

"All good writing," Fitzgerald says in a letter to his daughter, "is *swimming underwater* and holding your breath" (*Letters* 101). This image suggests, for one thing, smooth progression within a medium that allows the stages of the journey to "blend" into one another "indissolvably" (like "the thing you have to say" and the "way of saying it" in another of Fitzgerald's formulations [*Letters* 11]).[9] Like writing itself, of course, such underwater movement also implies silence.[10] The motif of holding one's breath recurs several times within *Gatsby*, each time associated with some near-sublime aspect of the telling-listening-writing-reading situation (14, 15, 18).[11]

Yet the notion of writing (or reading) as cool, quiet, frictionless "flow" indicates only the tip of the iceberg (to adapt Hemingway's famous metaphor). The underside may be glimpsed in my opening epigraph, Fitzgerald's outburst to Perkins: "[I]nk . . . the ineffable destroyer of thought that fades an emotion into that slatternly thing, a written-down mental excretion" (*Letters* 148). To juxtapose this comment with Fitzgerald's idea of writing as swimming underwater is to reveal two poles of the writing experience as Fitzgerald conceived it: timeless, seamless glide and time-bound struggle with resistant material; smooth, swimmable water and recalcitrant, even grossly repulsive ink. In the latter formulation, mental process is converted not only into a more opaque liquid than water, but into one that implicitly (as "excretion") seeps out through the body rather than supporting it. Within *Gatsby*, related tensions inform the act of face-to-face narration as well. The occasional "magic" of the living human voice is itself threatened by disjunctures of all kinds.

Nick's ambivalent responsiveness to Daisy's voice exemplifies the problem of verbal exchange. On the one hand, Daisy's voice is for Nick a "wild tonic in the rain" (86), a source of "warm human magic" (109), an elusive temptation, rivaled only by Gatsby's smile.[12] On the other hand, Nick's relationship to Daisy's voice is repeatedly subject to hesitation and doubt. The more completely Daisy's voice enchants him, the more intense is his eventual disappointment and mistrust.

In addition, despite his emphasis on the "inexhaustible" promise and "deathless" magic (97) of Daisy's voice, Nick's descriptions repeatedly include not only a sharp sense of inevitable endings, but also a finely differentiated sense of process or cycle in which Daisy's voice is seen to crystallize and fade, fade and reemerge. Nick's depiction of this process is informed by a highly concrete sense of stages and transitions (beginnings, middles, and endings) such as mark not only lives and human relationships, but, still more palpably, works of fiction. Thus, as recurrent motif, Daisy's voice is associated with the process of sustaining what Nick calls "attention . . . [and] belief" (18) through story telling, through the often spellbinding, sometimes highly crafted, and always relentlessly time-bound sequences of words, told and written, that join narrator and narratee in a dynamic and reciprocal relationship.[13]

To understand Nick's ambivalent responses to Daisy's voice is thus to clarify his relationship to narrative. Nick's recurrent cycle of involvement with and recoil from Daisy's voice provides a paradigm for the way readers and listeners become first implicated in, then detached from, a narrator's story.

The Vicissitudes of Narration: Listening and Reading

Whatever else Nick may be, he is (like Fitzgerald) a storyteller, more precisely the author of a book (2). Nick's status as a writer is explicitly, if intermittently, noted: he rereads what he has written, tries to correct any misleading impressions he might give (56), and explains his rationale for "put[ting] . . . down" particular bits of information when he does (102). We can take Nick at his word then: he is a writer and, like all writers, he is implicitly writing to be read, dependent on a reader for coherence.[14] Again like any writer, he is both hidden and represented by the story that he tells.

Nick's implicit stake in the act of narration is not confined to the art of telling (or writing) however. Nick repeatedly listens to stories, stories told by Daisy, Gatsby, Jordan, Myrtle. Presented not merely as writer and storyteller, but also as a recipient of other people's stories, the figure of Nick illuminates numerous facets of narration: its motivation, its impact, its rewards, and its dangers. Through metaphoric implication and analogy, the recurrent image of Nick as sometimes skeptical, but always intensely responsive, listener also provides a model for Fitzgerald's own wished-for, potential, ideal reader.

Nick and Daisy

For Nick, all narration involves a tension between open invitation and manipulated design. Nick's rendering of Daisy's voice epitomizes this tension. When Nick listens to Daisy, his reactions range from euphoric delight to the feeling, on the contrary, of being cheated and betrayed. Nick's first description of Daisy in East Egg emphasizes the attraction of "her low, thrilling voice": "there was an excitement in her voice that men who had cared for her found difficult to forget; a singing compulsion, a whispered 'Listen'" (9). Two vignettes in chapter 1 exemplify Nick's own "compulsion" to "[l]isten" to Daisy while projecting a paradigmatic contrast between two kinds of listener: one expectant and satisfied, the other suspicious and disappointed.

Early in chapter 1, Daisy asks Nick if he would like her to "tell [him] a family secret," the story of the butler's nose. Nick responds enthusiastically, and Daisy's tale affords Nick a highly satisfactory experience. He is repaid for his attention and willing participation with a sense of involvement, gentle separation, and closure. As Daisy ends her story, Nick feels a sense of loss—of regret—yet not of a painful rending:

[T]he last sunshine fell with romantic affection upon her glowing face, her voice compelled me forward breathlessly as I listened—

then the glow faded, each light deserting her with lingering regret,
like children leaving a pleasant street at dusk. (14)

"Compelled . . . forward . . . as [he] listen[s]," Nick is "breathless." Yet he is
enchanted not primarily by the peculiar content of the tale; he is "compelled"
by Daisy's whispering voice and "glowing face" until, "like children leaving
a pleasant street at dusk," Daisy's voice slowly fades, and Nick's attention is
gradually withdrawn.

These satisfying moments are soon followed, however, by a listening
experience that stirs anger and conflict in Nick. Toward the end of the section, when Daisy recounts her own "turbulent emotions," the process of telling culminates in a violent reaction on the part of the captivated listener:

> *The instant her voice broke off, ceasing to compel my attention, my belief,*
> I felt the basic insincerity of what she had said. It made me uneasy,
> as though the whole evening had been a trick of some sort to exact
> a contributory emotion from me. I waited, and sure enough, in a
> moment she looked at me with an absolute smirk on her lovely
> face. . . . (18; my emphasis)

Nick's feeling of being coerced, trapped, cheated into going along, staying
longer, or giving more than he had intended is absolutely characteristic of
him. In the context of the questions raised by telling, listening, and believing, however, the above passage points beyond Nick's character to the problems of sustaining and ending a narrative.

When Nick renders the last moments of Daisy's "confession," he at once
chronicles the breakdown of reciprocal attention and anticipates the final
passage of *Gatsby* itself with its Dutch sailors, who, Nick assumes, "must have
held [their] breath . . ." in the encounter with "the new world, *compelled* into
an aesthetic contemplation [they] neither understood nor desired" (182; my
emphases). Like the Dutch sailors, Nick himself is repeatedly "breathless"
when "compelled" into spellbound attention, not to "worlds," but to "words."
Unlike the breathless sailors, however, Nick generally bridles at the sense of
having been "compelled" into rapt admiration or trust.

A recurrent factor in Nick's sense of coercion and betrayal by a speaker
is the speaker's physical presence. Here, it is Daisy's smirk that remains when
her voice "breaks off." It is her voice and smile—not her words—that "compel [Nick's] attention [and] . . . belief" in the first place. It is her "smirk" that
convinces Nick he has been had. Nick's sudden awareness of Daisy's physical presence breaks the spell of her narrative, creating a sense of disjuncture. Such disjunctures—between words and the voice behind the words, the

smile behind the voice—are repeatedly underscored in the course of Nick's narration. If Daisy's voice often promises human contact, even intimacy, it intermittently detaches itself from the body it seems to represent, leaving Daisy (like her listener) disoriented, isolated, and exposed. Gatsby strains unsuccessfully toward Daisy's disembodied presence, "trying to touch what was no longer tangible, struggling . . . toward that lost voice across the room" (135) moments before the fatal car ride. At the New York Plaza, the motif of voice repeatedly dramatizes Daisy's warring impulses: whether to contain, conceal, or reveal an inner state. Here Nick's description of Daisy's voice again anticipates the closing passage of the novel: "Her voice struggled on through the heat, beating against it, molding its senselessness into forms" (118–19). Daisy's attempt to "mold . . . senselessness into forms" is a bid to use her voice as an effective shaping force. Failing to control the implications of her own words, however, Daisy betrays herself:

> "Who wants to go to town?" demanded Daisy insistently. Gatsby's eyes floated toward her. "Ah," she cried, "you look so cool."
> Their eyes met, and they stared . . . at each other. . . .
> "You always look so cool," she repeated. She had told him that she loved him, and Tom Buchanan saw. He was astounded. (119)

This is the exchange that impels Nick to call Daisy's voice "indiscreet." Daisy's physical presence here fills the gaps between voice, words, and meaning, turning the words "you always look so cool" into a declaration of love.

In an early passage Nick feels "as if [Daisy's] heart was trying to come out to you concealed in one of those breathless, thrilling words" (15). The suggestively vague concept of an "indiscreet" voice is partially concretized in this figure of "breathless . . . words" that at once conceal and reveal a heart trying to leave a body. Other characters find themselves similarly thwarted and disjointed in the effort to control words and voice, compelled by other aspects of their being to give themselves away. The novel suggests that we all struggle on, like Daisy's voice, "through the heat, beating against it" in a desperate effort to make (or conceal) meanings. In this context, Nick's famous last words suggest the typical disjunctures of all communication: "we beat on . . . against the current, borne back ceaselessly into the past" (182).

Nick and Gatsby

Throughout *Gatsby*, characters encounter the gaps between voice and body, intention and expression, expression and response. The frustration suggested by these encounters—ineffective human struggles "through the heat" or "against the current"—stand out sharply in relief against the imagery of primal unity or satisfaction that Nick associates with the culminating moments of Gatsby's dream. The well-known image of Gatsby waiting to "suck on the pap of life, gulp down the incomparable milk of wonder" (112) evokes a moment unusually free of the disjunctures that threaten all desire, all human interaction, and all efforts to make narrated meaning[15] in the novel.

In the suspended moment during which Gatsby holds back "a moment longer" before kissing Daisy, he is engaged in the activity of "listening": "alone" with the vibrations of "the tuning fork that had been struck upon a star" (112). A similarly sublime (and silent) "enchanted moment" (182) is projected in the final passage of the novel, where the Dutch sailors, having come upon the "green breast of the new world," are held in the grip of "aesthetic contemplation." An obvious source for Fitzgerald's sailors is relevant here. The final image of Keats's "On First Looking into Chapman's Homer" evokes the sudden, "wild surmise" of Cortez "and all his men / . . . Silent, upon a peak in Darien." When one recalls in this context that Keats's speaker renders the sublime silence of Cortez's men for the explicit purpose of representing the effects of a literary experience—reading Homer—a set of analogies emerges.

I have linked the image of Gatsby (listening to "the tuning fork that had been struck upon a star") with Fitzgerald's sailors ("compelled into . . . aesthetic contemplation"). To consider Keats's sailors in this context is to uncover additional connections among Fitzgerald's sublime moments. While only Keats's image points directly to the experience of reading, I suggest that Fitzgerald's sailors, like the figure of Gatsby (and Nick), are informed by the same concern.

Nick Carraway experiences no moment comparable to Gatsby's (or the sailors') silent epiphany. Nick tends to be extremely cautious and skeptical about giving himself over to experience of any kind. Yet nothing elicits Nick's own "capacity for wonder" more consistently than Gatsby himself. Like Daisy, Gatsby repeatedly solicits (or "compels") Nick's "attention [and] . . . belief." Despite his resistance, it is as a listener to and observer of Gatsby that Nick eventually achieves his own most satisfying, even ecstatic moments, moments linked by association and analogy to the paradigmatic experience of a reader. We have noted that Nick is explicitly figured as a "reader" of *Gatsby* in Fitzgerald's original manuscript. He remains, metaphorically, the quintessential reader.

Nick is necessarily a listener to and observer of Gatsby before he is a narrator. Before he can tell Gatsby's story, Nick suspends disbelief and enters Gatsby's world, accepting his terms of discourse. Still, Nick's relationship to Gatsby (as to Daisy) is informed by a pattern of alternating faith and doubt.

It is precisely by articulating both his faith and his doubt about Gatsby that Nick becomes a model for the reader in addition to being a writer and storyteller. For Nick, as for the reader of Fitzgerald's text, acceptance of Gatsby depends on the "transitory" condition of "enchantment" (182) or belief. Fiction itself, of course, is always something one simultaneously believes and disbelieves. That doubleness, like the fluctuation of Nick's belief in Gatsby, is an indispensable component of all fiction reading.[16]

In the course of narration, Nick presents himself not only as Gatsby's best believer, but also as one of Gatsby's biggest skeptics. While Nick's faith in Gatsby thus encourages the reader's own receptivity (Cf. Kenner 37; Michelson 570–71), Nick's reservations prevent the reader from going overboard, from accepting Gatsby's magic too naively, believing too completely in his smile. Like Nick's opening description of Daisy, his initial rendering of Gatsby suggests both the persuasiveness and the limits of Gatsby's appeal. Like Daisy's "thrilling voice" and charming murmur in chapter 1, Gatsby's smile implies intimacy and reciprocity. The smile disappears, however, just at the moment of its greatest promise. "[P]recisely at that point" it confronts Nick with a sense of strain, disjuncture, disbelief.

> It was one of those rare smiles with a quality of eternal reassurance in it. . . . It understood you just as far as you wanted to be understood, believed in you as you would like to believe in yourself, and assured you that it had precisely the impression of you that, at your best, you hoped to convey. Precisely at that point it vanished—and I was looking at an elegant young roughneck, a year or two over thirty, whose elaborate formality of speech just missed being absurd. (48)

When Gatsby's smile vanishes, doubt creeps in, subjecting Nick to a backlash of disappointment and anger. Whenever Nick doubts Gatsby, he feels exploited, taken for a ride, seduced by false pretenses. Nick's anger at Gatsby under these conditions recalls his earlier attraction to and recoil from Daisy's voice. With Gatsby, however, Nick's sense of betrayal, or doubt, is frequently offset by reaffirmations of faith. Where Gatsby is concerned, Nick's metaphoric elaborations and his narrative sequences repeatedly culminate in a burst of affirmation.

During Nick's first excursion with Gatsby, Gatsby decides to "tell [Nick] something about [his] life" (65). "I don't want you to get a wrong idea of me from all those stories you've heard," Gatsby says (65). As Gatsby outlines his career in the war, in Europe, at Oxford, Nick listens with increasing skepticism. Indeed, it is only with "an effort" that Nick "manage[s] to restrain [his] incredulous laughter" when Gatsby explains how he

'lived like a young rajah in all the capitals of Europe—Paris, Venice,
Rome—collecting jewels, chiefly rubies, hunting big game, painting
a little, things for myself only, and trying to forget something very
sad that had happened to me long ago.' (66)

Nick is particularly disturbed by what he sees here as the failure of Gatsby's
rhetorical power. Gatsby's "*very phrases*," he complains, "were worn so
threadbare that they evoked no image except that of a turbaned '*character*'
leaking sawdust at every pore as he pursued a tiger through the Bois de
Boulogne" (66; my emphases). When Nick is seen as a figure for the reader,
his criticism makes good sense. He has expected more of Gatsby, if not as
truth teller, at least as storyteller.

In due course, Gatsby does fulfill Nick's expectations. Nick's most satisfying moments are precisely those in which he can affirm his "renewed
faith" in Gatsby's image despite his lingering doubts or "disapproval." Nick's
moments of belief in Gatsby depend upon the rhythms of the story-telling
process, shored up by the personal interaction between speaker and listener.
As Daisy's glowing face and telltale smirk alternately entice and disillusion
Nick, so Gatsby's physical presence (voice, nodding head, radiant smile) is
indispensable to his narrative performance.[17] Fittingly, Gatsby clinches his
young rajah account with corroborating evidence (medals, photographs): two
bits of material "proof" that deal a final blow to Nick's defenses. In a sudden
leap of faith ("then it was all true"), Nick caps his acceptance of Gatsby's tale
with his own fanciful contribution to the story: "I saw the skins of tigers flaming in his palace on the Grand Canal; I saw him opening a chest of rubies
to ease, with their crimson-lighted depths, the gnawings of his broken heart"
(67). Nick's language here is at least as extravagant as Gatsby's claims, which
is perhaps as it should be, since Nick is participating in an account that has
precious little to do with logic, consistency, or "proof." As Weinstein puts it,
the issue is one of "belief rather than truth" (24; cf. 31), and if Gatsby is the
"consummate fiction maker" (38), Nick, by the same token, is the optimal,
responsive, participating reader.[18]

Nick intermittently functions, then, both as a lightning rod for the reader's disbelief and as a model for such reader response as Fitzgerald himself
may have sought. If discord between text and reader is represented metaphorically in the scene of Daisy's smirk, Gatsby's physical presence, especially
his smile, creates temporary harmony when words fail to persuade. Nick's
most gratifying moments as a listener are just those moments when Nick
(as in the "young-rajah" episode) can be persuaded by Gatsby, without necessarily believing him. Under these conditions, Nick is free to believe and
disbelieve at once, free (like a reader of fiction) to believe without regard for

verisimilitude. In these paradoxical moments, Nick's "attention" and "belief" are at once "compelled" and freely given.

Nick's final face-to-face confirmation of Gatsby reproduces the delicate balance of resistance and receptivity indispensable to the reading process and characteristic of Nick's relationship to Gatsby. As I have noted, Nick's fluctuating responses to Gatsby often culminate in a provisional assertion of love or loyalty. "They're a rotten crowd," Nick calls across the lawn at the moment of parting from Gatsby:

> "You're worth the whole damn bunch put together."
> I've always been glad I said that . . . because I disapproved of him from beginning to end. First he nodded politely, and then his face broke into that radiant and understanding smile, as if we'd been in ecstatic cahoots on that fact all the time. (154)

Like the "renewal of complete faith" in Gatsby that Nick experiences at the Plaza (131),[19] the sense here of Nick and Gatsby in "ecstatic cahoots" is striking, the more so because Nick's own responses so rarely suggest the "ecstatic." Nick's description of his final contact with Gatsby culminates in a sense of delight, reflected in Gatsby's familiar smile. Yet as we know, Gatsby's smile, buoyant source of "eternal reassurance" (48), tends to vanish in due course, giving rise to doubt in turn. Further consideration of this cycle can clarify Nick's wish to tell Gatsby's story in writing.

The Vicissitudes of Narration: Telling and Writing

If Nick experiences the pleasure of giving attention and approval only when he does not feel "compelled," coerced, it is not surprising that he validates Gatsby's story by telling it only after Gatsby's death. To Nick, sooner or later, presence always means coercion or deception: a smirk, a voice that "br[eaks] off," a smile that disappears.

Thus it is only after Gatsby's death that Nick feels fully committed to Gatsby—determined to invest himself—to "get somebody for him," to "reassure him" (165) as Gatsby's smile once reassured Nick. By telling Gatsby's story only after his death, Nick protects himself from all further demands or betrayals on Gatsby's part. By doing so in writing, Nick also protects himself from any awkward entanglements with the recipient of his tale. Alone with Gatsby's dead body Nick finds himself "on Gatsby's side, and . . . interested—interested, I mean, with that intense personal interest to which every one has some vague right at the end" (165). While Nick's story may be seen in this context as an effort to create "intense personal interest" on Gatsby's behalf, Nick's story telling also expresses considerable uncertainty about just whose tale this really is.

If according to Nick "everyone has some vague right [to intense personal inter-
est] at the end," we may well ask who bestows such interest on Nick Carraway
himself. Surely the answer is no one, no one, that is, within the represented
world of the text. Perhaps, then, Nick tells his story not just as a tribute to
Gatsby, but also to create some "intense personal interest" on his own behalf:
to "get someone" not only for Gatsby, but for himself as well. This hypothesis is
supported by the uneasy balance sustained throughout the text between Nick's
evocation of Gatsby and his own self-presentation in narrative.

A curious shift in focus toward the end of chapter 3 exemplifies the ten-
uous balance by virtue of which Nick's story telling (like Daisy's or Gatsby's)
raises questions about the relationship between the words of a story and the
articulating presence behind the words. After Nick's description of his first
party at Gatsby's, a typographical break in the text is followed by some retrospective reflections on Nick's part:

> Reading over what I have written so far, I see I have given the
> impression that the events of three nights several weeks apart were
> all that absorbed me. On the contrary, they were merely casual
> events in a crowded summer, and, until much later, they absorbed
> me infinitely less than my personal affairs. (56)

This assertion foregrounds the fact that Nick is writing a narrative, while
shifting the focus of interest from "The Great Gatsby" to Nick himself.
The figure of Nick takes shape here both as writer and as a man with his
own "personal affairs." The rest of this chapter, indeed, stresses Nick's
own activities, professional and personal. In the following chapter, Nick
reappears in the (by now familiar) position of spellbound listener. Here,
with Jordan Baker as storyteller, the pleasures and pitfalls of the "narrating
instance" (Genette 212) gain heightened corporeal reality: Jordan's narration
leads Nick to a rare moment of physical passion.

While chapter 4 begins with Gatsby's young-rajah presentation of himself,
it ends with Jordan Baker's account of Daisy and Gatsby as she had glimpsed
them before the war. Jordan's narrative is unique within the text not only
because of its length (over four pages) but also because it is rendered entirely in
Jordan's own words. Jordan ends her tale by linking Jay Gatsby of West Egg to
the officer whom she once glimpsed with Daisy in Louisville. "Gatsby bought
that house so that Daisy would be just across the bay," Jordan explains.

> Then it had not been merely the stars to which he had aspired on
> that June night [Nick comments]. He came alive to me, delivered
> suddenly from the womb of his purposeless splendor. (79)

Jordan's story brings Gatsby to life for Nick, giving "form" to "senselessness," bestowing or creating life, as direct personal contact has not. In addition, Nick's climactic sense of Gatsby "c[o]me alive" soon generates intimacy between Nick and Jordan:

> I put my arm around Jordan's golden shoulder and . . . [s]uddenly I wasn't thinking of Daisy and Gatsby any more, but of this clean, hard, limited person, who . . . leaned back jauntily within the circle of my arm. . . . Unlike Gatsby and Tom Buchanan, I had no girl whose disembodied face floated along the dark cornices and blinding signs, and so I drew up the girl beside me. . . . Her wan, scornful mouth smiled, and so I drew her up again closer, this time to my face. (80–81)

Jordan as storyteller is here replaced by Jordan as love object. If her story in a sense engenders Gatsby for Nick, making him "come alive," "delivered" from a "womb," her story telling subsequently engenders—and eroticizes— the figure of Jordan herself. To put this differently, if at first it is Gatsby who "c[o]me[s] alive" for Nick through Jordan's story telling, soon it is Jordan herself who comes alive for her listener.

This curious aftereffect of Jordan's story—a kiss for the storyteller— raises more questions about the function of narration, its rewards and dangers, not only for Nick but perhaps for Fitzgerald himself. Jordan's story not only "engenders" the figure of Gatsby, but generates new possibilities of contact as a result of the narrating situation, temporarily binding teller and listener in "ecstatic cahoots." What, then, we might ask in this context, are the implications for the story told by Nick or (for that matter) the story told by Fitzgerald?

One difference between Jordan's story and that of either Nick or Fitzgerald is precisely the difference between stories told and stories written: stories told by a voice emanating from a physical body, heard by an actual ear, and stories in which teller and listener are replaced by writer and reader, joined (but also separated) by the silent, printed page. Unlike Daisy's, Gatsby's, or Jordan's story telling, where narration depends upon the physical proximity of teller and listener, Nick's tale enables him to keep his distance even while soliciting "intense personal interest" and "getting someone" for himself. If, by writing his story for anonymous readers, Nick invites that "intense personal interest to which everyone has some vague right at the end," he is at the same time effectively protected from the risk that Jordan's story exposes her to.

By telling his story in writing and in retrospect, Nick can evoke Gatsby's presence and affirm his devotion most strongly just when there is no longer anything to fear from direct personal contact. Nick's written narrative thus enables him to finalize his separation not only from Gatsby, but from all the other participants in the summer's experience. Nick, that is, creates distance through his story, distance that makes, among other things, for safety.

The figure of Myrtle Wilson provides a further comment on this aspect of story telling, exemplifying some potential dangers of too little distance, too little separation, not only between teller and listener, but also between teller and tale. Nick first meets Myrtle when Tom "literally force[s him] from the car" of the train near Wilson's garage (24). A sense of entrapment pervades Nick's description of the evening he spends at Tom and Myrtle's New York apartment (chapter 2). Characteristically, Nick feels the wish, but not the ability, to escape: "each time I tried to go I became entangled in some wild, strident argument which pulled me back, as if with ropes, into my chair" (36). Nick's sense of entrapment reaches a climax when Myrtle forces him to be a captive audience: "[S]uddenly," as Nick describes it, "her warm breath poured over me, the story of her first meeting with Tom" (36), and Nick is compelled to listen to Myrtle's account of sexual attraction and involvement. According to her story, Myrtle (like Nick) is forced off a train by Tom but, unlike Nick, Myrtle is ready to enjoy being coerced:

> When we came into the station he was next to me, and his white shirt-front pressed against my arm. . . . I was so excited that when I got into a taxi with him I didn't hardly know I wasn't getting into a subway train. All I kept thinking about, over and over, was "You can't live forever; you can't live forever." (36)

Rendered still more passive than usual by the story Myrtle "pour[s] over [him]," Nick feels increasingly smothered and trapped. This is a far cry from Nick's best moments as a narratee. Too much insistence or intrusive presence on the storyteller's part only stimulates resistance in the listener.

The final image of Myrtle dramatizes the danger implicit for the teller in unmodulated, uncontrollable outpourings:

> her left breast was swinging loose like a flap, and there was no need to listen for the heart beneath. The mouth was wide open and ripped at the corners, as though she had choked a little in giving up the tremendous vitality she had stored so long. (138)

The question of storing "vitality" repeatedly surfaces in the course of *The Great Gatsby*. "The colossal vitality of [Gatsby's] illusion," Nick says after the Gatsby–Daisy reunion, "had gone beyond her, beyond everything. He had thrown himself into it with a creative passion. . . . No amount of fire and freshness can challenge what a man will store up in his ghostly heart" (97). If Myrtle is literally disembodied and mutilated in "giving up the tremendous vitality she had stored so long," "the colossal vitality of [Gatsby's] illusion" is inevitably diminished in the process of being released from "the ghostly heart" where it has been "store[d] up" and decked out with "creative passion." What, the novel seems to be asking, is a viable form in which to "store up" or transmit vitality: a heart, a body, a dream, a voice, a written story?[20]

"Vitality" seems inevitably to be lost—or at least diminished—in the process of being conveyed, released, or delivered. When Daisy's heart "tries to come out" of her body, "concealed in one of those breathless, thrilling words" (15), an "absolute smirk" is what remains of the attempt. Moreover, the transition can be treacherous: Myrtle's vitality bursts forth in violence, destroying the body that stored it. Gatsby, for his part, "throw[s] himself into" his "colossal[ly] vital" illusion, trying to live his dream as "son of God" (word made flesh?). He too dies in violence.

If, as Weinstein puts it, Gatsby himself is "the consummate fiction maker" (38), he is so primarily by making fiction in and of himself. No wonder he does not survive the attempt. Nick, on the other hand, through the distancing power of written narrative, can limit the "creative passion" (97) to words and safely "repeat the past," even while soliciting "intense personal interest" on his own behalf. What then of Fitzgerald? If, as I have suggested, Nick functions as a kind of "fall guy," deflecting the reader's resistance to Gatsby, he also functions as a ubiquitous presence, obstructing the reader's access to any embodied image of the novelist, surrounding the author with even more distance than Nick can establish.

We have repeatedly noted Nick's sense of being undermined by the voices and faces that surround him. When Nick kisses Jordan after her story telling, he implies that he does so because he himself has "no girl whose disembodied face floated along the cornices and blinding signs" (81). In the absence of a "disembodied" image, Nick makes do with physical presence. Over-involvement, passivity, betrayal—these are only some of the consequences of proximity. Distance thus emerges as an indispensable condition not only for safety, but for mystery, beauty, and hope: "The city seen from the Queensboro Bridge is always the city seen for the first time, in its first wild promise of all the mystery and beauty in the world" (69). Like the green light at the end of Daisy's dock or "the green breast of the new world," the city depends for much of its "promise" on the right amount of distance, imaginative and literal. A delicate balance is required to create an "enchanted object." With too little distance, Daisy's green light is only a light bulb; seen from closer yet it is a blur. Too much distance, on the other hand, and the green light disappears. Perception of an object in the distance requires a certain imaginative adjustment not unlike the act of reading (or writing) itself. To turn letters into words and words into "meaning" rather than "senselessness" requires what Edith Wharton, in a related context, calls "an adjustment of the mental vision" (*House of Mirth* 140).

Narrative Transactions: Reading and Writing

The act of reading—opening a book, perceiving words and sentences, turning pages, suspending "disbelief"—is an indispensable part of the process by which fiction manages to make any meanings at all.[21] *The Great Gatsby* is structured to elicit in the reader, through the process of reading, a condition that approaches Nick's intermittent "state of enchantment" in relation to Gatsby, or Gatsby's in relation to Daisy. Of course such a state depends upon many transformations beyond the conversion of letters into words.

We recall the pattern of Nick's belief and disbelief in the presence of various storytellers. We might say that Nick's difficulties listening to stories by Daisy, Gatsby, Jordan, or Myrtle are analogous to a problem encountered by every reader (or writer) of fiction: the problem of sustaining the "transitory" state of "enchantment," of "attention" and "belief." For Nick to sustain his illusion as a listener requires his imaginative or emotional disengagement from the smirk that betrays the voice, the smile that eventually vanishes, the storyteller who becomes more tempting than the story, the coercive and vitiating presence of the "warm breath that pours the story" over the listener.

Similarly, the illusion of a reader depends upon that reader's temporary disengagement from his or her own immediate circumstances and requires the reader to "forget"[22] the surrounding context and material conditions of reading, including the fact that writing is just black and white marks on a page. In addition, for Nick (or Fitzgerald) to sustain the fictional illusion, they must deflect attention from the presence in the story of, say, "appalling sentimentality," "threadbare" phrases, and "character[s] leaking sawdust": the very deficiencies that nearly subvert Gatsby's "young-rajah" account for Nick.

For a story to enlist the belief of its audience, the manipulations of plot and language—the presence of craft—must not be readily apparent. Fitzgerald, moreover, as a writer of fiction (unlike Nick) needs to deflect the reader's attention from any impulse that the novelist might have to elicit "personal interest" on his own behalf. Here again Nick serves the function of lightning rod, obscuring issues of prime concern to the real author of *Gatsby*: issues of distance, personal need, self-exposure, reader response.

To preserve its credibility, fiction in a sense must conform to Nick's definition of "personality" as "an unbroken series of successful gestures" (2). In order to "compel" a reader's "attention [and] . . . belief," the signs of welding, the craft, the "leaking sawdust" must not show.[23] Most important perhaps is to avert the reader's perception that, as a result of the reading process itself, the border between fiction and "reality"—the end of the book—is steadily approaching. How establish a sense of "ecstatic cahoots" between reader and text? How induce a reader to keep on reading? How avoid Nick's all-too-frequent sense of violent betrayal at the end?

One way, perhaps, is to deflect attention from the inevitable and painful fact that like people, dreams, and love affairs, novels "can't live forever." When does the end of a novel begin to become palpable? Certainly once the midpoint is reached, the end is virtually in sight.[24] As we have noted, Gatsby delays the first kiss he gives Daisy for as long as he can. He tries to prolong the vibrations of that "tuning fork . . . struck upon a star" because

> [h]e knew that when he kissed this girl and forever wed his unutterable visions to her perishable breath, his mind would never romp again like the mind of God. So he waited, listening for a moment longer to the tuning-fork that had been struck upon a star. Then he kissed her. At his lips' touch she blossomed for him like a flower and the incarnation was complete. (112)

"Unutterable visions" like "colossal vitality . . . store[d] up in a ghostly heart" seem unbounded by either time or space. But Myrtle knows "you can't live forever; you can't live forever"; and Gatsby knows that once the "unutterable" is given a local habitation or a name, the end is near. Once the "incarnation [is] complete," the dream embodied, mortality has set in.

No sooner is the climax of Gatsby's reunion with Daisy achieved in chapter 5—the very center of the text—than Nick produces his well-known formulation about Gatsby's diminished "count of enchanted objects." Once Daisy is present, able to "put her arm through his," "the colossal significance of [the green light has] . . . vanished forever."

> Compared to the great distance that had separated him from Daisy it had seemed very near to her, almost touching her. It had seemed as close as a star to a moon. Now it was again a green light on a dock. His count of enchanted objects had diminished by one. (94)

At the very moment of culmination (incarnation, embodiment), the dream begins to fade. But this is just the dynamic of reading (and writing) a novel as well. Gatsby is cleverly made to deflect our awareness that enchanted objects (like pages) are numbered, that the result of reaching the climactic

midpoint of the narrative is an inevitable vision of the end.[25] Once the center
is reached the remaining words and pages, like Gatsby's enchanted objects,
inexorably diminish. It is only a question of time before the reader—like
Gatsby—will be "watching over nothing" (146).[26]

"Do you always watch for the longest day of the year and then miss it?
I always watch for the longest day of the year and then miss it" (12). Thus
Daisy, in one of her seemingly arbitrary statements. The "two changes of the
year" are invoked again, however, in the incarnation-tuning fork passage itself
(112). And I suggest that if "watching over nothing" is a perfect description
not only of the reader's state at the end of a novel, but of reading fiction
altogether, then one of Fitzgerald's prime aims in this text is to get the reader
involved in "watch[ing] for the longest day of the year" and then missing it.

It is, in other words, the novelist's imperative to throw sand in the
reader's eyes lest the "unbroken series of gestures" that Nick takes for "personality" become a broken series of voices, gestures, "character[s] leaking
sawdust," "threadbare" phrases, diminishing enchanted objects. Fitzgerald's
triumph, through Nick, through the devious time scheme, and the metaphoric panache is precisely to locate all these dangers or failures elsewhere,
diverting our attention from the presence of any such flaws in his own text.
As a maker of images, enchanted objects, "colossal . . . illusion[s]," Fitzgerald himself is the "prime fiction-maker" even more than Gatsby, with whom
(of all the characters in the novel) Fitzgerald is all but directly identified.
All but directly identified, for if embodiment, incarnation, and "illusion" are
Fitzgerald's "business" throughout the text, *dis*-embodiment is his own position within it (*Letters*).

In this sense Fitzgerald seems more identified with what Frank Norris
called "the book, [the] manuscript, the page to page progress of the narrative"
(92) than with any single character or action represented in the text. Like
Nick, Fitzgerald makes his story out of words rather than (like Gatsby) out of
himself. We have seen how this move ensures a measure of safety, denied, say,
to Gatsby and Myrtle. Releasing vitality into a book, however, Fitzgerald (like
any novelist) encounters other problems. "I often think writing is a sheer par-
ing away of oneself," he reflects in a letter, "leaving always something thinner,
barer, more meager" (*Letters* 70). Working on his text and letting go of it at
last in the public arena, Fitzgerald himself becomes a voice without a body.

We have consistently pointed to the contrast between the concrete
physicality of persons (or texts) and their more mesmerizing or ethereal attributes. When Daisy's voice is represented as "a deathless song" (97), "glowing and singing" (15), it is the antithesis of a written text that inscribes the
inevitability of its own demise precisely as the culminating middle point is
reached. When words are sung—apprehended as "cymbal's song" or "siren's

song" instead of printed and bound upon numbered pages—the middle is hard to find, as hard to take hold of as the longest day of the year. Fitzgerald's presence in his text (unlike its material center) is equally hard to pinpoint, as diffuse as the "ripple of [Daisy's] voice . . . in the rain" (86). Authorial presence is at once palpable and invisible like the "definite, unfamiliar, yet vaguely recognizable" look that occasionally sweeps across Gatsby's face (121, 135).

I have been suggesting that the language of *Gatsby* reflects the multiple tensions between words and meaning, voices and bodies, tellers and listeners, readers and books. Many of Fitzgerald's formulations about particular characters and events in *Gatsby* seem uncannily applicable to the process of reading (or writing) itself. "I think [Daisy's] voice held [Gatsby] . . . most," Nick says, "with its fluctuating feverish warmth, because it couldn't be overdreamed" (97). Like Nick's responsiveness to Gatsby's smile or Daisy's voice, the reading process too is characterized by fluctuations. As Daisy's voice attracts and repels Gatsby and Nick, Fitzgerald's text elicits varying responses from readers: faith and doubt; receptivity and resistance; now a sense of contact, now of separation.

Fluctuations are inevitable wherever stories are told, whether by speakers to listeners or through the printed word. Fitzgerald knew that a story is never (like the hypothetical one Nick reads in Fitzgerald's draft) "climaxes only." However, Fitzgerald's very consciousness of the need for pacing and the tenuousness of illusion in fiction often comes dangerously close to deflecting attention from the events and the characters in his own story, all but foregrounding instead the very concern with artifice that a writer must hide in order to maintain the fiction. Thus, such manifest themes as "time" and "illusion," so familiar to every reader of *Gatsby*, are relevant not only to Gatsby's dream of Daisy or to that of the Dutch sailors, but also to Fitzgerald's own fiction-making procedures.

Indeed, *Gatsby* seems pervaded by a tension between the wish to project an effective illusion (a fiction) and the wish to call attention not only to that illusion as such, but to the illusion-making process itself. The fictional illusion seems repeatedly threatened by Fitzgerald's fear of revealing (or his impulse to reveal) the working procedures of the novelist, what Edith Wharton called "the threads on the wrong side of the tapestry" (*Backward Glance* 197, 324).[27] Benjamin's figure of the potter's handprints takes on further resonance in this context. For Benjamin, the "handprints of the potter on the pot" epitomize the culture of artisanship, of a craft tradition passed on from generation to generation. In a preindustrial culture, handprints on a clay vessel—traces of the making process—confirm the existence of that harmony between artisan and artifact that in Benjamin's view fosters oral narration as well. However, whereas the potter's handprints become for Benjamin a precious sign of continuity and community, a sign that human work has gone on, the modern novel—printed, advertised, marketed—is, on the, contrary, a finished product at some distance from its author (cf. Borus 67). In *A Backward Glance* (1935) Wharton's image of "the wrong side of the tapestry" (324) underscores not the continuity, but the division, between the making process and the finished work. Moreover, a glimpse of Wharton's tapestry threads (unlike Benjamin's handprints) disrupts the self-containment of the aesthetic object.

Unlike Benjamin's pot—and like Wharton's novel/tapestry—*Gatsby* comes perilously close to creating irreparable disjunctures by calling attention to itself as a "worked artifact."[28] Insofar as inadvertent (or self-conscious) illusion breaking occurs in a work of fiction, it undercuts the presumption of verisimilitude and exposes the way that the language of representation intermittently points to its own nature or its own methods of embodiment rather than to the represented world in the text. By the same token, self-reflexive elements generate flickering intimations of a novelist at work and foreground the existence of the writer.

We have seen how the "inexhaustible charm" (120) and "deathless song" (97) of Daisy's voice often seems antithetical to anything either mortal or material. Yet Daisy's voice is also seen as "indiscreet" and "full of money," highly earthbound attributes. Both the "indiscretion" and the moneyed "jingle" of Daisy's voice, moreover, point to additional aspects of novel writing. Fitzgerald certainly meant, so to speak, to fill his own "voice" with money and never more so than when working on *Gatsby*.[29] In pursuing that goal, Fitzgerald drew upon his own personality and private life both to write his novels and to promote them. Yet Fitzgerald often hesitated and even recoiled from the "indiscretion" of self-revelation and self-exposure in fiction.[30]

It may seem grossly reductive to link the figure of voice in *Gatsby* to the most material and personal details of authorship, but that is precisely the point. Fitzgerald himself was never sure whether he had transmogrified or merely incriminated himself in the texts that he offered to his "own personal public" (*Letters* 158). The character of Gatsby "started as one man I knew and then changed into myself," he wrote; "the amalgam was never complete" (qtd. in Weinstein 29). *The Great Gatsby* reflects Fitzgerald's sense of the fiction writer as both sublime alchemist and weary toiler, immortal artist and wage-earning scribbler, alternately transmuted and rudely exposed in the process of converting "a great dream" (*Letters* 32) into publicly accessible words "excreted" onto a page.

I have suggested that Gatsby also reflects Fitzgerald's uncertainty about the extent to which the time-bound process of "excretion"—the signs of a writer's craft—are hidden or accessible within the finished narrative. As we have seen, these uncertainties generate recurrent motifs within the novel, creating a tension between absent and present narrators, embodied and disembodied voices, sustained (or sustaining) illusions and abruptly disjointed ones. If then, as Weinstein says, the "energy and power" of *The Great Gatsby* "mocks both closure and exposure" (38), it does so because Fitzgerald in this text so intensely imagines and implicitly intimates the dynamic processes of both.

NOTES

1. For recent discussions of changes in the literary marketplace toward the turn of the century and thereafter, see Daniel Borus and Christopher Wilson.

2. Fitzgerald's letters to his editor are full of advertising and marketing ideas intended to make his books more attractive to a reading public with rapidly shifting tastes and expectations (see *Letters* 157, 168, 169, 172, 184).

3. Bakhtin uses strikingly similar language to suggest that words are always permeated by a sense of other people's being: "the word does not exist in a neutral and impersonal language . . . rather it exists in other people's mouths [and] . . . contexts . . . : it is from there that one must . . . make [the word] one's own" (294).

4. "I honestly believed that with *no effort on my part* I was a sort of magician with words," he writes to Scottie in 1937 (*Letters* 16; Fitzgerald's emphasis).

5. See Walter Ong on the difficulty of restoring the oral antecedents of language to a literate reading public. Ong suggests that the "pre-emptiveness of literacy" makes it virtually impossible for most readers to dissociate words from writing. See especially 13–15 and chapter 1.

6. Compare Michael Fried's emphasis on "the role of . . . the writer as corporeal being . . . in the production of writing" (140).

7. At least since Lionel Trilling, Gatsby's comment has been singled out as one of the few significant things he ever says in his "own voice" (112). Compare Arnold Weinstein's discussion of Daisy's voice (26–28).

8. Fried (esp. xiv, 100, 117–20), Walter Benn Michaels (esp. 3–28), and Mark Seltzer (esp. 3–21) have recently shown how late nineteenth-century American fiction is informed by uncertainties about the status of the material, particularly in relation to the idea of the self and the very possibility of representation. One aspect of this problem is realism's underlying concern with the "materiality" or "physicality" of writing itself.

9. The bid for seamless unity implicit in Fitzgerald's use of water imagery for the act of writing recurs. Compare his concern with stories that "flow . . . well in the reading" (*Letters* 93) and "sentences 'that never leak'" (*Letters* 518).

10. Compare Bakhtin's sustained emphasis on the novel as a genre dependent on "mute perception" (3) and his still greater emphasis on "voice" and even "sound" as a metaphor for what a writer writes (278).

11. In the pencil-draft of *Gatsby*, Nick "too h[o]ld[s] [his] breath" (like the Dutch sailors) while "brooding on the old unknown world" (qtd. in Eble 86).

12. See Weinstein on the analogy between voice and smile (29–30).

13. On the writer-reader relationship as dynamic and reciprocal see Wolfgang Iser (232, 274–75, 278–79) and Georges Poulet (47–49). Michael Steig provides a lucid rationale for the use of "a term like interaction or transaction" to describe the reading process (11–13).

14. As a fictional character, Nick is dependent on the reception of his story not only for coherence, but for existence: in more senses than one, he has no life apart from what he narrates.

15. Indeed, the imagery suggests a preverbal state of being.

16. Compare Weinstein's link between "the power of belief" (36) and "the power of the dream or . . . of fiction" (30). Compare also Norman Holland on the state of "belief" and the reading process (75, 80–83, 103).

17. Early in this scene when Nick suspects Gatsby of "pulling [his] leg," one "glance at [Gatsby], convince[s Nick] otherwise" (68). Soon Nick undergoes a further shift of mood from "incredulity to fascination." This transition occurs when Gatsby "lifted up the words and nodded at them—with his smile" (66). Fascinated now, Nick is ready to believe what he hears.

18. Reciprocity is inherent in oral story telling for Benjamin (91–92). Compare Ong (59–60). Brooks emphasizes narrative as gift, with contributions to the story affirming that the gift has been received ("The Tale" 290–91).

19. The Plaza scene (129–30) reproduces the pattern where Nick, after much hesitation, embraces Gatsby's version of himself. While Tom tries to expose Gatsby as a liar, the rest of the audience does not "mirror . . . his unbelief," as he had hoped. Nick's "renewal of complete faith," rather than Tom's "unbelief," is "mirrored" by the scene. The exchange ends in a rousing victory for Gatsby's version of himself (cf. Weinstein 33–37).

20. "I'm finishing my novel for myself . . . ," Fitzgerald writes Zelda in 1940. "It will be nothing like anything else as I'm digging it out of myself like uranium . . ." (*Letters* 131).

21. On the role of "disbelief" see Holland 80, 82–83. Reading theory has increasingly taken the material realities of reading into account. See Fish 74, 83, 85; cf. note 8 above. Fitzgerald's letters display his own recurrent attention to such material features of his books as their type (*Letters* 143, 144), their binding (*Letters* 157, 188), jacket design (*Letters* 153, 168, 189), and so on. Many of his letters also foreground their own typographical state by explaining or apologizing for Fitzgerald's use of a pencil, pen, or typewriter.

22. Fried would say "repress" (xiv). On related grounds Walter M. Kendrick stresses the need to "ignore" the fact that the realist text "is [made of] writing" in order for the reader to "look . . . through" the written page to the represented world (7).

23. Gertrude Stein's formulation about sentences that "never leak" is worth recalling in this context. While Fitzgerald cites the phrase itself only in a late letter (*Letters* 518), he often mentions Stein during his work on *Gatsby* (*Letters* 165, 166, 169).

24. On the link between narration and death, especially the reader's "resistance to the end," see Brooks, *Reading* 23, 95, 103–04, 107–08. See also D. A. Miller 195–264.

25. Fitzgerald's revisions reveal concern with the midpoint of the text (or its difficulties for him). Kenneth Eble notes variations in Fitzgerald's revisions: "the beginning and end are comparatively clean, the middle most cluttered" (85). Compare Fitzgerald's letters to Perkins regarding the middle of *Gatsby* (*Letters* 169, 170).

26. Compare Seltzer's concept of "the realist tautology," where the terminal point of realism is seen in a "minimalism that equates the consuming of paper and

of the novel itself" (79) or where the realist imperative of making things visible ends by "the making visible of writing itself" (111).

27. Compare Amy Kaplan's reading of this figure (100) as used by Wharton in an earlier form (*House of Mirth* 285) and Seltzer's sense that, in realism, both "narration and characterization are everywhere threatened by their exposure as merely effects of certain practices of writing" (107).

28. The phrase is from Fried's discussion of Thomas Eakins. Fried explores the tension between inviting a spectator into the represented space of the painting and, alternatively, drawing attention to the "worked artifact" as such (74). Compare the tension in "realist [narrative] theory" between what Borus calls an "industrial and preindustrial conception" of the work of writing. "The industrial conception," in Borus's terms, "took as natural the existence of a commodity divorced from . . . human action. . . . The preindustrial or artisanal mode stressed the individual human touches necessary to demonstrating that work had gone on" (67; cf. chapter 4).

29. See Fitzgerald's letter to Edmund Wilson quoted in Ernest H. Lockridge (105). Compare Fitzgerald's letter to Thomas Boyd dated June 23, 1924 in Matthew J. Bruccoli and Margaret M. Duggan 143. On Fitzgerald's finances prior to *Gatsby*, see Andrew Turnbull 141.

30. While Fitzgerald, as John O. McCormick puts it, was "a relentlessly autobiographical writer" (28), he often insisted on distinguishing between his characters' experience and his own. We know of Fitzgerald's resistance to having a figure that he felt resembled him on the cover of *Beautiful and the Damned* (*Letters* 153) and, in a letter to Scottie, of his disclaiming any connection between Zelda and a female protagonist she appeared to suggest (qtd. in Turnbull 131). More than most narrative devices, a first-person narrator might seem to "embody" the novelist's voice even while protecting it from being directly associated with the author. One can conceptualize the character of Nick without constructing an image of Fitzgerald himself. It is largely for this reason that the figure of Nick is so often given the credit for making Gatsby the most aesthetically "realized" of Fitzgerald's works. Such praise suggests that in his other novels Fitzgerald himself is too thinly veiled, too obtrusively "present" in the text.

WORKS CITED

Bakhtin, Mikhail. *The Dialogic Imagination*. Trans. Caryl Emerson and Michael Holquist. Austin: U of Texas P, 1981.

Benjamin, Walter. *Illuminations*. Trans. Harry Zohn. New York: Schocken, 1969.

Borus, Daniel. *Writing Realism*. Chapel Hill: U of North Carolina P, 1989.

Brooks, Peter. *Reading for the Plot*. Oxford: Clarendon, 1984.

———. "The Tale vs. the Novel." *Novel* 21 (1988): 285–92.

Bruccoli, Matthew J., and Margaret M. Duggan, eds. *Correspondence of F. Scott Fitzgerald*. New York: Random, 1980.

Eble, Kenneth. "The Craft of Revision: *The Great Gatsby*." *Critical Essays on F. Scott Fitzgerald's The Great Gatsby*. Ed. Scott Donaldson. Boston: Hall, 1984. 85–93.

Fish, Stanley. "Literature in the Reader: Affective Stylistics." *Reader Response Criticism*. Ed. Jane P. Tompkins. Baltimore: Johns Hopkins UP, 1980. 164–84.

Fitzgerald, F. Scott. *The Great Gatsby*. New York: Scribner's, 1953.

———. *The Letters of F. Scott Fitzgerald*. Ed. Andrew Turnbull. New York: Dell, 1963.

———. *This Side of Paradise*. New York: Macmillan, 1986.

Fried, Michael. *Writing, Realism, and Disfiguration: Thomas Eakins and Stephen Crane.* Chicago: U of Chicago P, 1987.

Genette, Gérard. *Narrative Discourse.* Trans. Jane E. Lewin. Ithaca: Cornell UP, 1980.

Hochman, Barbara. "A Portrait of the Writer as a Young Actress: Dreiser's *Sister Carrie.*" *New Essays on Sister Carrie.* Ed. Donald Pizer. New York: Cambridge UP, 1991. 43–64.

———. "The Rewards of Representation: Edith Wharton, Lily Bart, and the Writer/Reader Interchange." *Novel* 24 (1991): 147–61.

Holland, Norman. *The Dynamics of Literary Response.* New York: Norton, 1975.

Iser, Wolfgang. *The Implied Reader: Patterns of Communication in Prose Fiction from Bunyan to Beckett.* Baltimore: Johns Hopkins UP, 1974.

Kaplan, Amy. *The Social Construction of American Realism.* Chicago: U of Chicago P, 1988.

Keats, John. "On First Looking into Chapman's Homer." *The Poetical Works of John Keats.* Ed. H. W. Garrod. London: Oxford UP, 1956. 38.

Kendrick, Walter M. *The Novel Machine.* Baltimore: Johns Hopkins UP, 1980.

Kenner, Hugh. "The Promised Land." *A Homemade World: The American Modernist Writer.* New York: Morrow, 1975. 20–49.

Lockridge, Ernest H., ed. *Twentieth Century Interpretations of* The Great Gatsby. New Jersey: Prentice, 1968.

McCormick, John O. *The Middle Distance.* New York: Free P, 1971.

Michaels, Walter Benn. *The Gold Standard and the Logic of Naturalism.* Berkeley: U of California P, 1987.

Michelson, Bruce. "The Myth of Gatsby." *Modern Fiction Studies* 26 (1981): 563–77.

Miller, D. A. *Narrative and its Discontents.* Princeton: Princeton UP, 1981.

Norris, Frank. "The Novel With a Purpose." *The Literary Criticism of Frank Norris.* Ed. Donald Pizer. New York: Russell, 1976. 90–93.

Ong, Walter. *Orality and Literacy: The Technologizing of the Word.* New York: Routledge, 1991.

Poulet, Georges. "The Self and the Other in Critical Consciousness." *Diacritics* 2 (1972): 46–50.

Seltzer, Mark. *Bodies and Machines.* New York: Routledge, 1992.

Steig, Michael. *Stories of Reading.* Baltimore: Johns Hopkins UP, 1989.

Trilling, Lionel. "F. Scott Fitzgerald." *The Liberal Imagination.* New York: Doubleday, 1953.

Turnbull, Andrew. *F. Scott Fitzgerald.* New York: Scribner's, 1962.

Weinstein, Arnold. "Fiction as Greatness: The Case of Gatsby." *Novel* 19 (1985): 22–38.

Wharton, Edith. *A Backward Glance.* New York: Scribner's, 1964.

———. *The House of Mirth.* New York: Signet, 1964.

Wilson, Christopher. *The Labor of Words: Literary Professionalism in the Progressive Era.* Athens: U of Georgia P, 1985.

ALBERTO LENA

Deceitful Traces of Power: An Analysis of the Decadence of Tom Buchanan in The Great Gatsby

When Ernest Hemingway first published *The Snows of Kilimanjaro* in *Esquire* (1936), the story contained an explicit reference to F. Scott Fitzgerald's relationship with the rich:

> The rich were dull and they drank too much ... they were dull and they were repetitious. ... He remembered poor [Scott Fitzgerald] and his romantic awe of them and how he had started a story once that began, 'The rich are different from you and me.' And how someone had said to [Scott], Yes, they have more money. But that was not humorous to [Scott]. He thought they were a special glamorous race and when he found they weren't it wrecked him just as much as any other thing that wrecked him. ([1939] 1967, 72)

Having read the text and spent a sleepless night worrying about his part in it, Fitzgerald urged Hemingway not to print his name in the story.[1] Having required this of him, he also enclosed the following comment: "Riches have never fascinated me, unless combined with the greatest charm and distinction" ("Fitzgerald to Hemingway, August, 1936," in Fitzgerald 1963, 311). Hemingway's remarks about Fitzgerald clearly show the degree of bitterness that was now present in his relationship with his old Paris friend; moreover,

From *Canadian Review of American Studies* 28, no. 1 (1998): 19–41. © 1998 by the Graduate Centre for the Study of Drama, University of Toronto.

they also demonstrate his apparent forgetfulness, or, at least, his fragmentary knowledge of Fitzgerald's work. For in 1925, Fitzgerald had launched one of his sharpest and most devastating attacks on the upper classes, in the form of his character Tom Buchanan, the Long Island millionaire in *The Great Gatsby* ([1925] 1991). Shortly after finishing the novel, Fitzgerald expressed his satisfaction with the character in a letter to Maxwell Perkins: "I suppose he's the best character I've ever done—I think he and the brother in *Salt* and Hurtswood in *Sister Carrie* are the three best characters in American fiction in the last twenty years" ("Fitzgerald to Perkins, December 20, 1924," in Fitzgerald 1963, 173). Certainly, Tom Buchanan is one of the pivotal characters in Fitzgerald's *The Great Gatsby*. Whereas its eponymous central character embodies the stereotype of the self-made man who has risen from nowhere, Buchanan represents the type of millionaire that is anchored in a solid tradition of socially acceptable (because inherited) wealth, and of the power derived from it. As Tony Tanner points out: "Buchanan is no more grounded in, or significantly related to, ancient American history than Gatsby" (1990, xii). His social exterior, which primarily consists of an awareness of his own wealth and the respectability that he derives from it, provides him with a fixed identity, in sharp contrast to Gatsby, who is forever seeking to create his own personality afresh.[2] In many ways, Tom Buchanan embodies the decadence of the upper classes. As the twin notions of decline and decay lie at the heart of the novel, I suggest that an analysis of the various facets of Tom Buchanan's wealth and character are instrumental in understanding the limits of Fitzgerald's fascination with riches, and also the reasons behind an attraction that led Malcolm Cowley to denominate some of his works within the category of the romance of money (Cowley 1973, 19).[3]

The Imperfect Millionaire

At the beginning of the novel, Nick Carraway's description of Buchanan becomes a vehicle for cataloguing his status as a millionaire by inheritance:

> His family were enormously wealthy—even in college his freedom with money was a matter for reproach—but now he'd left Chicago and come east in a fashion that rather took your breath away: for instance he'd brought down a string of polo ponies from Lake Forest. It was hard to realize that a man in my own generation was wealthy enough to do that. (Fitzgerald [1925] 1991, 9–10)

In a few lines Carraway furnishes the reader with essential information by mentioning the source of Buchanan's income as well as his spending habits.

Thus, his enormous inheritance renders him the diametrical opposite of the self-made man, a concept forged at the end of the nineteenth century.[4] The concept of the self-made man lays emphasis on the fact that the millionaire is the product of the laws of natural selection and, in that struggle for survival, his money becomes a token of his successful adaptation to the environment. As Graham Summer argues:

> The Millionaires may fairly be regarded as the naturally selected agents of society for certain work. They get high wages and live in luxury, but the bargain is a good one for society. This assures us that all who are competent for this function will be employed in it, so that the cost of it will be reduced to the lowest terms. (1914, 90)

Unlike the social Darwinists who used Jean Lamarck's doctrine of inheritance to prove that the successful individual passed his economic virtues on to the following generation, the new millionaires emerging from the Gilded Age promulgated the myth of the self-made man. This myth stressed the notion that the most important goal was individual betterment. This could be achieved by a combination of sustained hard work and strength of character, no matter how obscure one's social origins were. As J. F. Wall said, it was an essential part of the American dream to believe that the most fit sons in the race for material success were sired by fathers who had failed in that race (1970, 380). The genius associated with the creator of wealth was a product of the slums rather than of comfortable colonial mansions.[5] Andrew Carnegie ponders on this idea in "The Advantages of Poverty":

> Let one select the three or four names, the supremely great in every field of human triumph, and note how small is the contribution of hereditary rank and wealth to the short list of immortals who have lifted and advanced the race. It will, I think, be seen that the possession of these is almost fatal to greatness and goodness, and that the greatest and best of our race have necessarily been nurtured in the bracing school of poverty—the only school capable of producing the supremely great, the genius. (1962, 64)

By and large, hereditary wealth had endowed its possessors with negative traits. With this in mind, Carnegie voices the following questions: "Why should men leave great fortunes to their children? If this is done from affection, is it not misguided affection?" (19). In fact, money earned without labour was an invitation to corruption in the eyes of a Republican nation and it was assumed that hereditary wealth had caused the decline of Europe. Drawing

again on Andrew Carnegie's writing we can understand the full implications of this issue. For he states explicitly that, "instances of millionaires' sons
unspoilt by wealth ... are rare" (20). What Carnegie had in mind was that
the millionaire, although by definition wealthy, should never forget the relationship between his wealth and the community from which his income was
derived; "the duty of the man of wealth: to set an example of modest, unos-
tentatious living, shunning display or extravagance" (25). The generation of
Carnegie, John D. Rockefeller, Enoch Pratt, and James J. Hill was aware of
the dangers of hereditary wealth because, as Wall points out, they feared the
consequences of dynastic wealth that would restrict the list of entrants more
than they welcomed the possibility of society evolving towards perfection if
social advancement depended upon a closed society (1970, 380). Dynastic
wealth was indeed seen as alien both to the productive process and to the
progress of society. In light of this tradition, we can appreciate that Carraway's first impressions of Tom Buchanan are designed to portray the latter,
because of his extravagant use of wealth as much as the fact that it is inherited
(the latter automatically renders him the antithesis of the self-made man). In
the 1920s, the hereditary millionaire had become simply a consumer who had
laid aside his role as a producer. As I shall show below, the novel develops this
aspect of Buchanan's personality in detail.[6]

Carraway's subsequent description of Buchanan's habits and features
serve to show the status of the latter as a millionaire. The first time that Carraway meets Buchanan, he appears "in riding clothes ... standing with his
legs apart on the front porch" (Fitzgerald [1925] 1991, 10). Both his sport
clothes and his relaxed pose suggest a way of life that has nothing to do
with the actual creation of wealth by means of productive labour. Indeed,
Buchanan's only real interests (his string of polo ponies, for example) seem to
be identical to those associated with the European aristocracy, men of gentle
breeding who maintain liveries of horses. Buchanan fits into the category
of the leisure class, a term coined by Thorstein Veblen (1934).[7] The leisure
class consists of a group of individuals who live on the fruits of the industrial
community rather than within it. Their main features, as depicted by Veblen,
are their manifest consumption and their equally obtrusive leisure. Both of
these features denote the respectability of the millionaire and emphasize that
he can allow himself to waste his money and time on idle amusements and
unnecessary goods, whereas the rest of the industrial population has to per-
form manual work in order to survive (Veblen 1934, 70).

The Instinctual Leisure Class

Carraway's subsequent descriptions of Buchanan's activities accentuate his
links with this class, especially in his association of Buchanan's life with

sports. A rugby player at the university and now a polo player, Buchanan's wealth allows him to play sports everywhere. In fact, sports rather than business seem to determine his activities and movements throughout the world. Thus, he "drifted here and there unrestfully wherever people played polo and were rich together" (Fitzgerald [1925] 1991, 10). Sports play an essential role in Veblen's description of the leisure class. According to his theory, this class had their origins in feudal society, when labour was no longer honoured by the community. In such a community, the leaders were hunters and warriors and, as such, they were excused from menial chores. Since this period, fighting had been a common way of life for this class, and Veblen insisted that the modern enjoyment of sports, especially athletic games, among the upper classes in the pecuniary age could be seen as evidence of a combative instinct: "Sports . . . afford an exercise for dexterity and for the emulative ferocity and astuteness characteristic of predatory life" (1934, 255). This explains why Buchanan is very often associated with physical violence. Thus, during a party in his New York apartment he breaks the nose of his mistress, Myrtle, in one of his outbursts of brutality. Moreover, when Carraway meets him walking on the street, he cannot fail to notice that

> he was walking ahead of me along Fifth Avenue in his alert, aggressive way, his hands out a little from his body as if to fight off interference, his head moving sharply here and there, adapting itself to his restless eyes. (Fitzgerald [1925] 1991, 166)

Carraway shows Buchanan in a permanently warlike attitude, like that of a predator even in a moment of apparent ease such as a stroll along the street. In Buchanan's descriptions, there is much to echo Veblen's reference to the leisure class as the class most likely to display bold aggression and an alert sense of status. Thus, Carraway refers to a conversation with Buchanan during their college days in which the combination of the latter's stance and tone of voice appear to convey the following message: "'Now, don't think my opinion on these matters is final,' he seemed to say, 'just because I'm stronger and more of a man than you are.'" (11). Buchanan is always eager to affirm his physical superiority over everyone else, although his affirmations are often expressed in terms that show evidence of a dubious sort of reasoning. For Veblen, behind the cloak of virtue with which the members of the leisure class envelop their lives, there lurks a type of person whose manners bear close resemblance to those of a barbarian. The explanation for this lies in the fact that in the past the sort of individual who had gained entrance to this class "was gifted with clannishness, massiveness, ferocity, unscrupulousness" (1934,

236). These were the qualities that counted in order to acquire full member-ship into the highest social class, and, for Veblen, these qualities still endure in the supposedly civilized members of the leisure class.

There are other factors of personality that Buchanan shares with Veblen's leisure class, and these also serve to highlight his chicanery, as the following description of the behaviour of Buchanan and his wife, Daisy, reveals:

> They were careless people, Tom and Daisy—they smashed up things and creatures and then retreated back into their money or their vast carelessness, or whatever it was that kept them together, and let other people clean up the mess they had made. (Fitzgerald [1925] 1991, 167)

This quote is interesting because it shows two levels of carelessness. Firstly, there is the carelessness shown by smashing things up, and then, a retreat into "vast carelessness." This retreat implies that they are careless of the consequences of their actions, which is a sign of social power. Thus, the initial thoughtlessness is compounded with the callousness of one who knows his actions hold no personal consequences for him, and is not capable of recogniz-ing the misery that he has inflicted upon others as such. The Buchanans behave irresponsibly and thereby bear out Veblen's opinion that force, fraud, and chica-nery are the province of the leisure class (1934, 273–74). These features survive in the leisure class during a pecuniary era. It is no wonder that Veblen believes that the man who belongs to this class may be treated as a delinquent:

> The ideal pecuniary man is like the ideal delinquent in his unscrupulous conversion of goods and persons to his own ends, and in a callous disregard of the feelings and wishes of others and of the remoter effects of his actions. (1934, 237)

Finally, Tom Buchanan's relationship with the economic forces of produc-tion strengthens his links to the leisure class, and draws attention to the perils presented by the power of the latter and the influence which it exerts upon all levels of society.[8] These issues are developed in an episode during which, after Buchanan has asked Carraway about his job, they engage in the following dialogue:

> "What are you, doing, Nick?"
> "I'm a bond man."
> "Who with [sic]?"
> I told him.

"[sic] Never heard of them," he remarked decisively.
This annoyed me.
"You will," I answered shortly. "You will if you stay in the
East." (Fitzgerald [1925] 1991, 13)

At the beginning of the novel, Carraway mentions that everybody he
knew was employed in the bond business; even his uncles and aunts have
heard of it and have recommended that he should get a job in it. Therefore,
within this context, Buchanan's answer puts him at the same distance from the
dealers, and probably in the same frame of reference as the aunts and uncles,
who know only slightly more about the bond business. Carraway shows the
narrowness of Buchanan's social sphere, and his lack of experience outside the
confines of the parochial world that he has been a part of until his move east.
Admittedly, Buchanan could be said to be looking after his own affairs by
only paying attention to the trading conducted by the big established firms,
who would be likely to give him the best long-terms returns (with the lowest risk) on his inherited wealth. However, Veblen emphasises the gulf that
separated the leisure class from the immediate productive process. This causes
him to designate the leisure class as predatory because its activities have little
to do with the actual creation of wealth through productive labour and, in
this respect, Buchanan certainly conforms to the criteria of the leisure class,
for, in all except the broadest terms, he clearly has no idea of the workings
of even secondary industries such as the bond trade. Veblen even goes so far
as to state that "the office of the leisure class in social evolution is to retard
the movement and to conserve what is obsolescent" (1934, 198). Therefore,
the preeminence of the leisure class represents a symbol of social decay, and,
in this light, Buchanan's aggressive manners, chicanery, and obsession with
sport prove not only his personal degeneration, but also highlight his place as
a handicap to the progress of society.

Prescriptive Morality and Decadence
Buchanan's muscularity provides us with a new context to understand the
novel. Carraway in his description of Buchanan, places considerable emphasis on his physical traits:

"Not even the effeminate swank of his riding clothes could hide the
enormous power of that body—he seemed to fill those glistening
boots until he strained the top lacing and you could see a great
pack of muscle shifting when his shoulder moved under his thin
coat. It was a body capable of enormous leverage—a cruel body."
(Fitzgerald [1925] 1991, 11).

Buchanan's main characteristic is precisely his muscularity, which makes him "a man of physical accomplishments" rather than a man of the mind. His strength serves to heighten his tendency towards brutality. Daisy describes him as "a big hulking physical specimen" (15). Throughout the novel, Buchanan is described as a massive body directed by a simple mind. Thus, Carraway refers to Buchanan's reaction when he discovers that his wife may have a lover by commenting: "There is no confusion like the confusion of a simple mind" (117). During his description of his last meeting with Buchanan, he stresses the latter's lack of mental maturity: "I felt suddenly as though I were talking to a child." In contrast, Gatsby is described as a man with "a lot of brain power[,]" engaged "in improving his mind" (157, 162). Judging by his "GENERAL RESOLVES [sic]," Gatsby appears extremely keen to learn useful knowledge after the fashion of Benjamin Franklin: "read one improving book or magazine per week" (161). In order to explain the disparity of mind and muscularity which these two characters display, I shall turn to Henry L. Mencken's interpretation of Nietzsche. Fitzgerald was familiar with Mencken's *The Philosophy of Nietzsche* (1908), and he read the book before writing *The Great Gatsby*.[9] In Mencken's book, as in the novel, the idea of civilization and the causes of its decay receive a great deal of attention. Mencken interpreted the concept of civilization in Nietzsche's writing as the dynamic tension between three castes: "The first class comprises those who are obviously superior to the mass intellectually; the second includes those whose eminence is chiefly muscular, and the third is made of the mediocre" (163). Common to each class is a particular notion of morality as well as of perfection.

There is much in common between Buchanan and the members of this second class. To the second class belong the guardians and keepers of order and security "—above all, the highest types of warrior, the judges and defenders of the law" (164). The novel shows that Tom Buchanan embodies a combination of warrior attributes (his brutality and muscularity), together with an obsessive 'lip-service' to law and order, in spite of his infidelity and the often criminal expression of its brutality. An example of this tendency is to be found in Buchanan's defence of family values: "Nowadays people begin by sneering at family life and family institutions and next they'll throw everything overboard" (Fitzgerald [1925] 1991, 122). In his attack on Gatsby, Buchanan emphasises the illegal sources which lie behind the former's wealth and flamboyance: "'Who are you anyhow?' broke out Tom. 'You're one of that bunch that hangs around with Meyer Wolfshiem'" (125). In his defence of the "status quo," which, as a useless millionaire, he depends on, Buchanan attempts to appear morally upright in a negative sense, by trying to unmask Gatsby's activities as a bootlegger, who collaborates with Wolfshiem, a paid-up member of the underworld.

Gatsby falls into the category of the first caste: that of the rulers. "Its members accept the world as they find it and make the best of it" and "their delight [lies] in self governing"(Mencken 1908,163). Like Gatsby, who breaks with his past by reinventing himself (as Carraway points out, "the truth was that Jay Gatsby, of West Egg, Long Island, sprang from his Platonic conception of himself" [Fitzgerald (1925) 1991, 93]), these individuals of the first caste are the creators of their own values and pay no heed to law and conventions. As Mencken said of this type of man, "his joy is in combatting and in overcoming—in pitting his will to power against the laws and desires of the rest of humanity" (1908, 169). In relation to the members of this first caste, the common man "is almost entirely lacking in this gorgeous, fatalistic courage and sublime egotism" (170). That Carraway perceives this spirit to be an integral part of Gatsby's character is demonstrated by the following description of him: "There was something gorgeous about him, some heightened sensitivity to the premises of life" (Fitzgerald [1925] 1991, 6). He represents an affirmation of life and all its possibilities without paying heed either to norms or to social prescriptions. Driven by his desire to possess Daisy at any price, his "vitalistic dream," Gatsby becomes a gangster, thus displaying his lack of "conventional" morality.

Efficiency is the other essential attribute of the ruling class. As I have mentioned, the novel emphasises that Gatsby is a highly efficient individual who even uses his spare time to study electricity; even at his parties, he is always alert to telephone calls relating to his business affairs, whereas Buchanan receives calls only from his mistress and seems to be reluctant to learn anything new about economic life. In Mencken's interpretation of Nietzsche, this attribute is essential in order to understand fully the differences between the first and second caste. The second caste are an inefficient class in terms of their control of the wealth of the world. The aristocracy belongs to the second caste, and, in order to protect its position,

> it hedges itself about with purely artificial barriers. Next only to its desire to maintain itself without actual personal effort was its jealous endeavour to prevent accessions to its ranks. (1908, 166)

Mencken also remarks that Nietzsche favoured what he considered to be the true aristocracy, which was a class with a high regard for efficiency. Moreover, what would prevent a society from falling into decadence was that "there should always be, . . . a free and constant interchange of individuals between the three castes of men" (166). Here we see the issue at the very heart of *The Great Gatsby*: the confrontation between a man of the second caste and a newcomer from the third caste now raised to the caste of the rulers. Nick Carraway's choice of Gatsby as the representative of the American dream implies that it is an amoral ideal, because Gatsby has acquired his wealth through criminal activities.[10] Moreover, he has no compunction about appearing in public with gangsters such as Wolfshiem.[11] Given this element of amorality at the core of the society depicted by Mencken and Fitzgerald, Gatsby's emergence as Buchanan's antagonist is justified. We can find the key to this issue, when at the end of the novel, Nick Carraway reflects upon Gatsby's failure by utilising the following description of Manhattan Island:

> As the moon rose higher the inessential houses began to melt away until gradually I became aware of the old island here that flowered once for Dutch sailors's eyes—a fresh, green breast of the new world. Its vanished trees, the trees that had made way for Gatsby's house, had once pandered in whispers to the last and greatest of all human dreams. (Fitzgerald [1925] 1991, 168)

Clearly, the beginning of the American civilization involved conquest, aggression, and destruction. There is an element at the very birth of the American civilization which goes hand in hand with amorality and dreams. The "fresh, green, breast of the new world" is connected with rape and aggressive masculinity. The vanished trees represent the dominion of man over nature as an limited will to power, while the fact that they "pandered in whispers" to this human dream shows how deeply the amorality of aggression and conquest is rooted: the trees, according to the narrator, almost invite their own end by simply growing there. As Tony Tanner says in his analysis of this paragraph, "Fitzgerald knows, of course, exactly what he is doing. He wants to show America desecrated, mutilated, violated" (1990, 1). Carraway links Gatsby with the American past by stressing elements of violent desire at the heart of the American dream. Implicitly, the source of Buchanan's riches are included in this, albeit that they are protected by law and morality, because, of all the characters in the novel, he is certainly the most grounded in and ancestrally related to American history. Critics have remarked on Fitzgerald's artistic success in transposing this paragraph from the first chapter of the novel to its end.[12] Yet it is significant that Fitzgerald had previously placed this paragraph at the beginning of the novel shortly after Nick Carraway had visited Buchanan's "red and white Georgian Colonial mansion," for this original placement serves to link the source of both Gatsby's and Buchanan's riches to forces of aggression and exploitation. Buchanan uses the defence of law and order to hide his decadence and, implicitly, his amorality. Additionally, the novel's representative of the American West, Dan Cody, shares the same lack of morality, which is portrayed as a feature of its original corruption. When he returns to the east, Dan Cody is "the pioneer debauchee, who during one phase of American life brought back ... the savage violence of the frontier brothel and saloon" (Fitzgerald [1925] 1991, 95). As C. W. E. Bigsby indicates, "the West has long since been corrupted by the forbears of Buchanan, Gatsby and even Carraway" (1971, 133). Moreover, the conclusion of the book suggests that the urge to conquer and dominate is endemic in the entire American psyche.

Appropriating Racism
Another piece of Buchanan's decay can be found in his defence of racist ideas.[13] In the course of a dinner at East Egg, he bursts out:

> "Civilization's [sic] going to pieces, ... I've gotten to be a terrible pessimist about things. Have you read 'The Rise of the Coloured Empires' by this man Goddard?"
> "Well, it's a fine book and everybody ought to read it. The idea is if we don't look out the white race will be—will be utterly submerged. It's all scientific stuff; it's been proved." (Fitzgerald [1925] 1991, 16)

As Mick Gidley (1973) points out, Goddard is an amalgam of the names of two race thinkers: Madison Grant (1865–1937) and Lothrop Stoddard (1883–1950).[14] The book that Buchanan is referring to is *The Rising Tide of Color*, written by the latter in 1920. However, during the course of the conversation quoted above, Buchanan appropriates the main points of Grant's argument: "This idea is that we're Nordics ... and we've produced all the things that go to make civilization—oh, science and art and all that. Do you see?" (16). The primacy of the Nordic race over all others had been put forward by Madison Grant in his book *The Passing of the Great Race* (1918). Grant argued that due to a process of natural selection, the Nordic race had achieved a status which made it entirely responsible for all progress and civilization. Its roots were in the Baltic regions where the harsh environment had imposed upon the inhabitants a rigid elimination of defects, which eventually created the fittest possible race. The Nordic race had expanded through the world, creating the roots of civilization in the south of Europe and America. Grant stressed that for any nation, the amount of Nordic blood was a fair measure of its strength in war as well as its standing in civilization. Wherever it went, the Nordic race marked a new vigorous period of higher civilization. The thesis of Grant rests upon the idea that "physical features" denote superior "mental and spiritual qualities," and that material success and political dominance are in themselves evidence of racial superiority (1918, 39, 43, 81–82, 188–97).[15]

Later in the novel, during his argument with Gatsby, Buchanan uses the "intermarriage between black and white" (Fitzgerald [1925] 1991, 122) as a sign of the decay of various social and cultural institutions. Buchanan seems to echo Stoddard's interpretation of the peril presented to America by the expansion in numbers of its black population, a thesis which made his reputation as the most popular American racist of the 1920s.[16] In *The Rising Tide of Color*, Stoddard expresses great concern as to the possibility that the United States might follow the same course as South America, where, in his view, the white race had degenerated by mixing its blood with that of the Indian. Using this paradigm, he envisioned the expansion of the black race as a return to primitive barbarism. Bearing this in mind, it is no wonder that Tom Buchanan is attracted to Stoddard's theories, since the latter associates mixed blood with political anarchy, using the examples of South America and the decline of the Roman Empire (Stoddard 1971, 168). As an unproductive member of society, Buchanan needs to defend his social position. As a hereditary millionaire, he is conscious of the importance of tradition and social order as devices by which to retain his position. His racist remarks also contrast with the eruption of the Harlem Renaissance and the search for wider recognition undertaken by many black intellectuals at that time who sought for dignity within American society. Buchanan simply cannot cope with the idea of change in society.[17]

Paradoxically, the fact that he appropriates this ideology only serves to underscore his weakness. The Nordic race may embody vigour as well as mental and spiritual energies in Grant's and Stoddard's peculiar interpretations, but the fact is that these qualities are totally absent from Buchanan's life, an irony which serves only to lampoon his apparent power. Indeed, the stark contrast between what Buchanan pretends to be (a vigorous individual who embodies the creativity of the Nordic race) and what he really is (a millionaire lacking in imagination and intellect who owes his privileged position in society to the efforts of previous generations), serves to throw his decadence into sharp relief. For Buchanan represents a type of man without a future, as Carraway describes him: "A national figure in a way, one of those men who reach such an acute limited excellence at twenty-one that everything afterwards savours of anti-climax" (Fitzgerald [1925] 1991, 9). This man who once possessed "an acute limited excellence" shows his deficiencies by appropriating this particular ideology. Stoddard emphasises that "an instinctive vitality" had put the Nordic race in its position of privilege because the "greater or less degree of vigour in people depends on the power of its vital instinct." (1971, 168). Yet that vital instinct, if not utterly lost, as it undoubtedly is in the case of the character Wilson, is certainly wavering in Buchanan's case.[18] He is not aware that the decadence of civilization lies not so much in the external threats of the new riches nor in the expansion of the blacks, as in himself and his own inefficiency.

When Order Unmasks Chaos

One of the greatest artistic achievements of the novel lies in the association of the main characters (Buchanan and Gatsby) with specific environments. On the one hand, Buchanan's East Egg Georgian mansion overlooking the bay represents order. Its French windows, sun-dial lawns, and brick walls suggest respectability and a continuity with the past. On the other hand, Gatsby's West Egg environment is closer to a "fantastic dream," a grotesque El Greco picture in which only drunkenness, carelessness, distortion, and chaos appear to thrive, and, moreover, with no sense of continuity. Yet, East Egg, behind its facade of order, is much closer to West Egg than it appears to be at first sight.

During the night of the car accident which kills Myrtle Wilson, Nick Carraway returns to Buchanan's East Egg mansion after an absence of three months. Looking through the blinds, he manages to spot Daisy and Tom "sitting opposite each other at the kitchen table with a plate of cold fried chicken between them and two bottles of ale" (Fitzgerald [1925] 1991, 136). It is a scene which denotes a strange intimacy, which becomes stranger because it has occurred shortly after, and, we infer, has been caused by the tragic death of an innocent woman. Buchanan is intently talking at Daisy, and the fact that neither of them have touched the chicken or the ale leads Carraway to believe that they are both "conspiring together" (136). The fact that neither has partaken of the superficially 'homely' element of the scene (that is, their supper) renders the meal an aesthetic rather than a functional requirement, contrived, like their conspiracy itself, to give their destructive relationship a veneer of stability. Thus, they are, ironically, alienated from the very substances which appear initially to convey a domestic cosiness. Finally, the conspiracy is acted out when Wilson kills Gatsby at the swimming pool and then commits suicide.

Carraway finds the proof of his suspicions when he accidentally and unavoidably meets Buchanan in the street, after everything has appeared to come to a conclusion. When he asks about what Buchanan said to Wilson during the afternoon of the accident, the latter's answer is revealing:

"I told him the truth" he said. "He came to the door while we were getting ready to leave.... He was crazy enough to kill me if I hadn't told him who owned the car...." He broke off defiantly, "What if I

did tell him? That fellow had it coming to him. He threw dust into
your eyes just like he did in Daisy's but he was a tough one. He
ran over Myrtle like you'd run over a dog and never even stopped
his car." (166)

By telling Carraway that he informed Wilson who the car belonged to,
Buchanan reveals his active role in Gatsby's holocaust. His complicity in the
crime shows the wealthy inhabitant of East Egg to be a covert agent of chaos
to a far greater degree than anyone from West Egg that we meet during the
course of the novel. Under the brick walls and colonial order lies the seed of
chaos. If West Egg is unconventional and grotesque in Carraway's eyes, East
Egg is no less disturbing, and is possibly more dangerous, since it has a misleading veneer of stable order. Moreover, Buchanan's revenge accentuates the
main features of his social decay. His destruction of Gatsby, which avoids any
direct confrontation through the subtle means that he employs, and his subsequent denial of any responsibility for his actions display a degree of cunning
and sophisticated contrivance which are the exclusive province of Nietzsche's
class of "*ressentiment.*" The theme of *ressentiment* was introduced by Nietzsche
in his *Genealogy of Morals* (1910), which Fitzgerald read during his composition of the novel (Sklar 1967, 151). For Nietzsche, *ressentiment* is directly
associated with decadence, being a revenge perpetrated by weak persons on
their superiors. This form of premeditated revenge represents a compensation
for their lack of any proper outlet for vital action (1910, 10).

Whereas, for the true aristocrat, self-affirmation springs from a triumphant affirmation of his own demands, the slave requires that all objective
stimuli be capable of action; therefore, "his action is a reaction" (35). During
much of the novel Buchanan acts as a passive individual. Even his eventual
action is only responsive, whereas Gatsby creates his own self in a burst of
initiative that marks the beginning of his social rise. Moreover, although a
gangster, Gatsby is still capable of an aristocratic form of honour. Although
he has the possibility of escaping to Chicago, he decides to stand by Daisy
after the accident. However, Buchanan, who is driven by a slave morality and
is obsessed with preserving his reputation and possessions, never runs risks.
Satisfied by his revenge, Buchanan returns to his former passive state, envel-
oped in the security of the comforts of his colonial mansion. In his revenge
and in his inability to forget, he shows his *ressentiment,* and the very essence
of the slave mentality which characterizes his decadence.

Tom Buchanan confirms Carnegie's suspicions of hereditary wealth as
an element of decadence in American society. In fact, heritage, in both a social
and a biological sense, represents the key to understanding his personality as
well as his place in the novel. His social heritage places him in the position

of a member of the leisure class, that is, mainly as a consumer rather than a creator of wealth for society. His own inefficiency explains his conservative position, for he is afraid of both the power of the newly rich, such as Gatsby, and of the political transformations which may emerge from the proliferation of new races in society. Above all, he is portrayed as a delinquent protected by social conventions which conceal his misdeeds, who tries to camouflage his misbehaviour by appealing to a moral order.

Buchanan, Gatsby, and Fitzgerald: Wealth and The American Dream

The features of Jay Gatsby's personality described in this article serve to contextualize his sudden arrival in a wider sense. Buchanan represents the individual who is unsuited to the labours of ordinary life. His extreme moral degeneration gives new meaning to the role that Gatsby plays. Although he is, in the broader terms of his society, a delinquent, Gatsby embodies a series of virtues that are totally lacking in the America of which Tom Buchanan is paradigmatic, such as vitality, efficiency, loyalty, and the necessity of a realisable dream. What the novel suggests is that in a world dominated by millionaires such as Buchanan, it becomes more and more difficult for men like Gatsby, whatever their mistakes and deficiencies, to climb the social ladder without partaking of the corruption that is associated with the leisure class. In the long run, it seems probable that Buchanan's class would dictate the rules of the society to which Gatsby aspires, thus making it hard for such self-made men to escape its corrosive influence.[19]

Tom Buchanan's brutal amorality overshadows Gatsby's selfishness and his disregard for any principles, and highlights the latter's eventual acceptance of responsibility (he chooses to stand by Daisy in the aftermath of the accident), which ultimately renders him vulnerable. Additionally, Buchanan's extreme, yet curiously unmanly brutality (exemplified when he breaks Myrtle's nose at the party) reveals him as a debauched member of the leisure class. This has the effect of making Nick Carraway stress the hints of honesty in Gatsby (as when he emphasises how "grateful" he feels when Gatsby makes it clear that he actually did go to Oxford) and of ignoring the more obscure aspects of the latter's past, but only in the company of Buchanan. Carraway's acceptance of his friend's dubious methods of captivating Daisy is another aspect of this personal loathing for Buchanan, and of his need to defend Gatsby against the brutality with which the former is synonymous within the context of the narrative.

Much of the novel's treatment of the power which is derived from money reveals the continuities in Fitzgerald's thought regarding the role of wealth in America, from *This Side of Paradise* (1948) to *The Great Gatsby*.[20] The position of Buchanan, as well as that of Gatsby, reveals the possibilities that wealth can

create in society, and that each individual is responsible for the uses to which
he puts his capital. Consequently, the inconsistency between what Buchanan
would like to be perceived as, and what he actually is, does not necessarily
imply that Fitzgerald condemns the importance of wealth in society. Preoccupied with this seeming dichotomy, Fitzgerald started to write the novel on
25 August 1924. In May 1921, he wrote the following letter from Rome to
Edmund Wilson:

> God damn the continent of Europe. [sic] It is merely antiquarian
> interest. Rome is only a few years behind Tyre and Babylon.... I
> think it's a shame that England and America didn't let Germany
> conquer Europe. It's the only thing that would have saved the fleet
> of tottering old wrecks.... You may have spoken in jest about
> New York as the capital of culture but in 25 years it will be just
> as London is now. Culture follows money and all the refinements
> of aestheticism can't stare off its change of seat (Christ! what a
> metaphor). We will be the Romans in the next generations as the
> English are now. (1963, 326–27)

Although these words have no direct reference to the stereotyped character who was later to become Buchanan, they show a number of similarities between Fitzgerald and his fictional protege; both uphold the power of
money and the idea of amorality and imperialism as the bases of civilization
and progress. However, if culture follows money, which implies the ability to
put the latter to imaginative use, Gatsby, rather than Buchanan, should be
associated with the highest social class. Fitzgerald's words show his internal
division when writing *The Great Gatsby*, which is illustrated by the opposing
qualities of Gatsby and Buchanan: the repellence of Buchanan as a character
sits well with the self-appraisal (shown above) of a reluctant imperialist who
hates the intellectual connotations of his own imperialism. My conclusion is
that, in *The Great Gatsby*, Fitzgerald has not broken free from his identifica-
tion of power, money, and amorality as the roots of progress and civilization.
Rather, in many respects, the book is a celebration of these elements of the
United States. However, it should also be seen as a criticism of the individuals
who wish to appropriate wealth without the concomitant cultural responsibility that Fitzgerald attaches to it, and the difficulties that this group create
for those who are directly below them and who are attempting to improve
their position, while also adhering to their moral code.[21]

In conclusion, *The Great Gatsby* can be seen not so much as an illustra-
tion of the decline of the Western world in general, or of American civilization in particular, but of individuals like Tom Buchanan, Daisy, and Jordan

Backer. After all, luck, rather than the system, sustains the Buchanans' "vast carelessness" and Gatsby's death is due to sheer accident, and not because he is too weak to continue his fight against Buchanan. The whole novel is pervaded by ambiguity as regards the idea of the decadence of the West. Thus, as C. W. E. Bigsby comments, New York in the novel represents "corruption and graft but, with its towering white buildings, it seems to contain the essence of that pure dream of national and self-fulfilment" (1971, 134).[22] These issues illustrate that whatever views of the American dream which Fitzgerald may have perceived during the writing of *The Great Gatsby*, he still adheres to his visions of 1921, to his celebration of amorality, power, and money. Nick Carraway's election of Gatsby as the representative of the American Dream is the greatest single proof of this. In this respect, *The Great Gatsby* occupies a position which is close to the halfway mark in Fitzgerald's intellectual development. In this novel, he is still far from attacking the corruption of the whole system and of the American dream with the all-pervasive bitterness of *Tender is the Night* (1934) and *The Last Tycoon* (1941). However, it would appear that by 1925 he had still not managed to rid himself of many of the ideas concerning the links between individualism, corruption, and capitalism which are present in *This Side of Paradise* and *The Beautiful and the Damned* (1950). This prompts me to conclude that *The Great Gatsby* represents a criticism of individual attitudes towards wealth rather than of the system itself, which, if it does not remain untouched, is not by any means completely destroyed.

NOTES

My thanks to Michael Wood for his encouragement, and to Juan José Coy, Mick Gidley, Alun Munslow, Joachim Stanley, Juan A. Merino for their comments and help.

1. In the 1967 reprint, the name "Scott Fitzgerald" was changed to "Julian."

2. Roger Lewis has stressed Gatsby's paradoxical position of having no external context with which to endow his sudden arrival to the world of wealth with meaning (cited in Bruccoli 1985, 47).

3. See Mick Gidley (1973, 171–72); Robert Sklar (1967, 135–56); Robert W. Stallman (1955, 5–12).

4. On social Darwinism in America, see Carl Degler (1991, 15–21); and Richard Hofstadter (1945, 25–36).

5. On Carnegie's use of Spencer's doctrines, see Alun Munslow (1992, 31–33).

6. For the importance of consumerism in that period, see Donald R. McCoy (1973, 116–26), and Roland Marchand (1985).

7. For relevant studies on Veblen, see John P. Diggins (1978), Clare Virginia Eby (1994), and David Riesman, (1953). On the influence of Veblen on Theodore Dreiser, an author close to Fitzgerald in respect of the importance he attached to wealth and consumer habits, see Eby (1993).

8. Richard Godden has also emphasised the relationship between the Buchanans and the leisure class focussing on Daisy (1990, 83).

9. Subsequent references will appear parenthetically in the text. On the influence of Nietzsche in America during the first decades of the century and specially on Mencken, see Patrick Bridgwater (1972, 149). On Mencken's exposition of Nietzsche's ideas, see Carl Bode (1969, 83–86); and Manfred Stassen's "Nietzsky vs. the Booboisie" in Manfred Putz (1995, 105–110). The relationship between Fitzgerald and Mencken is analysed in Fred Hobson (1994, 238 and 276–77); Fitzgerald's reading of Mencken's book was first pointed out by Sklar (1967, 61). On the idea of decadence in English literature, see Ian Fletcher (1979).

10. As Thomas H. Pauly has pointed out Gatsby as a gangster was the very product of prohibition's criminal conditions (1993, 225).

11. Susan Resneck Parr has particularly emphasised the lack of moral sense at the root of Gatsby's mannerisms and wealth (cited in Bruccoli 1985, 63).

12. Roger Lewis (cited in Bruccoli 1985, 55).

13. On racism and intolerance during the period, see John Higham (1992, 272–73).

14. Carl Degler has studied the scientific context from which the works of Grant and Stoddard emerged (1991, 48–55).

15. On details about Grant's life, see Fairfield Osborn (1958, 256). For a comprehensive analysis of American racist theories, see Thomas F. Gossett (1963).

16. For the importance of Stoddard in relation to the idea of decline of the West, see Lewis Turlish (1971, 442–44).

17. On the context of Buchanan's remarks in relation to the Harlem Renaissance, see Gidley (1973, 180). On Harlem and the Jazz Age, see Gilbert Osofsky (1965, 229–38). In 1927, there was an exchange between Leothrop Stoddard and Alain Locke (1927, 500–519); see as well, Mark Helbling (1994, 289–314).

18. Wilson represents the lowest degree of vitalism in the novel. As Nick Carraway comments on him after he has discovered that his wife might be having an affair with another man: "It occurred to me that there was no difference between men, in intelligence or race, so profound as the difference between the sick and the well" (Fitzgerald 1990, 116).

19. As Marius Bewley has commented of Gatsby: "A great part of Fitzgerald's achievement is that he suggests effectively that these terrifying deficiencies of Gatsby, . . . are deficiencies inherent in contemporary manifestations of the American vision itself—a vision no doubt admirable, but stupidly defenceless before the equally American world of Tom and Daisy" (1963, 140–41).

20. On racism and imperialism in Fitzgerald's early works, see Gidley (1973, 174–78).

21. For a liberal interpretation of the novel, see Lionel Trilling (1961, 251–54). On *The Great Gatsby* as a liberal tragedy, see Godden (1990, 96–97).

22. The image of New York in the novel has been studied by Roland Bergman (1994, 85–109).

Works Cited

Bergman, Roland. 1994. *The Great Gatsby and Modern Times*. Chicago: University of Illinois Press.

Bewley, Marius. 1963. "Fitzgerald criticism of America." In *F. Scott Fitzgerald: A Collection of Critical Essays*, edited by Arthur Mizener. New York: Prentice-Hall.

Bigsby, C. W. E. 1971. "The Two Identities of F. Scott Fitzgerald." In *The American Novel and the Nineteen Twenties*, edited by Malcolm Bradbury and David Palmer. London: Edward Arnold.

Bode, Carl. 1969. *Mencken*. Carbondale and Edwardsville: Southern Illinois University Press.

Bridgwater, Patrick. 1972. *Nietzsche in Anglosaxony: A Study of Nietzsche's Impact on English and American Literature*. Leicester: Leicester University Press.

Bruccoli, Matthew J. (ed.) 1991. *Some Sort of Epic Grandeur: The Life of F. Scott Fitzgerald*. London: Hodder and Stoughton.

———. 1985. *New Essays on the Great Gatsby*. Cambridge: Cambridge University Press.

Carnegie, Andrew. 1962. "The Advantages of Poverty." In *The Gospel of Wealth, And Other Timely Essays*, edited by Edwards C. Kirkland. Cambridge, MA: Harvard University Press.

Cawelty, John G. 1965. *Apostles of the Self-Made Man*. Chicago: Chicago University Press.

Cowley, Malcolm. 1973. *A Second Flowering: Works and Days of the Lost Generation*. New York: Viking Press.

Degler, Carl N. 1991. *In Search of Human Nature: The Decline and Revival of Darwinism in American Social Thought*. New York: Oxford University Press.

Diggins, John P. 1978. *The Bard of Savagery: Thorstein Veblen and Modern Social Theory*. New York: Seabury Press.

Eby, Clare Virginia. 1993. "The Psychology of Desire: Veblen's 'Pecuniary Emulation' and 'Invidious Comparison' in *Sister Carrie* and *An American Tragedy*," *Studies in American Fiction* 21 (August): 191–208.

———. 1994. "Thorstein Veblen and the Rhetoric of Authority," *American Quarterly* 46, no. 2 (June): 139–73.

Fitzgerald, F. Scott. [1925] 1991. *The Great Gatsby*. London: Scribners.

———. 1934. *Tender is the Night*. New York: Scribner.

———. 1941. *The Last Tycoon: An Unfinished Novel*. New York: Charles Scribner's Sons.

———. 1948. *This Side of Paradise*. New York: Scribner's.

———. 1950. *The Beautiful and the Damned*. New York: Scribner.

———. 1963. *The Letters of F. Scott Fitzgerald*, edited by John Turnbull. New York: Charles Scribner's Sons.

Fletcher, Ian. (ed.) 1979. *Decadence and the 1890s*. Stratford-upon-Avon: Edward Arnold.

Gidley, Mick. 1973. "Notes on F. Scott Fitzgerald and the Passing of the Great Race," *Journal of American Studies* 7, no. 2 (August): 171–81.

Godden, Richard. 1990. *Fictions of Capital*. Cambridge: Cambridge University Press.

Gossett, Thomas F. 1963. *Race: The History of an Idea in America*. Dallas: Southern Methodist University Press.

Grant, Madison. 1918. *The Passing of the Great Race or The Racial Basis of European History*. New York: Charles Scribner's Sons.

Helbling, Mark. 1994. "Feeling Universality and Thinking Particularistically: Alain Locke, Franz Boas, Melville Herskowits, and the Harlem Renaissance," *Prospects* 19: 289–314.

Hemingway, Ernest. [1939] 1967. "The Snows of Kilimanjaro." In *The Short Stories of Ernest Hemingway*. New York. Scribner.

Higham, John. 1992. *Strangers in the Land: Patterns of American Nativism*. New Brunswick, NJ: Rutgers University Press.

Hobson, Fred. 1994. *Mencken: A Life*. Baltimore: John Hopkins University Press.

Hofstadter, Richard. 1945. *Social Darwinism in American Thought, 1860–1915*. Philadelphia: University of Pennsylvania Press.

Locke, Alain, and Leothrop Stoddard. 1927. "Should the Negro be Encouraged to Cultural Equality?" *Forum* 77, no. 77 (October): 500–519.

Marchand, Roland. 1985. *Advertising the American Dream: Making Way for Modernity*. Los Angeles: University of California Press.

McCoy, Donald R. 1973. *Coming of Age: The United States During the 1920's and 1930's*. Harmondsworth: Penguin.

Mencken, Henry L. 1908. *The Philosophy of Nietzsche*. Boston: Luce and Company.

Munslow, Alun, 1992. *Discourse and Culture: The Creation of America, 1870–1920*. London: Routledge.

Nietzsche, Friedrich. 1910. *The Genealogy of Morals: A Polemic*, translated by Horace B. Samuel. London: T.N. Foulis.

Osborn, Fairfield. 1958. "Grant, Madison," *Dictionary of American Biography*, Volume 22. London: Oxford University Press.

Osofsky, Gilbert. 1965. "Symbols of the Jazz Age: The New Negro and Harlem Discovered," *American Quarterly* 17 (Summer): 229–38.

Pauly, Thomas H. 1993. "Gatsby as Gangster," *Studies in American Fiction* 21 (August): 225–36.

Putz, Manfred. (ed.) 1995. *Nietzsche in American Literature and Thought*. Columbia, SC: Camden House.

Riesman, David. 1953. *Thorstein Veblen: A Critical Interpretation*. New York: Charles Scribner's Sons.

Sklar, Robert. 1967. *The Last Laocoön*. New York: Oxford University Press.

Stallman, Robert W. 1955. "Conrad and *The Great Gatsby*," *Twentieth Century Literature* 1, no. 1 (April): 5–12.

Stoddard, Lothrop. [1920] 1971. *The Rising Tide of Color Against White World-Supremacy*. Westport, CT: Negro University Press.

Summer, William Graham. 1914. *The Challenge of Facts and Other Essays*. New Haven: Yale University Press.

Tanner, Tony. 1990. Introduction. *The Great Gatsby*. London: Penguin.

Trilling, Lionel. 1961. *The Liberal Imagination: Essays on Literature and Society*. London: Martin Secker's and Warburg.

Turlish, Lewis. 1971. "The Rising Tide of Color: A Note on the Historicisms of *The Great Gatsby*," *American Literature* 43 (Autumn): 442–44.

Veblen, Thorstein. 1934. *The Theory of the Leisure Class*. New York: Modern Library.

Wall, John Frazer. 1970. *Andrew Carnegie*. New York: Oxford University Press.

RICHARD LEHAN

The Great Gatsby—*The Text as Construct: Narrative Knots and Narrative Unfolding*

I have always been slightly puzzled about why a novel as carefully constructed as Fitzgerald's *The Great Gatsby* has so many inconsistencies within it. The novel takes on the verbal complexity of a poem, and Fitzgerald skillfully tells a compelling story at the same time as he brilliantly compresses elements involving American history and Western culture into the fifty thousand words that make up the novel. It is a novel, the meaning of which refuses to be limited: every reading offers a new insight, and seventy-five years after publication the criticism often offers us something new; and yet this is a novel in which Fitzgerald inconsistently describes a character, confuses key dates, compresses action to the point that it perhaps strains credulity, and offers statements that are often simply confusing in relation to each other. Moreover, it is a novel in which the motives of perhaps the most important scene in the novel are left vague, if not totally ambivalent, and in which the ending puzzles us by the behavior of the narrator as well as the difficulty of assessing that behavior in moral terms.

I will come back to these matters. But before I do, I should like to say a few words about *The Great Gatsby* as a constructed text. The idea of textual construct is fairly recent. Previously, most of the critics had brought a concept of organic form, the old New Criticism idea of the inseparable relationship between part and whole, to a reading of the novel. This assumption had

From *F. Scott Fitzgerald: New Perspectives*, edited by Jackson R. Bryer, Alan Margolies, and Ruth Prigozy, pp. 78–89. © 2000 by the University of Georgia Press.

proven to be a useful one, since so much of the meaning in *Gatsby* comes out of its imagery, its texture, and the complexity of its motifs, all of which establish constellations of meaning that make up the universe of the novel. And yet in looking at the novel rather obsessively in these terms, we have, until recently, been somewhat casual about the cultural meaning of the text.

In order to read *The Great Gatsby* as a textual construct we must realize that, like every text, it was first pretextualized—that is, it was first the product of literary conventions that were in place before it was written. Such conventions became codified and expressed as literary modes, creating their own system of literary reality. These modes were brought into being in a historical context and served cultural agendas (and are thus ideological). Since the narrative mode is always larger than the text to which it applies, we have variation between texts in the same mode, at the same time that no text will ever be identical with the way it exists conceptually.

To see *Gatsby* in this context is to see first the way it draws its being from modernism—that is, in what way it organizes itself within terms of the narrative discourses that Fitzgerald, as a modernist, had at his disposal. We know that there were really two narrative modes that Fitzgerald could have drawn from. One was an aesthetic tradition that owed much of its being to the romantic movement. As Edmund Wilson has told us, modernism was simply the second stage of romanticism, modifying the mythic with the symbolic, working in the main within cyclical theories of history, and foregrounding a sense of subjectivity and consciousness often connected with philosophies of consciousness such as Bergson's. The other tradition, of course, was literary naturalism, a realistic tradition that emphasized the deterministic effects of environment, heredity, and a pregiven temperament. Fitzgerald had never worked within the mainstream of either tradition. In *This Side of Paradise* he brought an aesthetic discourse to his novel, retelling Compton Mackenzie's bildungsroman *Sinister Street*, which allowed Fitzgerald to saturate Amory Blaine's consciousness in the high romantic poetry from Keats and Shelley to Pater and Dowson. In *The Beautiful and Damned* he moved in the other direction and told a story of physical decline in the manner of Norris and Dreiser that Mencken, whom he admired at the time, had advocated. In *Gatsby* he attempted to bring the two traditions together, creating a realm of personal romantic intensity and cultural destiny told against a world of physical force embodied by Tom Buchanan and the mechanics of the new city, the new megalopolis.

That *Gatsby* is a product of visionary romanticism is a point important enough to emphasize. We know of Fitzgerald's interest in the subject from the famous course in romanticism he took with Christian Gauss at Princeton, a course the subject matter of which Edmund Wilson comes back to time and time again in *Axel's Castle* to suggest the bedrock upon which modernism rests.

In Gauss's course, works like Pater's *Greek Studies* were read, especially Pater's famous essay on Dionysus. The Dionysus myth informs Western culture from Aeschylus and Euripides's *Bacchae* to Keats's later poetry and Nietzsche's *The Birth of Tragedy*. Historically, Dionysus was a re-presentation of the man-god figure that came out of Asia Minor embodied in Tammuz. The tradition was carried on in the Adonis figure, primarily Greek but with Hebrew origins, and was also inscribed in the Osiris figure in Egypt and Africa. In Greek legend, Dionysus is conceived by the God Zeus in the human Semele, the daughter of King Cadmus. When Semele dies she gives premature birth to her baby, who is brought to term by Zeus who sews the baby into the folds of his own flesh. Most of the readings of Dionysus connect him with vegetative and fertility rituals, with seasonal change, the earth renewing itself as do the vines of wine. But Dionysus was also connected with a cult organized around women who became frenzied to the point that they were capable of murder, as in Euripides when Agave murders Pentheus, her own son. Dionysus is usually seen as the opposite of Christ, since Christ calls for self-control rather than self-abandonment. But the connection between Christ and Dionysus is that both are born of woman/God—that is, they bridge the space between the earthly and the transcendent.

In the eighteenth century, the mythic nature of Dionysus was transformed, and his function was "re-presented" (that is, historically reembodied) by the carnival and later by the mysterious stranger and the man in the crowd. Joyce's Macintosh man carries much of the original meaning. Both Poe and Twain make use of such a figure in their fiction. While the vampire legend stems from a different mythology, its function is very much the same: Dracula, supported by at least three women, stalks the night, disrupting the ordered Victorian London that he has mysteriously entered. Fitzgerald's Gatsby embodies many of these elements: he emerges from the carnivalesque crowd of his own parties as a mysterious stranger, especially when seen at night. Fitzgerald cut eighteen thousand words describing Gatsby's childhood and background in order to give him this intensified sense of mystery. These elements play an important part in modernism in general, as we can see with poets like H.D., who translated from the Greek and used the Dionysus myth in her poetry, and dramatists like Eugene O'Neill, who employs a version of the Dionysus myth in *The Great God Brown*.

A slightly different use of the man-god figure informs *The Great Gatsby*: Gatsby is the embodiment of his own godlike vision, or as the text tells us, "He was a son of God."[1] Such a creation implies vision, and the novel keeps coming back to the matter of sight through the eyes of T. J. Eckleburg, the eyes of the owl-eyed man, and the eyes of Nick that get more myopic as the novel proceeds, until we end with the eyes of Gatsby whose sight is transformed from the resplendent to the ordinary the day he loses Daisy, and a rose simply becomes a rose.[2] Like Dionysus and Christ, Gatsby becomes the dual product of his own creation. Like both the Greeks and the early Christians, Fitzgerald realized that the real story of God is not in the heavens or on earth, but in the reconciliation of the two—in the romantic intensity that transforms the physical.

If such intensity makes up one-half of Gatsby's character in the novel, the other half is given over to the physical powers that undo it, and here the novel is played out in the physical realm of Tom Buchanan and the city. Henry Adams had discussed the connection between these two realms in his "Virgin and the Dynamo" chapter in *The Education of Henry Adams*. The Virgin is a mythic vision—the vision of self that Gatsby uses to create himself and that organizes the medieval culture according to Adams. The dynamo is the random physical power that feeds off the natural universe and goes beyond romantic containment, giving rise to the diversity and multiplicity that fragments self as well as culture. Fitzgerald's novel clearly takes place within these narrative parameters. Before it is anything else it is a romantic/naturalistic battle between the visionary and the physical realms. The visions that give direction to life are indeed perishable, Fitzgerald tells us, perhaps destined in materialistic America to fail because they soon become outworn, soon are taken over by the past, which means that we are often looking backward when we think we are looking forward: "So we beat on, boats against the current, borne back ceaselessly into the past" (182).

Such is the story of Gatsby who projects an image of Daisy five years too late to be realized. And such is the story of Gatsby's America. Just before Fitzgerald began writing *Gatsby*, Frederick Jackson Turner's book involving the frontier thesis was published, based on the famous paper he had read in 1893 at the meeting of the American Historical Society at the World's Exposition in Chicago. Turner argued, based on census figures, that the frontier was now closed, the frontier that made America unique by allowing the nation to accommodate the vision of what it could be. So long as the frontier was open, everything was in the realm of the potential, waiting to be realized. James J. Hill had gone to the frontier and remade himself, so had Dan Cody, whose name suggests the beginning and end of the frontier (Daniel Boone who entered the true wilderness and Buffalo Bill Cody who transformed the frontier experience into a Disney-like Wild West show). Gatsby models himself on both Hill and especially Cody, and takes his frontier vision not to the frontier but to the city, where he plays it out in a world of new physical force, the end product of which is the Valley of Ashes. Fitzgerald not only saw the vision as allowing new ways of seeing and creating new forms of energy but he saw the loss of the vision as leading to forms of cultural blindness and to the entropy that leaves us with physical waste. It is for these reasons that the blind eyes of T. J. Eckleburg look out over the Valley of Ashes, and for these reasons that its custodian is the burnt-out, sickly George Wilson, whose name suggests another burnt-out visionary (Woodrow Wilson) and who blindly becomes the agent of Gatsby's death when he looks into the eyes of T. J. Eckleburg, tells us that God knows everything, and then goes out and kills the wrong man.

As a constructed text, *Gatsby* takes its meaning from the play between romantic and naturalistic narrative modes, between a belief in the visionary and the limits set on such transcendent desire by a realm of physical force. And clearly Fitzgerald felt that these motives took us to the very heart of what was meant by America—the world to which the Dutch sailors brought a new-world vision and the corruption of that vision from the end of the Civil War when the idealistic views of Jefferson, who carried so much of the visionary meaning for Fitzgerald, gave way to the more materialistic views of Hamilton.[3] Fitzgerald, of course, saw that other writers had anticipated him in this theme, especially Mark Twain in works like *A Connecticut Yankee in King Arthur's Court* and *The Gilded Age*, but also critics like Van Wyck Brooks who saw idealized and materialized elements at war within America like viruses might war within the physical body.

The critics who have made the connection between Fitzgerald and Twain anticipate what I mean by the constructed text—a text that takes its being from what is dominant at a historical moment in narrative modes. My only objection is that those critics seldom make the connections in these terms. Robert Sklar, in *F. Scott Fitzgerald: The Last Laocoön*, takes us to Twain with what seems to me the misguided belief that Fitzgerald was playing out the genteel ideals that pervaded late-nineteenth-century America. What someone like Sklar misses is how close, if not identical, Fitzgerald's view of culture came to that of the old historicism—the belief that every culture has an inbred meaning, a spirit or *geist* that gives it identity, a kind of essential being organized in terms of a period of time (as in Burkhardt's history of the Renaissance) or in terms of a national culture (as in von Ranke's history of Bismarck's Germany).

Fitzgerald, I believe, did see America in historicist terms, but they were the terms of Spengler, who saw American destiny as part of the larger destiny of the West. Within this destiny the process of decay and degeneration had already set in, a theme that Max Nordau and Cesare Lombroso made abundantly clear, suggesting that historical evolution had become inverted as Adams did in his theory of entropy, and which twilight poets like Dawson and Pater reinforced. From Adams's dynamo to Eliot's wasteland, to Fitzgerald's valley of ashes, to Pynchon's Trystero is a straight line in the development of this idea. The flip side of visionary history is the entropic, and both are built into the workings of the old historicism, to which Fitzgerald gave consent when he gave consent to Spengler, an idea I have documented elsewhere and which Fitzgerald documented himself in a long interview that he gave in April of 1927 to Harry Salpeter of the *New York World*.[4] Vision and decline, energy and waste—here are the key elements that Fitzgerald brought to his fiction, not only in the novels that precede *Gatsby* (*This Side of Paradise* and *The Beautiful and Damned*) but also in the novels that follow (*Tender Is the Night* and *The Last Tycoon*, as well as in the series of long short stories that make up the novella "Philippe, Count of Darkness").[5]

Along with a sense of the mythic/symbolic, and a historicist's sense of time, the modernist had a theory of consciousness (that is, subjectivity) that also becomes embedded in a novel like *Gatsby*. Clearly it is a tradition of thought that moves through Henry James and Joseph Conrad before it informs the mind of Nick Carraway. In his preface to *The Nigger of the Narcissus*, Conrad discussed his own aesthetics of fiction. Fitzgerald was moved by Conrad's critique, and it led to his idea of the "dying fall," the term he used to convey the sense of sadness and melancholy that came about when the intensity of the romantic visionary was deflected by opposing materialistic forces. Such romantic intensity stemmed in turn from special moments of experience that lived sharply in memory, informed our very sense of self, and which gave time a quality of being—or so Bergson said in his modernistic theory of time. And while Fitzgerald did not know Bergson directly, he certainly did indirectly, at least to the extent that he knew that the same experience could never be repeated. Once informed by consciousness, such an experience could never again be innocent of such consciousness. When Nick tells Gatsby, you can't repeat the past, he is unlocking another modernist truth.

Once we posit Fitzgerald among the moderns, we can begin to see how the narrative elements of *Gatsby* (what I have been calling the constructed text) supply a source of power beyond themselves, allowing Fitzgerald to draw from the strong spring and diverse currents of modernism itself. But most looks at *Gatsby* do not begin from this end of the telescope; instead, they examine particular scenes and passages within the text on the assumption that such matters have meaning in their own right. In the hope of suggesting how matters of critical indeterminacy might be mediated by the idea of the constructed text, I would like now to return to some of the questions that I raised initially, and to look specifically at *Gatsby* in terms of some of the more obvious narrative problems we encounter.

One of the more obvious problems in the novel involves the discrepancies of Daisy's hair.[6] At one point, Daisy refers to her daughter's "yellow hair" and says, "She's got my hair and shape of face" (117); but, at another point, when Daisy and Gatsby first fall in love, we are told "he kissed her dark shining hair" (150). Obviously, this inconsistency was not intentional; my guess is that Fitzgerald had two women in mind as he wrote about Daisy, and that she began as Ginevra King (who had brown hair) and was transformed on occasion into Zelda (who had blond hair). But the problem here has much larger ramifications, and points to the fact that Daisy's physical characteristics are left vague throughout the novel. Daisy lacks physical presence because it is more important that she embody romantic expectation and lost time.

Daisy's vagueness and impalpability led to mistakes in accounting for her chronology. We are told that Daisy and Gatsby fall in love in the summer and autumn of 1917 when Daisy is eighteen years old. The next autumn, 1918, she makes her debut "after the armistice" (November 11, 1918), is engaged to a man from New Orleans in February 1919, and in June 1919 she marries Tom Buchanan (76–77). Tom and Daisy honeymoon in the South Seas through June and July of 1919 and in August they are in Santa Barbara, where Tom gets into an accident on the Ventura highway with a chambermaid from the hotel (78). The next April, 1920, Daisy gives birth to her child. The novel, we know, takes place in the summer of 1922, and we are told that the child is three years old. But if the child was born in April of 1920, it would be two years and two months old.[7] Such a significant mistake has no meaning in and of itself, but it does suggest to me that Fitzgerald was far more concerned with symbolic rather than physical chronology in this novel. Movement from spring to autumn, from youth to adulthood, from romantic expectation to disillusionment, from life to death, from pastoral to tragic, from the ideal to the grotesque, from the spiritual to the material—these are symbolic elements that get narrative priority in *Gatsby* and literary modernism.

Once within the discourse of modernism, Fitzgerald could write at a physical distance from the world he was describing, even if it led to certain inconsistencies, even incredulity in plot. This happens when Fitzgerald revises the order of his narrative. In an earlier draft, Fitzgerald put the scene at Gatsby's party before the scene involving Tom and Myrtle Wilson in the apartment on 158th Street. This order gives Tom a slightly longer time to renew his acquaintance with Nick. By reversing these scenes, we have Tom taking Nick almost immediately into his confidence and inviting him to a moment of his lovemaking in New York. We know that Tom has not seen Nick for at least seven years, and we also know that Nick is Daisy's cousin. Such behavior on Tom's part does not seem very credible, but Fitzgerald braved it anyway, because he wanted to delay the appearance of Gatsby until the present chapter 3 in order to make Gatsby more mysterious and to make his eventual presence more strange in keeping with the mythic nature of the novel.

It is this desire for mystery, as well as the desire to give Gatsby a dual nature, that gets Fitzgerald into more narrative trouble. He has really created two Gatsbys: One is the man who has turned himself into God, the other is the Dakota farm boy who is still a roughneck. The latter tells Nick he is from San Francisco in the Midwest, while the former has been around the continent three times in Dan Cody's yacht and surely knows where to find San Francisco. Here the realistic and romantic elements of the novel pull the character away from any kind of consolidated meaning. Fitzgerald did not want us to bring these narrative elements together because they were not always in narrative synchronization with each other, as we can see if we allow Gatsby's account of the accident that killed Myrtle Wilson to get too detailed. To be sure, Daisy was driving, but Gatsby does manage to stop the car with the emergency brake. He clearly has the option of returning to the scene of the accident, but as Gatsby tells Nick, Daisy "fell over into my lap and I drove on" (145). Gatsby's participation in Myrtle's death gets almost no attention from the critics because, I would argue, they have been caught up in the sweep of Fitzgerald's romantic modernism and read this scene very differently than they do a comparable scene in Dreiser's *An American Tragedy*, when the car wreck near the beginning of the novel realistically establishes the meaning of Clyde Griffiths as a character.

But these are minor discrepancies in contrast to those that involve Nick. We never come to understand, for example, how Nick knows in such detail what went on in Wilson's garage the night and morning after Myrtle's death, since Nick was not there. And, more important, we never really come to know whether Tom Buchanan knew that Daisy was driving the car when he allows George Wilson to believe that Gatsby had run over Myrtle. And despite the fact that much of the meaning of the whole novel turns on how you answer this question, no critic, to my knowledge, looks upon it as a major narrative problem, but all instead assume either that Tom knows or that Tom does not know. Perhaps the latter interpretation is in the ascendancy, although to read the novel this way gives a certain justification to Tom's actions that reverses (at least for me) the narrative force and meaning of the novel. I believe Fitzgerald gives us an answer of sorts when he sends Nick around to the back of the Buchanans' house where he observes Tom and Daisy talking at the kitchen table over an uneaten plate of chicken and untouched bottles of ale. He tells us they looked as if they were "conspiring," a word that suggests Tom is aware of Daisy's involvement in the accident. On this one word, then, so much of the meaning of the novel turns, because if Tom sends Wilson to Gatsby's house knowing that Daisy was driving the car, then Tom is as responsible for Gatsby's death as is Wilson. The fact that Fitzgerald can let so much of the meaning of his story ride on the ambiguity of one word tells us as much about the narrative mode in which he was writing as it does about the story itself.

What is equally puzzling is the passage Nick gives us before he witnesses Tom and Daisy at the kitchen table: "A new point of view," he tells us, "occurred to me. Suppose Tom found out that Daisy had been driving. He might think he saw a connection in it—he might think anything" (145). What can this mean? What is the connection? Possibly that Daisy had intentionally run over Myrtle? Possibly at an inquest that his own name will become linked to Myrtle as her lover? The ending of the novel is not much more helpful in answering some of these questions. Here Nick confronts Tom and asks him directly what he told Wilson. His question stems from a guess—a correct guess—that Tom had sent Wilson in pursuit of Gatsby. But Tom insists that he told Wilson "the truth": "I told him the truth. . . . He was crazy enough to kill me if I hadn't told him who owned the car" (180). Tom lets Nick believe that he did not know that Daisy was driving: "He [Gatsby] ran over Myrtle like you'd run over a dog and never even stopped the car" (180). That Tom says this means nothing, since he does not know that Gatsby has told Nick that Daisy was driving. But what is more puzzling is Nick's response: "there was nothing I could say, except the one unutterable fact that it wasn't true" (180). Why is this fact unutterable? What has Nick to gain by letting Tom think that he has acted correctly, finally shaking hands with him as they part? This scene makes the actual ending of the novel all the more ambiguous. Nick leaves the East and retreats back to the West, the scene of his youth, with all the nostalgia that Fitzgerald brings to that world. Nick, in other words, seems intent on repeating the past, just what he told Gatsby he could not do, and the novel supposedly ends on a note of both contradiction and defeat.

Such inconsistencies are a part of the ending of *The Great Gatsby*, and yet they have seldom been discussed as serious lapses in the novel. While they must remain lapses, I think they are softened in their effect and can be explained by the modernist intentions that Fitzgerald brought to his novel, especially his desire to end the novel on a note of the "dying fall": he wanted to increase the sense of sadness and pathos that come with Gatsby's death, a pathos that in part also stems from Nick's feeling of helplessness in the face of Tom and in the East—that is, in New York—the realm and source of Tom's power. His desire to create a dying fall, a sense of life sadly running out for both Gatsby and Nick, is also the reason that Fitzgerald tells his story against the seasons of the year, moving from late spring (the novel begins on June 7, 1922) to late autumn (Nick last meets Tom "one afternoon late in October" [179]). That the fate of Gatsby is inseparable from the seasons of the year only intensifies his mythic character and suggests another parallel to the Dionysus story—and another connection to modern narrative discourse. While reading

Gatsby as a modernist text does not wash away the narrative blemishes it may have, it helps explain those blemishes and allows us to see better the narrative problems Fitzgerald had to encounter in writing this brilliant novel.

In suggesting that Fitzgerald had access to a narrative realm that preceded his writing of the novel, I am, of course, coming very close to an aspect of Michel Foucault's theory of discourse. While I am willing to acknowledge this debt, I also want to say, by way of conclusion, that there are many differences between Foucault and me: the most important would be my insistence on the need to historicize discourse, lock it into a historical moment, into a specific culture, and into the diachronic. *The Great Gatsby*, like so much of modern American fiction, is a postwar novel that comes with the closing of the frontier and the rise of urban America, written at a time when romanticism still had mythic import and when a historicist sense of the past could still inform creative consciousness. Also, unlike Foucault, I make no claim for the death of the author; I argue just the opposite: that *The Great Gatsby* becomes *The Great Gatsby* only when the elements of modernism are filtered through the special consciousness of Fitzgerald himself. I have no desire to eliminate agency from history or from the act of creating fiction but insist on seeing how an author and a historical moment come together. Whatever blemishes we may find in *The Great Gatsby*, whatever may be its narrative knots and its puzzling unfolding, Fitzgerald gave life to a historical moment of which he himself was also the product, and produced a modernist text that we have long recognized (and I hope—in this time of canon reformation—we will continue to recognize) as one of the supreme achievements of American literature.

NOTES

1. Fitzgerald, *Great Gatsby*, 99. All subsequent page references to *The Great Gatsby* are to the 1957 edition and appear parenthetically in the text.

2. The wording here suggests Gertrude Stein. Stein's intent was to deflate the romantic vision, and her theory is the basis for another tradition of language in modernism—namely, imagism and later the idea of the vortex, although in trying to find an equivalent to the cubism of art, she broke company with Pound and especially Wyndham Lewis, whose *Time and Western Man* is a direct attack on modernist theories of time and consciousness—simultaneity and durée.

3. The dispute between Jefferson and Hamilton runs deeply throughout American literature, especially in the modernist period. Pound, Faulkner, and Dos Passos all shared Fitzgerald's sympathy for the Jeffersonian over the Hamiltonian vision.

4. Lehan, "*The Great Gatsby*": *The Limits of Wonder*, 80–90; Salpeter, "Fitzgerald, Spenglerian."

5. "Philippe, Count of Darkness" is a sequence of short stories, originally published in *Redbook Magazine*, October 1934 ("In the Darkest Hour"), June 1935 ("The Count of Darkness"), August 1935 ("The Kingdom in the Dark"), and posthumously in November 1941 ("Gods of Darkness").

6. Joan S. Korenman has pointed out the inconsistency in the color of Daisy's hair in "'Only Her Hairdresser.'"

7. In the new Cambridge edition of *Gatsby*, Matthew J. Bruccoli silently changes the dates in the text to bring them into synchronization with each other. Such an editorial policy, I believe, is dangerous, because it hides from the reader the various time lines Fitzgerald confused. The text Fitzgerald gave us seventy-five years ago has an integrity that should not be violated by modern editors, especially when there are no notes to reveal that an editor's hand—and not Fitzgerald's—is at work.

Works Cited

Adams, Henry. *The Education*. 1918. Ed. Ernest Samuels. Boston: Houghton Mifflin, 1973.

Detienne, Marcel. *Dionysus at Large*. Cambridge, Mass.: Harvard University Press, 1989.

———. *Dionysus Slain*. Baltimore: Johns Hopkins University Press, 1979.

Deutsch. Helene. *A Psychoanalytic Study of the Myth of Dionysus and Apollo*. New York: International University Press, 1969.

Ebel, Henry. *After Dionysus*. Rutherford, N.J.: Fairleigh Dickinson University Press, 1972.

Evans, Arthur. *The God of Ecstasy: Sex Roles and the Madness of Dionysus*. New York: St. Martin's Press, 1988.

Fitzgerald, F. Scott. *The Great Gatsby*. 1925. New York: Scribners, 1957.

———. *The Great Gatsby*. 1925. Ed. Matthew J. Bruccoli. New York: Cambridge University Press, 1991.

———. *The Last Tycoon*. New York: Scribners, 1941.

———. "My Lost City." In *The Crack-up*. Ed. Edmund Wilson. New York: New Directions, 1945. 23–33.

———. ["Philippe, Count of Darkness"]. "In the Darkest Hour," *Redbook Magazine* (October 1934): 15–19, 94–98; "The Count of Darkness," *Redbook Magazine* (June 1935): 20–23, 68, 70, 72; "The Kingdom in the Dark," *Redbook Magazine* (August 1935): 58–62, 64, 66–68; "Gods of Darkness," *Redbook Magazine* (November 1941): 30–33, 88–91.

———. *Tender is the Night*. New York: Scribners, 1934.

Foster, John Burt. *Heirs to Dionysus: A Nietzschean Current in Literary Modernism*. Princeton, N.J.: Princeton University Press, 1981.

Korenman, Joan S. "'Only her Hairdresser . . .': Another Look at Daisy Buchanan." *American Literature* 46 (1975): 574–78.

Lehan, Richard D. *F. Scott Fitzgerald and the Craft of Fiction*. Carbondale: Southern Illinois University Press, 1966.

———. "F. Scott Fitzgerald and Romantic Destiny," *Twentieth Century Literature* 26 (1980): 137–56.

———. *"The Great Gatsby": The Limits of Wonder*. Boston: G. K. Hall, 1990.

Salpeter, Harry. "Fitzgerald, Spenglerian." *New York World*, April 3, 192: 12M.

Spengler, Oswald. *The Decline of the West*. 2 vols. Tr. Charles F. Atkinson. 1918; 1922. New York: Knopf, 1926; 1928.

Taylor, George Rogers. *The Turner Thesis*. Boston: D. C. Heath, 1956.

Turner, Frederick Jackson. *The Frontier in American History*. New York: Henry Holt, 1920.

Wilson, Edmund. *Axel's Castle: A Study in the Imaginative Literature of 1870–1930*. 1931. New York: Scribners, 1959.

JOHN HILGART

The Great Gatsby's *Aesthetics of Non-Identity*

> The test of a first-rate intelligence is the ability to hold two
> opposed ideas in the mind at the same time, and still retain the
> ability to function.
>
> F. Scott Fitzgerald, *The Crack-Up*

Like Nick Carraway's two most direct and famously perplexing statements of simultaneous approval and disapproval of Jay Gatsby, the whole
of *The Great Gatsby* is strung tautly on apparent self-contradiction (6, 162).[1]
While the novel employs the strategic ellipses of modernist narrative, it
also complicates its own provocative ambiguity—piling up surprisingly
blunt declarations of "fact" that are immediately or eventually undercut by
other declarations or other evidence. The question of Nick's reliability that
has prompted so much critical ink undershoots the mark; Nick seems to go
out of his way to make us a dubious audience, from his opening invitation
to look for the "obvious suppressions" in "the intimate revelations of young
men," to his claim of unique and absolute honesty at a moment of patent
deception, to the novel's final lines, which caress us seductively as they
declare that we are all doomed to repeat the tragedy we have just finished
reading (6, 64, 189).

Arguments that attempt to correct Nick's account are often provocative in revealing just how difficult it is to attach certainty to much in his

From *Arizona Quarterly* 59, no. 1 (Spring 2003): 87–116. © 2003 by the Arizona Board of
Regents. Revised by the author.

narrative, but they inevitably attempt to build something solid on what they simultaneously acknowledge is shifting sand. *Gatsby* becomes a sort of detective novel, with one critic concluding that Gatsby was indeed, as he lamely claims, driving the car that killed Myrtle Wilson, while another asserts that Daisy knew that Myrtle was Tom's mistress and ran her down intentionally (Edwards, Cartwright). In another account, it is not Wilson who kills Gatsby but Wolfshiem's thugs (Lockridge). One critic judges Nick to be "slow-thinking, sentimental, and occasionally dishonest," but proceeds to separate the reliable from the unreliable with sufficient confidence to judge Nick's favorable comments on Gatsby "ultimately quite humorous" (O'Rourke 58).

After a certain point, the sheer volume of correcting-for-Nick arguments, contradicting each other as they do, persuade us that contradiction must be very much the point, but correction beside it. A more productive approach to the novel's overt dissonance considers it to be less a matter of "the facts" than a function of Nick's own conflicted character and divided loyalties. Scott Donaldson carefully accounts for Nick's competing evaluations of Gatsby by showing Nick to be both obsessively concerned with propriety (bad for Gatsby) and a victim of a romantic imagination much like Gatsby's. However, the richest mystery of contradiction concerns the apparent ideological divide between Nick's thorough expose of commodified materialism and the degree to which he still seems to be seduced by it. Richard Godden is representative in his judgment that it is Nick's unmodified bourgeois identity and class affiliation that accounts for his "averting his eyes from Gatsby's dramatization of contradiction," even as he seems so smart about it (365). Janet Giltrow and David Stouck argue that at the level of plot, the novel is quite critical of materialism, but that at the level of prose—especially in the lyrical passages—Nick falls prey to the allure of commodity culture.

We have agreement, then, that the narrator, narrative, ideology, and style of *The Great Gatsby* manifest pervasive tensions and contradictions. At the center of this is, of course, Nick himself; the criticism is always finally about Nick, who is the text's surrogate author, and who is generally judged to be limited in his capacity to see what we, the readers, see. In this essay, I resist the conclusion that contradiction in the novel defines Nick's limitations, arguing on the contrary that contradiction is very much Nick's overt technique, serving not to undercut his critique of commodity culture but to mount it. I am interested in several insistent themes of *The Great Gatsby* that have, in recent years, come in for sophisticated critical treatment without coming together fully: the novel's concern with the commodity form, its powerful study of desire, and its aesthetics.

Several arguments are particularly relevant. John T. Irwin develops a Freudian reading of desire in the novel with a focus on figuration, concluding that the ultimate concern of the text is desire *per se*, unhinged from the possibility that its figured objects might actually be consumed or satisfy that desire. Irwin judges Nick to be pursuing desire itself by means of a circular dance of deferral. Irwin's concern with figuration implies a reading of the novel's aesthetic dimension, but this is outside of the scope of his article. In separate pieces, Lois Tyson and Ross Possnock give more attention to the novel's aesthetics, as they explore the novel's juncture of desire and the commodity form. Tyson examines at length the transformation of individuals into commodities in *Gatsby*, arguing that the American Dream is portrayed as "a commodity— in this case, a sign invested with the desire for consumption as the principal mode of production" (41). While she finds the novel's understanding of the reifying force of commodity culture to be penetrating, she (with Giltrow and Stouck) ultimately finds Nick himself to be co-opted by this force, seduced by Gatsby's dream and reproducing the allure of the commodity in his aestheticized representation of both the dream and the material manifestations of it.

Similarly, Possnock demonstrates the degree to which Lukacs' model of reification—the complete permeation of consciousness by the (il)logic of exchange value in commodity culture—is played out complexly in the novel, focussing, like Tyson, on the centrality of exchange (rather than intrinsic qualities) in the valuation of people and objects. And like the others, Possnock views Nick as "implicated in the commodification of reality under capitalism," locating this complicity in Nick's language—"Nick's 'aesthetic contemplation'"—but also pointing to Nick's "deeply divided evaluation of Gatsby" (Possnock 210–211). Possnock concludes his essay by tossing off an astute suggestion that can serve as the starting point of the present argument. Possnock invokes a central tenet of Theodor Adorno's critical theory to suggest that "the blatant contradictions in Nick's response" reflect the inherent contradictions of capitalism: "Only an understanding rooted in the acceptance of contradiction can defy the reductionism of reification and discover the 'antagonistic whole' of life under capitalism" (212). Possnock cuts the Gordian knot, transforming the individual matter of unreliability into the social symptom of contradiction.

Most of these arguments attend to some formal aspect of the novel, often the apparent complicity of Nick's lyrical flights with commodified culture. The more delicious his language becomes, the more he seems to be an apologist for the material and historical amnesia of Gatsby's dream. We look for the decisive counter-statement, the luminous line or paragraph that contains the stabilizing thesis we want from Nick. It doesn't exist. The rebuttal to commodity fetishism as viable equipment for living is embedded in every turn of the plot, but the narrative fabric refuses to name a winner. It manifests an almost granular resistance to fixation, piling self-contradiction on top of indeterminacy. What Nick gives with one hand, he takes away with the other, making his narrative not so much unreliable as insistently unresolvable. This, I would suggest, is the primary and overarching aesthetic that governs the book—a persistent act of assertion and negation that is itself the dialectical critique that *The Great Gatsby* offers up. Nick is not the representative dupe of commodity capitalism, but rather the systematic purveyor of contradictions that reveal its inner workings.

Adorno's aesthetic theory speaks to exactly this formal phenomenon. The affective stylistics of a text, he argues, produce a readerly experience of *non-identity*, the negation of the insistence on identity that is fundamental to the exchange economy of the commodity form. To the extent that art contradicts our naturalized cultural assumptions, art contradicts us—disclosing the contingent ideologies of the world that we inhabit and that inhabits us in turn. And because the core ideology of capitalism is the exchangeability of all things—creating an essential identity among all things—contradiction itself becomes the fundamental critique. If certain lyrical passages in *Gatsby* encode the autonomous allure of the commodity, then the novel's contradictory representations undo that autonomy, privileging difference and negating identity. Aimed at commodity culture, this negation directs us away from the apparent autonomy of reified objects toward a larger material matrix. The reader's uneasy experience of incessant cancellation of one representation by another—and of pleasure, cancelled by discomfort—is evidence of our own reified consciousness. There is, then, a utopic dimension to Nick's aesthetics—an implication that a different kind of subject, here conjured in the space of our dissonant reading experience, might have produced a different kind of society.

This brings us back to the matter of the novel's construction of reified consciousness itself—of human desire thoroughly mapped by and trapped in the circular logic of commodity fetishism and the unlimited exchangeability of objects. While Irwin accuses Nick of pursuing desire *per se*—figured but deferred, and therefore falling into Gatsby's own trap—we can view Nick's drive inward toward absolute desire as part of the utopic dimension of his aesthetic of negated figuration. The horizon of desire is continually reduced by the novel's characters to commodity fetishism, but the text's pattern of evoking our desire in seductive representations of commodities, only to strip away the adequacy of those objects, serves to dislocate our own desire in the reading experience. The text exploits us as the subjects of reified desire, then dismantles the objects with which it has seduced us. It seems to say again and again, "Yes, desire, but not for this," the friction of conflicted representation setting desire loose in the text and in the reader.

The particular formal means by which this effect is produced suggests Jacques Lacan's structural model of the subject and of desire as wholly constructed by and within language. Language and desire are inseparable, and language drives the individual ever onward in an attempt to signify that which would complete the subject, while in its very nature measuring lack, the parsing of that hypothetical whole *by* language. Lacan's structurally deferred subject would seem at odds with Adorno's historically deferred subject, but just as Lacan emphasizes our construction not merely by language but by *a* language, reified consciousness is disclosed in *Gatsby* in the form of a particular cultural *cul de sac* of signification The characters Nick studies and the larger signifying economy he has inherited struggle to signify desire outside of the commodity's logic of identity—the exchanges of cars for wives, shirts for love, houses for dreams, and so forth. Lacan argues that our pursuit of desire through language forms a metonymic chain of signifiers—parts taken for the elusive whole—which we see manifested in the functioning of metaphor. Metaphor is "the superimposition . . . of signifiers," and through metaphor a "creative spark . . . flashes between two signifiers one of which has taken the place of the other in the signifying chain, the occulted signifier remaining present through its (metonymic) connexion with the rest of the chain" (Lacan 160, 157). The "sliding of the signified under the signifier," causes "that veering off of signification that we see in metonymy" (Lacan 160). The actual signified of these superimpositions, slippages, and metonymic traces is quite distinct from what we imagine ourselves to be naming; we are, Lacan says, "caught in the rails" of metonymy, "eternally stretching forth towards the *desire for something else*" (167). The space of the subject exists not in discursive intent, but where meaning necessarily fails, "flee[ing] from our grasp along the verbal thread" (166). Though there is for Lacan no escape from this chain, and no tangible subject beyond language, he suggests that contrary to the automatic functioning of language, which maintains the status quo of meaning and understanding, metaphor's spark, flying between distant signifiers, brings the subject briefly into view and disrupts habituated understanding. A new meaning is brought forth through new metaphors and hence a modified subject position.[2] It follows, then, that we are victims of whatever metaphors prevail—which become naturalized, thereby losing their spark of difference—and of whatever productive metaphors are occluded as a result.

In *Gatsby*, we see figuration so reified, so circumscribed by identity thinking that successive figurations of desire do not form chains extending outward so much as they circle back upon themselves impotently. The relationship of identity, upon which commodification insists, becomes a problem of signification in *Gatsby*; the successive metaphors of desire may vary in their particulars, but they and their metonymic play are curtailed by cultural habituation. Desire is ultimately what Gatsby, as individual and as cultural representative, is aiming at with his many colorful and often desperate conceits, but this signified is so preconditioned by his acculturation into consumer culture that the metaphoric spark of difference is snuffed out by the logic of identity in exchange.

The problem with which Nick's narrative contends is how to circumvent the impasse of commodified desire, extending desire's horizon by exceeding the means by which his culture signifies it. By re-representing the objects, people, ideas, and judgments of his text in contradictory fashion, Nick's aesthetic of negated figuration produces baffling metaphors; the reader is thrown into a paradox, in which the relatedness implied by metaphorical connection (superimposed figurations of the same thing) is pitted against apparent mutual cancellation. The autonomous guise of the commodified object cannot withstand refiguration in terms that involve labor or history, and this ideologically dissonant metonymy, apparent at the level of word and phrase, is raised to the level of the novel's dominant formal effect. This breaking of the boundaries of reified patterns of signification, corresponds to Adorno's theory of an artistic negative dialectic, in which formal dissonance encodes the contradictions inherent in commodity culture and its pervasive guise of identity. As signifiers of desire in a reified sign-system are cancelled out by contrary figurations, the empty space of the signified is that which would be occupied by a transformed consciousness; it is the modernist lacuna as utopic possibility. When Nick reports that the East had become "distorted beyond my eyes' power of correction," he might as well be describing his own narrative, which the reader is forced to view as if through mismatched lenses (185). Our critical eyes do not, in the end, have the "power of correction"; rather, we are to accept the contradiction as a negation suggesting an absent alternative.[3]

This then is a reading in which Nick does indeed come to grips with the phenomena he encounters in his summer out east. Certainly, we could read the revelatory dissonance of his narrative's aesthetics as a manifestation of an unconscious reaction against capitalism's contradictions (Adorno) or as an equally unconscious struggle with language to exceed his own fixation *vis-à-vis* desire (Lacan), but Nick's evident self-consciousness about *writing* a narrative and structuring it just so, as well as moments in his text that consolidate his insights, cause me to find it more appropriate to credit Nick (as Fitzgerald's surrogate) than language or the unconscious with the narrative's broader revelations.

Negated Figuration

I used to launch my class discussions of the novel by asking the students what they thought of Nick's first evening at the Buchanans' and of his first party at Gatsby's. The results pointed to the narrative's cognitive dissonance, with some students seduced by the Buchanans' vaulting lawns and room full of floating women in white, while others were frankly horrified by the tense domestic unhappiness and the clamor of adultery calling on the telephone. The same split applied to Gatsby's parties, and in the close readings that followed my "poll," both factions were proved correct. There are the fantastic, lyrical conceits, formally enacting the novel's thematic concern with vast desire—the prose equivalents of Daisy herself, "gleaming like silver, safe and proud above the hot struggles of the" narrative (157). And then there is everything else in the novel, the incessant disappointments, compromises, self-deceptions, and casual bad driving. *Gatsby's* objectified world is made ineffably appealing and absolutely crass in turns, with nothing mediating the discrepancy and neither perspective ever gaining dominance in the novel. The "boom" of Tom shutting the windows, which terminates the fantastic early image of floating women in a wind-filled room, is a figure for these affective stylistics (12). Just as some object is conjured up for us in all of its impossible potentiality, Nick shuts the window, and the reader drops back to the floor. Our own desire is provoked only to have its objects erased, causing desire itself to become disembodied, de-figured.

The party in Chapter Three is a set piece for this phenomenon, shifting between the famous figurative passages—which are shiny, alluring promises of everything and of nothing in particular—and frank demonstrations that the parties hold disappointment at every turn. They are firmly rooted in the material world and far more demonstrative of failed human connection than of the ecstatic consummation the guests seem to hope for. As is the case at several points, Daisy is our barometer of contradiction. She is "offended" because the party is characterized not by the formal "gesture" but by raw "emotion" (113). At the same time, she is drawn into "the very casualness of Gatsby's party," where "there were romantic possibilities totally absent from her world" (115). The chapter's rhythm of assertion and negation is established in the first few paragraphs, which detail Nick's voyeuristic perspective as non-attending neighbor.

> There was music from my neighbor's house through the summer nights. In his blue gardens men and girls came and went like moths among the whisperings and the champagne and the stars. At high tide in the afternoon I watched his guests diving from the tower of his raft or taking the sun on the hot sand of his beach while his two motor boats slit the waters of the Sound, drawing aquaplanes over cataracts of foam. (43)

Here Nick's language piques our desire as the remote perspective piques Nick's, but within a sentence, there is an abrupt shift to the labor force that supports this vision, "with mops and scrubbing-brushes and hammers and garden shears, repairing the ravages of the night before" (43). This material foundation of the ethereal is elaborated in the next two sentences:

> "Every Friday five crates of oranges and lemons arrived from a fruiterer in New York—every Monday these same oranges and lemons left his back door in a pyramid of pulpless halves. There was a machine in the kitchen which could extract the juice of two hundred oranges in half an hour, if a little button was pressed two hundred times by a butler's thumb."

What is interesting about this minimalist account of commerce, labor, and waste products (and wasted labor) is the absence of the moment of consumption, the party itself, which is reduced to a midsentence dash. We can retroactively insert the "blue gardens" and "moths," but they no longer function the same way. Gatsby's parties can be the free-floating promise of desire fulfilled only when they are detached from the material and labor that go into them and the waste that comes out the other end. Nick gives us two parties, mutually exclusive, and he will continue to oscillate between them, without mediation, for most of the chapter. In this way, the formal pattern of Nick's narrative mimics the disconnection it documents, splitting the reader's experience between commodified desire and those things that reveal its material contingency and its obligatory forms of amnesia.

Following the image of the butler's thumb, Nick immediately returns to the lyrical evocation of the party, shifting tense strategically to draw us inside it:

> By seven o'clock the orchestra has arrived.... The lights grow brighter as the earth lurches away from the sun and now the orchestra is playing yellow cocktail music and the opera of voices pitches a key higher. Laughter is easier, minute by minute, spilled with prodigality, tipped out at a cheerful word.... Suddenly one of these gypsies in trembling opal seizes a cocktail out of the air, dumps it down for courage and moving her hands like Frisco dances out alone on the canvas platform.... The party has begun."
> (44–45)

When Nick actually attends a party in the next paragraph, the duality of promise and disappointment becomes more insistent. As a man alone, Nick is intensely uncomfortable, lingering by the cocktail table on his way to getting drunk. Jordan provides him with a warm body to attach himself to, eliminating Nick's sense of being "purposeless and alone" (46). As he follows Jordan through a pair of vapid conversations—no moths, no opera of voices—Nick apparently remains silent, while his prose does little more than to document the encounters (47). However, when Nick is in transition at the party, as he is between these first two conversations, he can resume his voyeuristic perspective and reclaim the party's alluring potential. As we move from the specific to the abstract, from discomfort to pleasure, the prose changes accordingly:

> "You've dyed your hair since then," remarked Jordan and I started but the girls had moved casually on and her remark was addressed to the premature moon, produced like the supper, no doubt, out of a caterer's basket. With Jordan's slender arm resting in mine we descended the steps and sauntered about the garden. A tray of cocktails floated at us through the twilight and we sat down at a table with two girls in yellow and three men, each one introduced to us as Mr. Mumble. (47)

Supper comes fully formed from a magical basket, and cocktails float in the twilight. While the commodification of experience is encoded here, characterized by the autonomy of material goods, the prose duplicates and caresses this autonomy, pitting experience against knowledge. Again it is the army of laborers who are absent, the caterers themselves and the people who carry the cocktails. Then begins the second empty conversation, but Nick's near silence reveals his preference for the intermission—his position as spectator, the remarks addressed to no one, and individuals who remain interesting to the degree that they remain anonymous. At one point, in the midst of another table full of crass conversation, Nick's exposition becomes almost sociological, and his reference to East Eggers being "carefully on guard against" the West Eggers' "spectroscopic gayety" is an indication of Nick's own double vision (49). As the party disintegrates into crashing automobiles, it is only in the slowly evolving mystery of Gatsby himself that Nick can sustain his romantic interest, though it too is polarized: Gatsby gives Nick the most flattering and alluring smile Nick has ever known, while, at virtually the same moment, striking Nick as nearly "absurd" (53).

It is apparent that *Gatsby*'s self-negating aesthetics have two axes, the one concerned with desire in its own right and the other with desire as it is channeled into and structured by material commodification. Gatsby and his parties are a locus for libidinal energies writ large, yet they rely on the power of wealth to create a scenario sufficiently incredible to support an illusion of ineffability. Nick goes about poking holes in the illusion, pulling back the curtain to reveal the otherwise invisible people and contraptions that make the show possible. In the Valley of Ashes passage, Nick makes clear that this curtain of invisibility is not simply an effect of Gatsby's "Belasco" productions but a deep seated social symptom—the amnesia of reified consciousness itself (27–28). Nick's conceit of a land made entirely of ash is also a history of material relations, moving from the agricultural "ridges and hills" of "wheat" to a factory town of "chimneys and rising smoke," to the final dehumanized image of masses of indistinguishable men "who move dimly and crumbling through the powdery air." Importantly, what this "swarm" of men *does* is hidden from view behind "an impenetrable cloud which screens their obscure operations from your sight." What one *can* see—what is visible above the obscured field of labor—is an advertisement.

The optometrist's billboard becomes the novel's central image for the blindness that commodity culture depends on, if its products are to be successfully positioned as the avatars of dreams. Advertising is the leading edge of capitalism's transmutation of things that have been made by someone into things that will make you into someone. Commodities are perfect lovers, and advertising is their come hither glance. Thus, Fitzgerald's choice of spectacles as his advertisement's product is both astute and ironic. This advertisement captures your gaze, returns your gaze, and promises to improve your gaze. It is spectroscopic gayety as a closed loop, a desirous voyeurism that sees only itself. The real men on the ground are no match for the advertisement of the man in the sky.

The Valley of Ashes passage embodies this idea of blindness as another of the novel's formal paradoxes, its lyric beauty contrasting with the horror of what it signifies, but more essentially struggling in its tenuousness to figure forth, "with a transcendent effort," that which it points out is finally invisible. The novel's geography drives home the point, using actual proximity to demonstrate conceptual distance: The Valley of Ashes is the shared toilet of the two adjacent geographic manifestations of rich promise and massive consumption—the neighborhood with lawns that jump over sun dials on one side and the city on the other, "rising up across the river in white heaps and sugar lumps all built with a wish out of non-olfactory money . . . [always seen] in its first wild promise of all the mystery and the beauty in the world" (73). When Nick delivers this rhapsody on the city, he has just passed through the Valley of Ashes.

Desire and Figuration

The fact that Daisy and the dream are revealed as inadequate to each other just halfway through the novel, in the first reunion of Daisy and Gatsby, is an indication of just how powerfully the novel leverages our readerly desire.

Half of the plot is post-mortem, yet our awareness of this does not diminish the compelling, sensuous quality of the reading experience. The story is about desire only up to a point, beyond which it simply *is* desire. Peter Brooks describes plot as "an activity, a structuring operation elicited in the reader trying to make sense of those meanings that develop only through textual and temporal succession. . . . Narratives both tell of desire—typically present some story of desire—and arouse and make use of desire as [a] dynamic of signification" (37). Employing Lacan's metonymic slippage, Brooks writes that "if narrative desire keeps moving us forward, it is because narrative metonymy can never quite speak its name" (56). It is, then, not so much Gatsby's desire but our own, and language's, leveraged by the text's aesthetics, that keep us reading eagerly, long after the death-knell of Gatsby's dream is struck.

If, as readers, we are simultaneously seduced by the lyrical evocations of autonomous material objects—that is to say by the prose duplication of the material as commodity—and repelled by the actual social context and significance of these objects, revealed in separate representations of them, then our own desire becomes problematic. Nick makes us want the party, the Buchanans' living room, New York City, etc., but soon enough the objects become sullied and our pleasure in them guilty. The unmediated contradictions of representation, however, serve to maintain and continually re-invoke this desire in one spectacular passage after another, rather than simply setting us up and then setting us straight. What, we must wonder, are we to do with this disembodied surplus of readerly desire?

According to Lacan, desire inaugurates a parade of objects—shifting figurative loci—but it has no accessible Object. Desire points, finally, not at things that it wants and that will satisfy it, but in the other direction, at what we lack. This is a lack produced by the advent of desire and the overwriting of a hypothetical, seamless Real with the Symbolic—language. Language separates the world into pieces, thereby turning the whole—an undifferentiated world that is retroactively felt to have been complete and unalienated—into discrete objects. Those objects cannot be constituted or differentiated except through symbolization, and therefore language is a symptom of loss—of literally losing the whole in the parts. This loss itself is desire-producing, but Lacan locates the arrival of loss and desire somewhat farther back, suggesting that the subject's alienation is precipitated by an initial fixation upon the *desirousness* of others—the fact that others, around a child, are apparently lacking—the observation of lack and desire themselves. This is the "cause" of desire (Lacan's *objet a*), which inaugurates a series of metonymically-linked attempts to signify the elusive object of desire, thereby perpetuating the partitioning of existence in the very attempt to (re)gain the fullness that desire is imagining. Bruce Fink explains this cogently:

Desire is fundamentally caught up in the dialectical *movement* of one signifier to the next, and is diametrically opposed to fixation. It does not seek satisfaction, but rather its own continuation and furtherance: more desire, greater desire! It wishes merely to go on desiring. (90–91)

Unable to quash desire, language perpetuates it through an endless chain of substituted signifiers and the objects they constitute. In this sense, Nick's study of Gatsby's desirousness is necessarily also a study of Gatsby's figurations and their failures—his circumscribed signifiers. His portrait shows Gatsby's consciousness to be so completely reified that desire's substitutional, symbolic process has become a kind of loop, repeatedly attempting to exceed itself yet ever diverted back to the signifiers of the commodity. Gatsby, to appropriate Lacan's description of Freud's Hans, "is left in the lurch . . . by his symbolic environment," and develops "all the permutations possible on a limited number of signifiers" (168).

During the summer, Nick moves from a near-duplication of Gatsby's circular predicament to an understanding of it. Just as Gatsby wishes to "recover some idea of himself" and "repeat the past," Nick's move to the East is an attempt to return to his own undergraduate self, now some ten years past (117, 116, 8–9). His fascination has much to do with the fact that Gatsby maintained Daisy as an unsullied object of desire for five years, because Nick has developed his own strategies for investing desire in objects and then deferring disappointment indefinitely. He laments the pattern of life at home in the "West where an evening was hurried from phase to phase toward its close in a continually disappointed anticipation," and he engineers fantasies the jouissance of which is dependent on holding back (17). He says that he picked out women in the street, and "in my mind, I followed them to their apartments on the corners of hidden streets, and they turned and smiled back at me before they faded through a door into warm darkness" (61). The ineffable parting smile is enough, even in fantasy. Following the women inside would produce the routine disappointment—the consummation that replaces an object's promise with its objective limits. Likewise, Nick's dance of dishonesty with the real women in his life is an effort to almost have a relationship, but not quite. In his supreme act of desire courted against disappointment, he is disgusted by what is going on in Tom and Myrtle's love nest and projects himself outside, looking in:

Yet high over the city our line of yellow windows must have contributed their share of human secrecy to the casual watcher in the darkening streets, and I was him too, looking up and wondering.

I was within and without, simultaneously enchanted and repelled by the inexhaustible variety of life. (40)

Undeterred by his repulsion, Nick can turn himself into an imaginary voyeur who is able to recapture the mystery and promise of that line of windows by pretending to know nothing about what is behind them. He finds it more exciting to see himself than to be himself. We might here recall Lacan's structural model of the infant confronting its reflection in the mirror: While the infant's physical capacities, such as motor skills, remain limited, the mirror image conveys an integrity, a wholeness, that the infant associates with the other bodies it sees. In the apartment, the disappointed, fractured Nick recovers the jouissance of desire, the fantasy of wholeness, by imaging a satisfied version of himself behind the glass.

This passage also illustrates the distinction to be made between the Nick who experienced the events of that summer and the Nick who later writes the narrative intended to disclose their significance. On the one hand, the passage is an extremely poignant disclosure of Nick's unhappiness. On the other, it follows the narrative's deliberate pattern of prosaic ugliness countered by lyrical reclamation of possibility—of Nick forcing us to hold two opposed ideas in our minds at the same time, simultaneously enchanted and repelled. It is Nick's study of Gatsby that helps him gain this critical distance on his own predicament, transforming the blind drives and decoy objects of his summer out East into his narrative's devices for capturing lightning in a bottle. Specifically, Nick studies Gatsby's failed attempts to figure his desire. That figuration itself is the issue for Gatsby and for Nick is apparent in the summary of Gatsby's earliest attempts to articulate his dream:

> The most grotesque and fantastic conceits haunted him in his bed at night. A universe of ineffable gaudiness spun itself out in his brain.... Each night he added to the pattern of his fancies until drowsiness closed down upon some vivid scene with an oblivious embrace. For a while these reveries provided an outlet for his imagination; they were a satisfactory hint of the unreality of reality, a promise that the rock of the world was founded securely on a fairy's wing. (105)

Here Nick enacts a certain stage of Gatsby's pursuit of desire through a chain of vague figurations—fantastic conceits whose referents are other fantastic conceits, language in search of a perfect object it will never find. Gatsby comes across as in a direct struggle with the elusive Real, working feverishly to symbolize that which he senses is there, somewhere outside and beyond. He can only hit at it with solipsistic metaphors that materialize and dematerialize their object simultaneously—ineffable but gaudy, unreal but real. As Nick depicts this moment in Gatsby's life, Gatsby is not yet completely subsumed by the allure of the commodity; desire and figuration remain free, flitting here and there "on a fairy's wing."

However, by the time Gatsby visits Daisy's house, Nick is describing Gatsby's desire in concretely reified terms.

> There was a ripe mystery about it, a hint of bedrooms upstairs more beautiful than other bedrooms, of gay and radiant activities taking place through its corridors and of romances that were not musty and laid away already in lavender but fresh and breathing and redolent of this year's shining motor cars and of dances whose flowers were scarcely withered. . . . (155–156)

This house is a space of great potential, the commodity as a literal structure to house a promise, a mystery, a hint. When we are told in advance that "what gave it an air of breathless intensity was that Daisy lived there—it was as casual a thing to her as his tent out at camp was to him," the emphasis of the second half of the sentence is not that *Daisy* lived there but that Daisy *lived there* (155). While the house's promise is elaborated as the paragraph proceeds, Daisy only appears again in the context of the excitement gener- ated by the fact that "many men had already loved Daisy," and that Gatsby "felt their presence all about the house" (156). Daisy occupies the central space here, within the house and certifiably desirable, but as a place-holder, not as a person. Daisy appears virtually arbitrary; her house has framed the ineffable, so Daisy herself becomes an ideal self, defined within that house. Daisy's arbitrariness climaxes with the exchange of the "mind of god" power of freely migrating desire for "this girl." Daisy becomes the "incarnation" of "a secret place above the trees—he could climb to it, if he climbed alone, and once there he could suck on the pap of life, gulp down the incomparable milk of wonder . . ." (117). This is, of course the decisive moment when the "unutterable"—that which can only be hinted at by means of "fantastic conceits," most notably this one—is traded for a more, but not permanently enduring object, Daisy. We have the image of a return to maternal pleni- tude, here with the added structural imagery of having to climb to it, like a child staring longingly upward at his mother's inaccessible breast. The divorce between these conceits and Daisy points to her role as mere place- holder object; Gatsby has not advanced his quest, merely transferred it to the illusion of the commodity—incarnated in Daisy's house—and thereafter to Daisy herself as its idealized consumer, Daisy. Gatsby wants *to be* Daisy.[4]

Two days later, the limitations of the physical Daisy as incarnation are already apparent, as Gatsby refines the promise of Daisy to her voice, which gives luster to the other, limited material signifiers. This voice will be glossed as something that "couldn't be over-dreamed—that . . . was a deathless song," and Nick describes it early on in terms that revert to the promise of Daisy's house; it conveys "a promise that she had done gay, exciting things just a while since and that there were gay, exciting things hovering in the next hour" (101, 14). This is the most perfect and durable form of Gatsby's dream, and a natural emphasis, because the voice, like the gaze, is posited by Lacan (and Derrida) as something like the perfect object of desire—perfect insofar as it cannot be pinned down, killed by the symbolic, or over-dreamed. It offers the promise of durable desire. The voice and the gaze "are unspecularizable: you cannot see them per se, they have no mirror images, and they are extremely difficult to symbolize or formalize. They belong to the register of what Lacan calls the real, and resist imaginarization and symbolization" (Fink 92).

However, underlining Gatsby's reified consciousness, he *does* immediately exchange the voice. Unable to resist the habituated reifying drive of desire in capitalism, Gatsby figures this experience of desire unhinged from the symbolic and material order in the most predictable way. In its initial and most sublime moment, he already reads Daisy's voice as signifying "the youth and mystery that wealth imprisons and preserves, of the freshness of many clothes and of Daisy, gleaming like silver, safe and proud above the hot struggles of the poor" (157). He will eventually say simply that Daisy's voice "is full of money," for what better objective form for pure promise commodified than the expansive, non-specific promise of currency. It is a particularly charged placeholder, the alluring undifferentiated potential of which always outstrips that for which it is exchanged, but which *insists* upon exchange as the culmination of its promise. A voice, as Lacan's Object, holds out the possibility of perceiving desire apart from habituated social figurations—a potentially revelatory unmasking for Gatsby—but he cannot resist or exceed such figurations and is thus led back to his starting point: A voice "full of money" burns a hole in reified desire's pocket, and demands to be spent. From here, his unstoppable advance into fully commodified figurations and descent into reified consciousness proceeds apace, as he amasses money, a house, a new identity, and a great many beautiful shirts with the intention of exchanging them all for Daisy. The sublime discovery of Daisy's voice might have made this a love story, but Gatsby's circumscribed figurative universe makes it a shopping trip instead. At the end of the first affair, Daisy remains the incarnation, but she has already been displaced, out of figuration by her voice, then refigured as (and exchanged for) a multitudinous background of purchasing power and luxury goods.

In contrast to Gatsby's misguided figurations, Nick's formal strategy of negated figuration concerns Lacan's elusive *objet a* in an absolute sense—as the desire for desire itself—for its "continuation and furtherance." As it is pure desire that demarcates the lack signified by *objet a*—that surrounds it, discloses its absence—desire itself can be understood as that which comes closest to accessing the fundamentally inaccessible lack that caused desire in the first place and that drives it onward and outward. Desire is the dream of fullness, and while that is a vain dream in its absolute Lacanian sense, it is a critical and utopic dream in the context of Nick's narrative, in which he seeks a formal means by which to dislodge desire from its reified figurations. Nick's aesthetics of negation put figuration itself into question, and what is at stake is an ideologically particular figuration and the particular subjectivity constituted by it.[5] As we have seen, figuration in the novel is inseparably bound up with and limited by the logic of the commodity—at the parties, in the Valley of Ashes, in Gabsy's successive constructions of Daisy. When Daisy herself attempts to represent what is desirable about Gatsby, she can only manage to say that he "resemble[s] the advertisement of the man. . . . You know the advertisement of the man" (125).

So, Nick depicts the fundamental structural nature of desire and figuration as tightly circumscribed by the historical and material figurations of commodity capitalism, while the formal techniques of his narrative free up desire by disrupting this disabling *cul-de-sac*. By isolating or setting loose desire in its own right, he is attempting to extricate the fundamental human drive from a limited, blinding context. The space he clears out is occupied by the specter of utopic social transformation—something that can only be represented as an absence, as an implication inherent in the narrative's irreconcilable differences.

However, Nick does attempt to figure this hypothetical alternative in the Dutch sailor passage near the end of the novel, in which he represents a fleeting moment outside of reification and outside of language. When the sailor catches sight of what we now know as North America, he is momentarily caught in a sublimely terrifying experience of the unfigured Real that is historically and ideologically potent. Once again, Nick provides two distinct and competing figurations. First Nick represents the Dutch sailor's speechless moment this way: "A fresh, green breast's" "trees" "pandered . . . to the last and greatest of all human dreams." The closest we come on the final page to a gloss of this "dream" is "the orgastic future." What is striking here is the relative crassness of this figuration when contrasted with the more elusive and valorizing language Nick uses in an alternative attempt to convey the sailor's experience, which evidences a resistance to figuration itself. Nick refers to what the sailor is literally looking at as "this continent," but even this is figuratively removed from the experience of the sailor, who would not know he was looking at a "continent"; to him it was neither "breast" nor "continent" but rather "something commensurate to his capacity for wonder." *Something.* If the sailor experienced the vista as an object of desire in the usual sense (e.g. as a breast or a continent to be plundered) his response would be pleasurable, but it is not.

In this "transitory enchanted moment," he is "compelled into an aesthetic contemplation *he neither understood nor desired,* face to face for the last time in history with something commensurate to his capacity for wonder" (189). It is commensurate because it is baffling and disturbing in its sheer overpowering vastness. It is uncomfortable because it cannot be assimilated. "Aesthetic contemplation" is not up to the task. It is unfigurable. Figuration will follow upon landing of course, as the continent is claimed, named, cleared of its inhabitants, and ultimately covered with the houses and social orders of East Egg, West Egg, and beyond. That is the course of history, betraying what was a moment of ambiguous potential, a moment that asked *how* this "something" would be figured, and what that would mean for those who would become the subjects of that figuration. Here as elsewhere, Nick intimates that desire—now on a national level—might have built a better home than Daisy's or Gatsby's own "huge incoherent failure of a house," one that would have emerged from a different historical trajectory and that would have produced a differently oriented desiring subject (188). Such a subject would not figure a pimp with a breast to sell as commensurate to the human capacity to wonder. Nick's representations work against each other, toward an absent alternative. This is his more adequate "aesthetic contemplation."

Metaphor and Non-Identity

Bruce Fink defines the Lacanian subject as "that which creates a *breach* in the real as it establishes a link between two signifiers, the subject . . . being nothing but that very breach" (69). The subject is essentially metaphor itself, "a spark flying from one signifier to another, creating a connection between them" (69).

> As metaphor's creative spark, the subject has no permanence or persistence; it comes into being as a spark flashing between two signifiers. As the result of new meaning brought into the world, however, the subject . . . remains fixated or subjugated, and acquires a kind of permanence as such. . . . We can provisionally view symptoms as having . . . a substitutional structure, wherein the subject as meaning persists indefinitely in its subjugated state unless

a new metaphor is achieved. In that sense, analysis can be viewed, in Lacan's theory, as requiring that new metaphors be forged. For each new metaphor brings with it a precipitation of subjectivity which can alter the subject's position. Given that the symptom itself is a metaphor, the creation of a new metaphor doesn't dissolve the symptom but reconfigures it or creates a new one, or a modified subjective position with respect to the symptom. (Fink 70)[6]

In Lacan's view, "understanding" in the conventional sense is a rather impotent capacity, as it indicates the insertion of something new into the existing chain of signifiers. "True understanding . . . is actually a process which goes beyond the automatic functioning of the symbolic order and involves an incursion of the symbolic into the real" (Fink 71). Metaphor precipitates such an incursion—"a new *order* in the signifying chain, a shakedown of the old order" (71). We can therefore view Gatsby's figurative trap as one of metaphorical illusion; while he keeps changing his metaphors, the relation of identity which his reified consciousness imposes upon them prevents productive disruption and reordering. In other words, the substitutional logic of commodity thinking, of identity through exchange, precludes a fruitful substitutional functioning of figuration, and Gatsby's subjective position cannot be modified.

Adorno identifies a similar stalemate in contemporary language, which he describes as having decayed into "that bilge of self-alienation, at once stereotyped and defective. . . . The second language of those who have fallen silent, an agglomeration of insolent phrases, pseudo-logical connections, and words galvanized into trademarks, the desolate echo of the world of advertisement . . ." ("Trying" 262). His subject here is Beckett's *Endgame*, which, in contrast to this scathing denunciation, is "the language of a literary work that negates language" (262). He argues that an interpretation of the play requires not assigning it a meaning but "understanding its unintelligibility, concretely reconstructing the meaning of the fact that it has no meaning" (243). While *Gatsby* does not go so far as the absurdist play, the enigma presented by the novel's aesthetic of negation is analogous, in the sense that Adorno's reading of Beckett stresses the text's determination to avoid making meaning as its essential critique of inherited and banal understandings of existence, culture, and history.

Gatsby's technique is more properly understood as a productive collision of incompatible meanings, and Adorno speaks to this in his aesthetic theory. He defines understanding as something that is achieved when the status quo of social meaning is disrupted by the dialectical relation of form and content. For Adorno, the essential power of artworks is their nondiscursive character, which prevents their subsumption within the existing rational order, which for Adorno is the *irrationality* of capitalism's rationalization of human capacities—the Enlightenment *telos* of human emancipation gone horribly wrong. Here we substitute for the Lacanian Real a society free of contradiction—an intimation of utopic transformation. For Adorno, form is the way in which artworks "both oppose society and communicate with it. Unresolved social antagonisms return in the artworks as the immanent problems of artistic form" (Zuidervaart 123).

> Moreover, the artistic dialectic of content and form is a liberating agent of revelatory contradiction and illusory reconciliation. . . . On the one hand, form enables artworks to oppose current society in a way that makes us aware of the implicit mediation of immediate and chaotic contradictions. On the other hand, form enables artworks to arrange society's scattered elements into a world that would differ from one where blind domination and exchange prevail. . . . Artworks are reconstellations rather than copies of social reality. The nondiscursive knowledge they provide is a determinate negation of contemporary society. (Zuidervaart 130)

> As a nondiscursive ordering or logic of content, artistic form sublates the discursive order of society and daily experience." When the "empirical social categories" that enter art begin to follow "artistic laws" of "space, time, or causality, their lawfulness is shown to be alterable, and the liberation of society from subjectively dictated lawfulness becomes a concrete possibility. (Zuidervaart 129)

In Shierry Nicholsen's account, this dialectic of form and content is put into action by Adorno's model of how art is experienced, which involves a dialectic of the mimetic and the discursive. The mimetic refers to the abeyance of the reader's discursive or rationalist capacities when fully subsumed in the movement of the work of art. Absorbed by the text, the reader becomes a mimetic reflection of it. The mimetic experience of art resists the imposition of homogenizing categories of rationality, thereby preserving the artwork's particularity and its deformation of existing social logic.[7] Full mimetic immersion allows the text to enact its own non-rational rationality, but it poses the danger of entrapping the reader; the relationship of identity between reader and artwork is one of sensuous disclosure, but that disclosure cannot become clear without discursive reflection (Nicholsen 149–151). By discursive, Adorno means a more distanced meditation upon the text, in which the reader steps back from the mimetic experience and tries to account for its nondiscursive meaning. What prompts this meditation is the enigmatic character of art—enigmatic *because* art is nonconceptual and nondiscursive and because, "as Adorno says, art cannot answer the question, 'What are you for?'" (Nicholsen 150). While the mimetic dimension establishes the reader's affinity with the text, the enigmatic quality establishes otherness.

> Enigma is ... the difference between what is experienced from completely outside the work of art and what is experienced from completely inside it.... [Adorno] is not talking about two separate mental activities, experience and theoretical reflection. Rather, he is attempting to specify a reflection that takes place on and perhaps within that enigmatic zone of difference, a zone of experience in which the enactment and assimilation of the other that constitute mimesis are inseparable from—but also distinct from—the rationality of philosophical reflection. (Nicholsen 151)

Let us then use these concepts to consolidate the case being made for *Gatsby*: metaphor as productive reconfiguration of the signifying chain; form as the disclosure of the social contradictions imbedded in content; and the disruption of the mimetic experience of a text by a non-discursive enigma calling for discursive reflection. The reader's mimetic experience of *Gatsby* is disorienting, stretched between two ways of seeing and two Nicks—the one who himself held a mimetic relationship to Gatsby's reified dream and the one who carefully structures its representation into a formal experience of dissonance. It is in the text's non-systematic presentation of the multiple faces of the commodity that our mimetic absorption into the text's movements becomes difficult, and the quality of enigma emerges.

The lyrical eruptions are, in Lacanian terms, *The Great Gatsby*'s crippled metaphors, those that are exchanged for each other without exceeding reified consciousness to connect with a wider signifying matrix. As we have seen, they are disconnected even from the surrounding prose on the page. They are Adorno's "desolate echo of the world of advertisement." Yet, when Nick juxtaposes these passages with his contradictory re-representations of the same phenomena, he creates the narrative's *functional metaphors*. His aesthetics simultaneously point to the connections between things and enact the ideological insistence that they are unrelated. The metaphorical spark is set loose, yet those things it connects cannot reconcile themselves into a relationship of identity—in which one subsumes or replaces the other. The autonomy of the commodity is there, on the page and in the reading experience, but its undoing is there too, in the form of the real connections among all the things of the world—labor, consumption, national history, personal history. The reader becomes the subject-as-breach, left to contend with the ideological enigma of this intra-metaphorical gap. If we retain Adorno's dialectical relationship to the text, simultaneously mimetic and reflective, we cannot remove the text's dissonance. We can, however, perceive its formal resistance to figurative identity as a formal resistance to the seductive sway of reified thinking itself.[8]

Endgame: Non-Identity

The night Myrtle Wilson is run down, Daisy chooses to be with Tom rather than Gatsby. In his imaginative reconstruction of the next day, Nick depicts Gatsby's annihilating confrontation with non-identity, after "living too long with a single dream."

> He must have looked up at an unfamiliar sky through frightening leaves and shivered as he found what a grotesque thing a rose is and how raw the sunlight was upon the scarcely created grass. A new world, material without being real, where poor ghosts, breathing dreams like air, drifted fortuitously about . . . like that ashen fantastic figure gliding toward him through the amorphous trees. (169)

This is of course Wilson, and the decisive phrase is "ashen fantastic figure," which connects this "ghostly" killer to those men of ash who do something invisible at the bottom of the world, beneath the advertisement and just beyond the shiny autonomous promise of the mansions and the city. This "figure" for the repression of the material relations hidden within the commodity emerges from the bushes to conclude the nightmare of non-identity into which Gatsby awakes—the determinate "material" negation of Gatsby's socially-constructed, illusory "real"—its assassin.

Following immediately on the heels of Gatsby's funeral, Nick's recollections of journeys home from college for Christmas begin a series of discrete passages that make up the final pages of the narrative: Nick's Midwest, his "El Greco" nightmare vision of the East, his break with Jordan, a scene with Tom outside a jeweler's shop, and the Dutch sailor meditation. In his Gatsby-like plan to start over, Nick came east hoping to "bring back" his undergraduate days, but he gives that up to return to a midwest no longer viewed as "the ragged edge of the universe" (7). The "my middle-west" he valorizes is a place where "dwellings are still called through decades by a family's name"—"Are you going to the Ordways'? the Herseys'? the Schultzes'?" (184). While this certainly indicates a bourgeois identity within a commodified culture, it also reverses what has become the conventional direction of identity in the novel;

whereas the house objectified the person, most dramatically in Gatsby's conception of Daisy, the house is now subordinated to the person. This is emphasized by the fact that this signifying system only works if the houses *are not* exchanged as commodities. More important, though, is Nick's comment on the moment during each train trip when he and the others became "unutterably aware of our identity with this country for one strange hour before we melted indistinguishably into it again" (184). A complete "identity with this country" would preclude an awareness of itself, would *be* indistinguishable melting, so Nick is actually describing a liminal sense of *non*-identity—a one-hour ride through the zone of difference that renders identity discernable. This might be the ultimate distillation of his narrative's purpose, and it is certainly an appropriate overture to the novel's final sequence of passages.

The "El Greco" vision of the East's commodified identity stands in direct contrast to the Ordways and Schultzes and their homes; men characterized only by their "dress suits" carry a woman characterized only by her "white evening dress" and a hand that "sparkles cold with jewels" into the "wrong house," which is one of "a hundred houses, at once conventional and grotesque" (185). Here interchangeable people and interchangeable homes signify a cultural situation in which the differences among people and things are superceded by the interchangeable commodities of clothing, jewels, homes, and finally people themselves: "No one knows the woman's name, and no one cares."

Nick's break with Jordan shows Nick acting on the above contrast. He renounces the "lie" he has been living, his variation on Gatsby's dance of deferral, in which he pursued the jouissance of desire by changing one woman for another, while keeping his distance (the woman back home, the stenographer, Jordan, and the cast of fantasy women). He and Jordan have functioned for each other as social currency; as a couple they could comfortably move through the social circles and events of the summer, while they carefully ignored each other as individuals. (Consider Nick's famous reaction to Jordan's incurable dishonesty: "I was casually sorry, and then I forgot" (63).) In the final conversation, Nick breaks a commitment that he and Jordan had studiously avoided ever making to each other. This suggests a new commitment to commitment itself, just as the deliberate rejection of a particular person suggests implicit criteria for someone with whom Nick could have a satisfactory relationship. Love objects for Nick are no longer freely exchangeable.

In the case of Nick's final meeting with Tom, we see the now wiser Nick's final word on the apparent autonomy of commodities—a kind of coda that fills in the absence within the Valley of Ashes figuration. Nick imagines that Tom is about to purchase some cufflinks (188). There is no indication of what Tom might actually be about to buy, but Nick is connecting whatever Tom buys or owns to Meyer Wolfshiem's cufflinks, manufactured to order from the molars of a man who made a pass at his wife (77). The parallel to Tom's by-proxy killing of Gatsby, his wife's lover, is obvious. Nick did not appear to catch the life history of Wolfshiem's sinister ornaments during his lunch with him, but here we see one of Nick's more important conclusions about his summer out East. Far from holding a vast and abstract promise—far from being almost magical and certainly autonomous vessels of immanent and imminent satisfaction—commodities have a compromising history. Nick's sidelong observation resists the amnesia of exchange—the laundering of history enacted by exchange though money; "the youth and mystery that wealth imprisons and preserves" is rewritten as the ruthless history that it conceals.

As we have already seen, the Dutch sailor's confrontation with the continent works to evoke pre-figured desire, a confrontation with the absolutely non-identical, with its intimation of a different possible history and of a subject outside of a (signifying) economy depicted as a pimp selling illusions to the human capacity for wonder—the national history obscured in the Valley of Ashes, and fronted by an advertisement. What is striking as we move to the final page's next metaphor is its puniness compared with the preceding anti-figure of the sailor's "something commensurate"; it is Gatsby gazing at the "green light at the end of Daisy's dock." In contrast to the non-identity confronted uncomfortably by the sailor, the green light is simply part of the loop of "pandering" signifiers ruled by exchange: Daisy's "house and its "rooms," "Daisy," "money," "Jay Gatsby," "beautiful shirts," "the green light," the "green breast." At this point, and certainly by the time Nick transforms "Gatsby" into "us" in the final three sentences, we should begin to feel uncomfortably implicated in an endless reduplication of Gatsby's misguided and fatal dream, for at the same time Nick spells out for the reader the precise nature of Gatsby's mistake, the spectacular language of his elegy for a doomed future once again produces a contradictory pleasure.

> Gatsby believed in the green light, the orgastic future that year by year recedes before us. It eluded us then, but that's no matter—tomorrow we will run faster, stretch out our arms farther. . . . And one fine morning—
> So we beat on, boats against the current, borne back ceaselessly in to the past.

This is the final moment of dissonance in the novel, superimposing seduction and the cancellation of satisfaction. As a conclusion it is Nick's challenge to the reader, an insult, a test. The question is, can we be pandered to? In the rapid-fire sequence of the last six pages, Nick has shown himself to be embracing a very different kind of past than Gatsby, one characterized by distinctions, commitment, historical depth, and an understanding of the commodity's lie. He has certainly not depicted *himself* in the way that he depicts "*us*" in the final lines, and we are obliged to choose between Nick and Gatsby as we confront the future and society. If we accept Nick's description of the nature of desire, will we go reflexively on inside of Gatsby's reified dream, or has the assault of the text's dissonance, its courting of non-identity, changed *our* subject position sufficiently that we will react negatively to this final accusation that we are all exactly the same, that we are Gatsby? We are being asked if the text has produced an experience akin to Nick's on the train—a consciousness of identity with this phenomenon, which is therefore a liminal sense of *non*-identity—a transitory experience that allows us to differentiate ourselves from the doomed consciousness Nick attributes to us in the final two paragraphs. Will we melt indistinguishably into it again, or will the productive quality of distortion persist?

Notes

1. An earlier version of this essay was published in *Arizona Quarterly* in 2003 under the same title.

2. Here I invoke Bruce Fink's gloss of metaphor in Lacan, to which I will return in more detail further on.

3. For a thorough account of Fitzgerald's own stated, partial allegiance to the ideas of Marxism, see Gervais. Possnock concludes his essay by saying that Fitzgerald "knew just what he was about when he declared himself to be 'essentially Marxian'" (212).

4. It is worth noting that in "Winter Dreams," the story from which Fitzgerald lifted many of the passages having to do with Daisy's house and voice, Dexter eventually and explicitly separates Judy and the dream from material goods and even ceases to want to possess Judy herself; what remains is more purely the desire to preserve intact the sense of having once believed in the dream. The past itself becomes the dear object. In adapting the material and prose for *Gatsby*, Fitzgerald was clearly interested in carrying the reification of the dream to the limit.

5. I am in agreement with John T. Irwin, who has argued that in *Gatsby* the foremost concern is "the attempt to preserve a self-sustaining image of desire, the category of Desire *per se*." But for Irwin Nick can't come to terms with "the persistence of the illusion that the original object of Desire is something physical" (536, 540). Irwin stylishly terms the phenomenon Nick courts as "compensatory prefiguration"; an object is figured forth, but "it is freed from questions of the attainability or reality of the imagined object of desire, and forever immune from disillusion because this capacity knows how to keep itself always in 'readiness' to act without ever committing itself to action" (541). Irwin ultimately judges that Nick has figured Gatsby in this way, making Gatsby Nick's inadequate but carefully sustained object. I am arguing that Nick extricates himself from this illusion, modifying "compensatory prefiguration" to compensatory *defiguration*.

6. I am circumspect about invoking, in an analysis of a text, the clinical dimension of Fink's interest in Lacan, but as the critical history of the novel manifests a consistent engagement with the reader response to figurative dissonance, it seems appropriate to acknowledge that what we are talking about here is, finally, the effect of forcing the reader into new metaphors and a new subject position.

7. See especially *Aesthetic Theory*, 53–56.

8. Adorno did not whittle down the contradictions of capitalism to the commodity, nor did he assert that formal manifestations of society would point exclusively in that direction. Therefore, I must acknowledge that while *I* am extracting a singular "rational" meaning from *Gatsby's* "nondiscursive enigma," the terms of my theoretical model insist that there are others.

WORKS CITED

Adorno, Theodor W. *Aesthetic Theory*. Ed. Gretel Adorno and Rolf Tiedemann. Trans. Robert Hullot-Kentor. Minneapolis: University of Minnesota Press, 1997.

———. "Trying to Understand Endgame." *Notes to Literature* (vol. 1). Ed. Rolf Tiedemann. Trans. Shierry Weber Nicholsen. New York: Columbia University Press, 1991.

Brooks, Peter. *Reading for the Plot*. New York: Knopf, 1984.

Cartwright, Kent. "Nick Carraway as an Unreliable Narrator." *Papers on Language and Literature* 20:2 (1984): 218–33.

Donaldson, Scott, ed. *Critical Essays on F. Scott Fitzgerald's* The Great Gatsby. Boston: G. K. Hall, 1984.

———. "The Trouble With Nick." Donaldson 181–89.

Edwards, Duane. "Who Killed Myrtle Wilson, A Study of *The Great Gatsby*." *Ball State University Forum* 23:1 (1982): 35–41.

Fink, Bruce. *The Lacanian Subject: Between Language and Jouissance*. Princeton: Princeton University Press, 1995.

Fitzgerald, F. Scott. *The Great Gatsby* (The Authorized Text). New York: Collier Books, 1992.

———. *The Crack-Up*. New York: New Directions, 1956.

Gervais, Ronald J. "The Socialist in Silk Stockings: Fitzgerald's Double Allegiance." *Mosaic* 15. 2 (1982): 79–92

Giltrow, Janet and David Stouck. "Style as Politics in *The Great Gatsby*." *Studies in the Novel* 29:4 (1997) 476–89.

Godden, Richard. "*The Great Gatsby*: Glamor on the Turn." *Journal of American Studies* 16 (1982): 343–71.

Howells, William Dean. *The Rise of Silas Lapham*. New York: Penguin, 1987.

Irwin, John T. "Compensating Visions: *The Great Gatsby*." *Southwest Review* 77 (1992) 536–45.

Lacan, Jacques. "The Agency of the Letter in the Unconscious or Reason Since Freud." *Écrits*. Trans. Alan Sheridan. New York: Norton, 1977.

Lockridge, Ernest. "F. Scott Fitzgerald's *Trompe l'Oeil* and *The Great Gatsby*'s Buried Plot." *Journal of Narrative Technique* 17:2 (1987): 163–81.

Nicholsen, Shierry Weber. *Exact Imagination, Late Work: On Adorno's Aesthetics*. Cambridge: MIT Press, 1997

O'Rourke, David. "Nick Carraway as Narrator in *The Great Gatsby*." *International Fiction Review* 9.1 (1982): 57–60.

Possnock, Ross. "'A New World, Material Without Being Real': Fitzgerald's Critique of
    Capitalism in *The Great Gatsby*." Donaldson 201–13.
Tyson, Lois. *Psychological Politics and the American Dream: The Commodification of Subjectiv-
    ity in Twentieth-Century American Literature*. Columbus: Ohio State University Press,
    1994
Zuidervaart, Lambert. *Adorno's Aesthetic Theory: The Redemption of Illusion*. Cambridge: MIT
    Press, 1991.

JANET GILTROW AND DAVID STOUCK

Pastoral Mode and Language in The Great Gatsby

In an account of style in *The Great Gatsby*, George Garrett observes that the created language of the book "allows for the poetry of intense perception to live simultaneously and at ease with a hard-edged, implacable vulgarity" (Bruccoli, *New Essays* 111). He amplifies this observation by stating that "stylistically *Gatsby* is a complicated composite of several distinct kinds of prose, . . . a composite style whose chief demonstrable point appears to be the inadequacy of any single style (a single means of perception, point of view) by itself to do justice to the story" (114). This broad summary accommodates the ways in which *The Great Gatsby* has traditionally been read—as a romantic version of the American dream, as an ironic assessment of American values, and as an elegy for something that has been lost in time.[1] But Garrett's essay, like other studies of Fitzgerald's style, offers little more than general impressions on the subject. Here, and in an earlier essay (Giltrow and Stouck), we respond to Jackson R. Bryer's call for a focus on "small units" of style (Donaldson, *Critical Essays* 127–28) in order to describe the unique voice of Fitzgerald's "composite" prose. In our first essay we examined the endings of Fitzgerald's sentences, where so often the indefinite excitements of ambition and romance are recorded lyrically in syntactically unnecessary appositive structures. We have considered there as well how the materials of romance are undercut by Nick Carraway's ironic representation of other

From *F. Scott Fitzgerald in the Twenty-first Century*, edited by Jackson R. Bryer, Ruth Prigozy, and Milton R. Stern, pp. 139–52. © 2003 by the University of Alabama Press.

voices around him, the sounds of the age. In this essay we shall look at how Nick attends to yet another order of experience, one beyond his immediate social habitat, an order stable, profound, and original, which we shall here equate with the pastoral mode. To describe the language of pastoral, we use, in addition to traditional accounts of English syntax, techniques from discourse analysis and linguistic pragmatics that will help us to investigate features of Fitzgerald's style that operate beyond the sentence, in the arena of language as socially situated, as utterance addressed and received both within the text and as an exchange between reader and writer.[2]

* * *

At the beginning of his story, Nick tells us of his unusually close relationship to his father and conveys a certain pride in the Carraway clan, said to be "descended from the Dukes of Buccleuch" (7). He also turns over in his mind a piece of advice from his father: "Whenever you feel like criticizing anyone . . . remember that all the people in this world haven't had the advantages that you've had" (5). Nick amplifies this counsel in a snobbish generalization, claiming that "a sense of the fundamental decencies is parcelled out unequally at birth" (6). Mr. Carraway's homily, his word of caution, has made a strong impression on his son. And it seems that it is the form as much as the content of the homily that impresses Nick, for although his amplification somewhat distorts his father's intention, his speech habits often exactly preserve the voice of the father. Despite his relative youth and his taste for partying, Nick makes a number of similar generalizations about life: "There is no confusion like the confusion of a simple mind" (131); "No amount of fire or freshness can challenge what a man will store up in his ghostly heart" (101); "there [is] no difference between men, in intelligence or race, so profound as the difference between the sick and the well" (131). In linguistic terms, such statements are maxims, that is, proverbial generalizations about human nature and human experience drawn from long reflection on the order of things. Occasionally they occur in *The Great Gatsby* as independent clauses, as in the second example above, but more frequently they are embedded in longer sentences, sometimes compressed into referring expressions, as when Nick says that he is going to become "that most limited of all specialists, the 'well-rounded' man." Insisting on the wisdom of this paradoxical observation, he continues to generalize, adding: "This isn't just an epigram—life is much more successfully looked at from a single window, after all" (8–9). In a sober mood he reflects on the lack of interest in the deceased Gatsby—"that intense personal interest to which everyone has some vague right at the end" (172). Such statements and expressions are not only general in reference ("most," "a man," "life," "everyone"), they have no specific time reference, their truth being neither particular nor contingent. They are somehow above, or beside, the narrative order of events, and they establish in the text the speaker's recourse to an order of permanent values beyond the resounding "echolalia" of the present.

Maxims also convey a speaker's claim to knowledge, his or her access to established authority and steady truths; in recognition of this, Aristotle said that while maxims were an effective tool for orators, young speakers should not use them.[3] Aristotle's advice acknowledges an incompatibility between lack of experience and wise sayings, yet Nick is very prone to thinking in maxims, despite his youth and his resolve to stay all judgments. Their incongruence draws our attention to that very divided nature of the novel's narrator, who on the one hand is a heedless partygoer, imagining glamorous encounters with women in darkened doorways, but on the other hand is an apprentice in the banking and bond business and a judicious observer of human behavior. Nick describes this doubleness when he says of himself at the squalid party in Myrtle Wilson's apartment: "I was within and without, simultaneously enchanted and repelled by the inexhaustible variety of life" (40). The voice of the maxim, grounded in paternal authority and wisdom, is a regulating device for Nick—solemn, stable, even magisterial—negotiating the extravagance and moral confusion of West Egg and New York, those "riotous excursions" to which he is so irresistibly drawn. When trying to understand Jordan Baker's behavior early in their relationship, Nick observes that "most affectations conceal something eventually, even though they don't in the beginning" (62). And reflecting on the rumor that she has cheated in a major golf tournament, he makes the sexist claim that "Dishonesty in a woman is a thing you never blame deeply" (63). Nick most often speaks in this voice when under pressure; he says of himself, "I am slow thinking and full of interior rules that act as brakes on my desires" (63–64). The posture of the maxims, distributed in the text beyond particular sentences and situations, signals for the reader something socially conservative in Nick's character—his close relation to his father and his anxieties in terms of class—which in turn has a powerful shaping influence on his narrative. Nick's tie to his personal past, so different from Gatsby's rejection of family and home, is a direct link to another dimension of the novel, a yearning for what is stable and originary but has been lost through time, an aspect of the story that has been described in terms of pastoral elegy.[4]

* * *

Nick's story is a lament, a mourning interpreted in terms of gardens and the passing of the seasons, and situated in the history of the imagination in

America. We use the term "pastoral" here not to evoke Theocritus's idyllic landscape, Schiller's maturing child, or Empson's social encounter of courtier and rustic,[5] but to suggest another representative anecdote, that of the abject memoirist, and the idea of pastoral not as a rural subject but as a mode of art based on memory. Nick himself says, "That's my middle-west—not the wheat or the prairies or the lost Swede towns but the thrilling, returning trains of my youth" (184). At the center of that memory is the human dream of a harmonious life from which are eliminated the complexities of social ills (greed, poverty, and wars) and natural process (change, decay, and death). What the pastoral imagination seeks to recover (to remember) is an existence when there was no conscious division of self from the rest of the world, no separation of subject and object.

For the study of literary texts, the drama of pastoral is probably best described by language-centered myths of human culture. In Jacques Lacan's rewriting of Freud in terms of language development, infancy is described as an "imaginary" state centered in the mother where no clear distinction yet exists between the self and the external world. The child initially experiences the world as whole or unitary and communicates directly with the mother through the body and through non-representational sounds, what Julia Kristeva calls the semiotic process (124–47). In pastoral writing this state is the "original relationship to the universe" described by Wordsworth and Emerson as pre-speech, wherein Wordsworth can describe himself as "a Babe, by intercourse of touch / [holding] mute dialogues with my Mother's heart" (*The Prelude* 267–68). But as the child necessarily grows apart from its mother, becoming aware of its separateness and at the same time acquiring speech, it begins to use language as a means to bridge the gap that has grown between self and other. Consequently, language is haunted by its origins in difference and absence, for to enter the symbolic order of language is, in Lacan's formulation, to be severed from the "real" (*Écrits* 1–7, 281–91) or, as Nick Carraway phrases it, to be convinced of "the unreality of reality" (105). If mode, as Northrop Frye argues, encodes views of human strength relative to the world (33–34), then pastoral is the particular mode that articulates a hero's powerlessness and sense of loss. After his neighbor's death, Nick broods over what has happened, then returns to his home in the Midwest, wanting no more parties, no more "riotous excursions," giving up his bid for power in the world of eastern finance and social advancement. It is from this position that he tells his story.

Nick is acutely sensitive to the evocative power of language, to the overtones of words, and especially to their power to evoke feelings of loss. As he listens to Gatsby rehearsing his past one evening, he reflects: "Through all he said ... I was reminded of something—an elusive rhythm, a fragment of lost words, that I had heard somewhere a long time ago. For a moment a phrase tried to take shape in my mouth and my lips parted like a dumb man's, as though there was more struggling upon them than a wisp of startled air. But they made no sound and what I had almost remembered was uncommunicable forever" (118). Gatsby has been telling Nick about the autumn night, five years before, when he first kissed Daisy. The scene as Nick recounts it lies at the crux between pastoral and romance, for as Gatsby approaches Daisy he recognizes that he is making an irreversible choice. Before he actually kisses Daisy, he imagines that the blocks of the sidewalk, visible in the moonlight, form a ladder and that if he were to climb it *alone* to a secret place above the trees, like Wordsworth's "Babe," he "could suck on the pap of life, gulp down the incomparable milk of wonder" (117). Gatsby's story, however, is not a pastoral; it is a romance quest, and accordingly he kisses Daisy, realizing "his unutterable visions" in this girl of his dreams. But Gatsby's desire for Daisy is thwarted by his lack of riches, and after she marries Tom Buchanan he is left with the painful memory of his loss and a determination to relive the past and set things right. "You can't repeat the past," Nick cautions Gatsby in one of his frequent maxims, but in fact Nick's counsel probably has more relevance to himself than it does to Gatsby.

This need to repeat the past, we would suggest, is the closest bond between Gatsby and Nick, but it reflects two very different ways of experiencing the past. Gatsby lives in the past, but his dream is still about future prospects; for Nick, on the other hand, the dream is retrospective, linked to some lost, more perfect place and time, some place of origins. Nick's rendering of Gatsby's life at this point, with its intimations of a story that will remain incommunicable forever, tells us much about Nick's imagination and about an elegiac refrain in his narrative. Nick also has set out on an adventure, the path of romance and self-invention; but when the summer of his story is over he can no longer go forward and returns to the "warm center" of his beginnings in the Midwest, where he wants "the world to be in uniform and at a sort of moral attention *forever*" (6; emphasis added).

That powerful undertow in Nick's imagination, which drags him back to his midwestern origins and an ideal of restored innocence, is manifest in the visual surface of his story, wherein the characters and events are repeatedly imagined in terms of summer and childhood and an absence of passion. At the story's opening dinner party, Daisy and Jordan are nostalgic about their "beautiful white girlhood" (24), and Nick continues to see the two women in this abstracted light: seated on a couch, they appear buoyed up in their white dresses as if floating on balloons (12). An ethereal, sexless quality in both women is suggested again when they are described later in the text as lying on an enormous couch, "like silver idols, weighing down their own white dresses against the singing breeze of the fans" (122). Nick refers several times to the complete lack of passion or desire in these women: "Sometimes [Daisy] and Miss Baker talked at once, unobtrusively and with a bantering inconsequence that was never quite chatter, that was as cool as their white dresses and their impersonal eyes in the absence of all desire" (16–17). Jordan says to Nick that perhaps Daisy "never went in for amour at all" (82). Jordan is Nick's potential love interest, but he sees her as even more cool and impersonal than Daisy. Both women are given androgynous qualities: Jordan is described as small-breasted with the hard, tanned, athletic body of a young cadet; and in the city, when Daisy is trying to escape the entanglement of Gatsby's attentions, she says that if they are looking for her, she will be the man on the corner of the street smoking two cigarettes (132). As an observer of women, Nick focuses his attention not on physical sensuality but on what is new and fashionable: "hair shorn in strange new ways," the latest style of dress, the neat, sad little waltz popular that summer.

At Gatsby's parties there is food—buffet tables "with glistening hors d'oeuvre, spiced baked hams crowded against salads of harlequin designs and pastry pigs and turkeys bewitched to a dark gold" (44). But more important in this text is drink, a thirst likely sharpened by Prohibition, but in Nick's pastoral imagination fraught perhaps with the primal pleasures and disappointments of oral gratification: "We drank in long greedy swallows" (124). Drinking is described in almost every major scene in the narrative, and at Gatsby's parties its originary status is evoked: "In the main hall a bar with a real brass rail was set up, and stocked with gins and liquors and cordials so long forgotten that most of his female guests were too young to know one from another" (44). This is linked to Gatsby's desire to "suck on the pap of life, gulp down the incomparable milk of wonder" and anticipates Nick's final revision of Long Island as "a fresh, green breast of the New World" (189).

There is attention to another breast in the novel, that of Myrtle Wilson, torn open in the car accident, letting her life pour away. Myrtle, who "carrie[s] her surplus flesh sensuously" (29), embodies the physical, sexual passion that Nick appears to evade. Her carnal nature is invariably linked to confusion and violence: the party Nick wanted to avoid ends with Myrtle's nose being broken and blood everywhere; her presence in the story concludes with her death on the road, which sets off a chain of events that ends in Gatsby's death as well. Her death takes place on a day that unleashes the passage of time (the enemy in pastoral): it is the last day of summer, Nick observes, humid and hot. For Nick the magic spell of summer is broken: he watches the perspiring passengers on the commuter train and wonders how "anyone should care in this heat whose flushed lips he kissed, whose head made damp the pajama pocket over his heart!" (121). Nick also reflects wryly that it is his birthday, that he has turned thirty, and that he must look forward to both thinning hair and a thinning list of single friends and enthusiasms. Old age and death follow as Gatsby's enfeebled father appears, not to reveal that the hero is of distinguished birth, but to attend his funeral.

* * *

In his essays and letters, as well as in his fiction, F. Scott Fitzgerald was obsessed by impermanence. Style was its counterforce, he argued: "material, however closely observed," he wrote, "is as elusive as the moment in which it has its existence unless it is purified by an incorruptible style" (*Afternoon of an Author* 263). Keats's "fine excess" was his model: Keats's greatest poems, Fitzgerald wrote to his daughter, are "a scale of workmanship for anybody who wants to know truly about words, their most utter value for evocation, persuasion or charm" (*Letters* 88). In a letter to Hemingway, he cites Conrad's preface to *The Nigger of the "Narcissus"* as providing him with a theory of fiction: "the purpose of a work of fiction is to appeal to the lingering after-effects in the reader's mind as differing from, say, the purpose of oratory or philosophy which respectively leave people in a fighting or thoughtful mood" (*Letters* 309). And in a letter to Maxwell Perkins about *The Great Gatsby*, he writes that he "selected the stuff to fit a given mood or 'hauntedness' or whatever you might call it" (*Letters* 551). "Evocation," "lingering after-effects," "hauntedness": at the core of these statements is a poetics of suggestion and allusiveness to describe high quality in writing. Focusing on style per se, Fitzgerald identifies it as this exchange between loss and impermanence on the one hand and abiding persistence on the other—or, we might say, the regret of pastoral elegy on the one hand and its unappeasable longing on the other.

Our thinking so far about pastoral and style in *The Great Gatsby* has been limited to considering patterns of imagery in the text, visual references of a nonlinguistic order. As we ask how Fitzgerald gave his prose this quality of "hauntedness," we will turn to another aspect of language—the nonreferential capacity of words to call to mind other words, thereby making a text both expansive and cohesive.[6] Pastoral art is invariably distinguished by a style that is evocative of loss. In *The Great Gatsby*, style serves this essence by cultivating a feature of language operating through and then beyond syntax: cohesion, the quality of sentences depending on one another for their interpretation, their quality as text, or their "texture."[7] Of the various conditions that have been identified as producing *text*—or texture—*lexical cohesion* is the one that works through words' basic materiality, their substance as words rather than as reference items indicating a nonlinguistic entity, or as operators in the syntax of propositions. Of the five types of lexical cohesion, straight *lexical repetition* is the one most open to traditional measures of style. A particular word can recur in a text—in different localities, with different reference—and concordance techniques can calculate these recurrences, which create a network of interdependencies beyond plot, or argument, or image. So a concordance to the novel lists, for example, 21 occurrences of "road," 16 instances of "dream[ed]," 14 of "flower[s]" (Crosland 272, 93, 121), and, according to Bruccoli's preface to the authorized text of *The Great Gatsby*, some 450 words having to do with time (xv). "Flower," reappearing after fifteen pages, or fifty pages, evokes not only its single instance but its earlier instance(s) as well, however irrelevant at the discursive level. Words acquire a "textual history" (Halliday and Hasan), and the reader's memory is the archive of this history. To straight repetition—a sort of cohesive bedrock—the linguistic taxonomy of lexical cohesion adds three types of *synonymy*.[8] These are less open to traditional concordance techniques, although their operation may comprise distinctive stylistic features. Finally, measures of *collocation* calculate the ties between words that have a tendency to appear together, societies of words that have a history of accompaniment—prior to a specific textual occurrence but activated by their textual configuration.

The category of collocation registers the potential energies resting in words themselves, residual from their use. Textual collocations transform that potential to kinetic energy. In Fitzgerald's representation of Nick's storytelling, such transformation can accompany Nick's surges of enthusiasm for moments that might leave others untouched. During Daisy's afternoon visit to Gatsby's mansion, Nick's faithful attention to time and place—his work as witness and reporter—suddenly expands to an embracing vision of weather and the time of day:

> Outside the wind was loud and there was a faint flow of thunder along the Sound. All the lights were going on in West Egg now; the electric trains, men carrying, were plunging home through the rain from New York. It was the hour of a profound human change and excitement was generating on the air. (101)

At one level this passage is cohesive on basic, practical grounds: a geographical template develops through the collocation of place-names—*the Sound/West Egg/New York*—and a chronological template develops through the collocation of time words—*note/hour*. These ties serve the substantive needs of plot, anchoring time and place. But just as hour expands to something more than just the time of day, other collocative ties draw the passage beyond itself. With *electric* (*trains*) a tie forms with *lights*: these are words that tend to co-occur. Nick doesn't have to say "electric trains"—"trains" would have done as well—but the choice, reactivating "lights," intensifies a reminder of the technological organization of this epoch. Beyond this immediate tie, another cohesive link connects *electric* with *thunder* in the first sentence, striking a latent association between these words, like a flash of lightning itself, illuminating in a second of exposure the domain these words share. Then, in the third sentence, *generating*, collocative with *thunder/lights/electric*, extends this circuit of sensation. Exploiting the properties of words as words, these collocations seem to make possible the claim about "profound human change and excitement" in a paragraph about commuting on a rainy afternoon. Turning away from the awkward conversation surrounding Mr. Klipspringer's hesitant performance at the piano, Nick finds a thrill of apprehension in the significance of the everyday moment beyond the room. At a level of intensity that could hardly be accounted for by plot, or character, or the social destiny of individuals, Nick, with his finger on some original pulse, expresses a vision of charged simultaneity between humans and their world, sensing even in metropolitan commuting a link between humans and nature. In this passage, the thrill—indefinite or not quite communicable, for, after all, what is this expected change?—rises from a dense nest of local collocative links that tie these sentences together beyond their propositional content. But the passage also echoes other parts of the novel, spanning expanses of narrative by reminding us, through "train," of incessant traffic in this book, comings and goings, transportation, even on the most universal level, of human migration itself, the discovery of the New World, or the rediscovery of an original "fresh green breast" (189).

Other passages in *The Great Gatsby* also exploit this potential for long cohesive spans. Take a sentence describing Daisy's and Gatsby's reactions to each other at the hotel party in New York, where the words seem to draw reverberations from the whole text: "But with every word she was drawing further and further into herself, so he gave that up and only the dead dream fought on as the afternoon slipped away, trying to touch what was no longer tangible, struggling unhappily, undespairingly, toward that lost voice across the room" (142). For the reader who already knows the text and has an ear for language, "fought on" anticipates the novel's last sentence, "beat on . . . against the current" (189), so that we hear "boat" in this sentence even though the word is not there. But we have already been conditioned to hear "boat" because of a textual history of sea words. In the beginning of his story, Nick tells us that at the Buchanans' waterfront home the breeze "rippled over the wine-colored rug, making a shadow on it as wind does on *the sea*" and that Jordan and Daisy on the couch "were *buoyed up* as though upon an *anchored* balloon" (12; emphasis added). And carrying the association of the boat from these crucially situated sentences, "across the room" picks up an echo of across the bay, and Daisy's lost voice becomes one with the green light, one of Gatsby's "enchanted objects." In this context, "trying to touch" recalls Gatsby's hands stretched out across the bay at the end of the first chapter, which in turn recalls Gatsby trying to reconnect with the past "just out of reach of his hand" (117). This elusiveness, not only of object but of language as well, returns with the account of Gatsby's departure from Louisville: "He stretched out his hand desperately as if to snatch only a wisp of air, to save a fragment of the spot that she had made lovely for him" (160). Some of the words of this sentence ("wisp of air," "fragment") echo their own use, although with different reference, from the sentence on page 118; but most powerful is the word "stretch," which gathers up the aspiration of romance and the longing of pastoral and yields their full force in those lines of the resonant penultimate paragraph: "tomorrow we will run faster, stretch out our arms farther" (189).

Words tracings, the imprint they make on a reader's memory, some connection audible but not quite understood—these "lost" but persistent fragments need to be examined as they reach across spans of text. For they create in the attuned reader the sensations we identify as Nick's unique way of speaking; they touch off fleeting and nearly "uncommunicable" recognition of the largest designs in the novel, its mythic dimension, referring us to light and dark, to nourishment, to strange and exotic gardens, to human migrations, to the sea, and to death. It is language deployed in this way that allows the reader of pastoral to hear "an elusive rhythm, a fragment of lost words," from an order of experience before speech and memory, that remains, in Nick's phrasing, "uncommunicable forever" (118). On the whole, sentence endings are the preferred sites for these collocations and haunting echoes. When Nick is first told of Gatsby's dream of reclaiming Daisy, he says: "He came alive to me, delivered suddenly from the womb of his purposeless splendour" (83). The word "womb" takes us back to the fourth page of the novel and a series of beginnings—the rebirth of summer, "new money," Nick's quickly acquired status as "pathfinder, an original settler" (8). It also anticipates the end of the novel and America first seen by Dutch sailors' eyes—"a fresh, green breast of the new world" (189).

But pastoral innocence evoked in these words is complicated by another account of origins in a sentence describing Dan Cody, which extends by means of appositives to invoke the sweep of American history: "I remember the portrait of him up in Gatsby's bedroom, a grey, florid man with a hard, empty face—the pioneer debauchee who during one phase of American life brought back to the eastern seaboard the savage violence of the frontier brothel or saloon" (106). Here, original settler, or pioneer, is redefined in terms of violence and debauchery, and in terms of hardness and emptiness, implicating by word association Nick's own family's pioneer beginnings, the Dutch sailors, the very beginnings of America's European history and its consequences. It also encapsulates all the elements of the story that are finally Gatsby's undoing. At this point we are made to recognize that words have lives of their own and that in a narrative of mixed modes (in this case romance and pastoral) words can evoke conflicting narrative intentions. "Pioneer" and "frontier" evoke innocence and origins at one point in the text and then are linked to crime and the underworld in the next. Fitzgerald's style is "composite" indeed: its language can sound a magisterial voice addressing snobbish concerns of class, then turn and gesture in an evocative phrase to a timeless order of origins; Gatsby is described in terms of his romance quest for Daisy, then suddenly in terms of a return to the succor of infancy. The tensions and complexities of the novel are everywhere resonant in the language.

Contemporary critical theory demonstrates that a literary text emerges from the historical conditions of its production and reception, bearing the imprint of social and historical practice by the users of words. Our analysis, however, suggests that another way of regarding works of literature may be equally valid, that the language of literary texts is also deeply tied to essential, radical motives, orders of experience we have conceptualized as mode. This study of *The Great Gatsby* in the light of pastoral has been concerned with the intersection of the temporal, "the hour of . . . human change and excitement," and the ahistorical—or, in Nick's words, with the "voice" that was "a deathless song" (101). We would argue finally that *The Great Gatsby* continues to resonate with meaning for readers at the beginning of the twentieth-first century not simply because of its retelling of the oldest story—the fairy-tale romance of the princess and the soldier—but equally and maybe more because of its way of singing to, its murmuring consolations to, our radical nostalgia.

NOTES

1. These readings were established in the criticism of the 1950s and remain a point of departure for subsequent studies. R. W. Stallman identifies Gatsby as a mythic hero representing America; Marius Bewley argues that the novel offers a damaging criticism of the American dream; while Arthur Mizener, Fitzgerald's first biographer, refers suggestively but vaguely to the novel as a "tragic pastoral" (*The Far Side of Paradise* 192).

2. Descriptions of style involve controversial issues; these include not only deciding what parts of a writer's work to analyze and how to conduct the analysis, but perhaps more importantly how to interpret the data and what empirical status to claim for the interpretation. One of the major criticisms of stylistics, voiced strongly by Stanley E. Fish, is that observable formal patterns are in themselves without value, or else they are given value in a wholly arbitrary fashion, unless they are situated in a context of reception and reader expectations (Freeman 70). To provide a context for our findings, we describe here and in our earlier essay the different modes

in which *The Great Gatsby* is written—naive and ironic romance, pastoral—for it is our claim here that features of style are engendered by mode and consequently they are inseparable from any reading that may be given to the text.

3. Aristotle describes the use of maxims as "suited to speakers of mature years, and to arguments on matters in which one is experienced. In a young man, uttering maxims is—like telling stories—unbecoming; and to use them in a realm where one lacks experience is stupid and boorish" (152). Interestingly, Aristotle's continuation of this advice on maxims also associates their rhetorical efficacy with a certain class sensitivity: "An adequate sign of this is that rustics are especially given to coining maxims, and always ready to vent them" (152). To us, this observation of Aristotle's relates to Nick's strong sense of identity with his midwestern origins, his tie to his father, and his pastoral longings for the "dark fields of the republic" (189).

4. The idea of pastoral has teased critics since Mizener's description of *The Great Gatsby* as "a kind of tragic pastoral" (*The Far Side of Paradise* 192). Several critics, including Ornstein and Barry Gross, have tried to expand on this observation by focusing generally on the matter of East versus West in the novel. More specific studies of pastoral and *The Great Gatsby* in terms of mode and genre can be found in essays by Kuhnle and Gervais and in Leo Marx's *The Machine in the Garden* (354–65).

5. Paul Alpers provides in *What Is Pastoral?* a comprehensive history of pastoral criticism; he argues, using Kenneth Burke's terminology, that herdsmen and their lives constitute the representative anecdote that most accurately describes the conventions of pastoral that remain stable from Theocritus to the modern novel. Alpers describes at length the poetry of Theocritus (137–53) and Virgil (161–69) and the ideas of Schiller (28–37) and Empson (37–43) about pastoral.

6. Donald Monk, in an essay with interests like our own, has raised the following question: How does F. Scott Fitzgerald make his prose evocative? Monk's answer is to examine the imagery of the text and show how patterns artfully interconnect with each other. Our interest here in the nonreferential dimension of language in *The Great Gatsby* is rejected by Monk as something excessive in Fitzgerald's prose: the "dependence on stylistic effects is . . . responsible for the quasi-hallucinatory sense of words becoming their own substance, their own *raison d'être*, which one can feel when in a mood unsympathetic to [Fitzgerald]" (79).

7. Halliday and Hasan's original and still unassailable work on cohesion identifies five types of cohesion. Three types (reference, substitution, and ellipsis) depend on grammatical systems, and one (conjunction) is semantic. The fifth type, lexical, is the one that concerns us here, although further study of Fitzgerald along these lines could reveal the relevance of the other types to understanding his style in representing Nick's storytelling.

8. These are (a) equivalents (e.g., dream/reverie); (b) hypernyms (e.g., oak/tree); and (c) general terms (e.g., place/city).

WINIFRED FARRANT BEVILACQUA

"... and the long secret extravaganza was played out": The Great Gatsby and Carnival in a Bakhtinian Perspective

> The supreme ruse of power is to allow itself to be contested ritually
> in order to consolidate itself more effectively.
>
> Georges Balandier[1]

From antiquity, Mikhail Bakhtin argues, literary history has been shaped both by "serious" genres such as tragedy and epic and by serio-comic genres like Menippean satire which constitute the carnivalistic line in Western literature. Petronius' *Satyricon* is a foundational text in the carnival tradition of the novel for its disenchanted portrayal of a changing contemporary society, its use of laughter to defamiliarize approved ideologies and ideas, and its roots in folklore and festive rituals. Behind its scenes and events, "there glimmers more or less distinctly the carnival square with its specific carnivalistic logic of familiar contacts, mésalliances, disguises and mystifications, contrasting paired images, scandals, crownings/decrownings, and so forth. [. . .] in fact the very plot of the *Satyricon* is thoroughly carnivalized" (*PDP* 133–34).[2]

Fitzgerald entitled a late version of his novel *Trimalchio* and in the published work he retained Nick's observation that after Gatsby realized Daisy did not enjoy his parties, "his career as Trimalchio was over." Various elements link these two works.[3] Both Trimalchio and Gatsby are *nouveaux riches* and invent elements of their own biographies. Each has a luxurious home, owns

From *Connotations* 13, nos. 1–2 (2003/2004): 111–129. © 2005 by Waxmann Verlag GmbH.

an impressive library, gives lavish parties attended by socially heterogeneous groups. Their festivities, where food is a form of play and often disguised so that its original nature is unrecognizable, unfold against a musical background and are so well-staged that Trimalchio is described as the "director, producer, main actor"[4] of his party while Gatsby is termed "a regular Belasco." Both are obsessed by the passage of time. An astrologist has revealed to Trimalchio the exact length of his life so he installs a big clepsydra in his dining room and has a uniformed bugler blow a horn every hour to remind him of how long he has left to live. Gatsby's story contains a myriad of references to time, and details such as the broken clock that almost falls off the mantelpiece during his reunion with Daisy symbolize his desire to stop or even reverse the flow of time. Crucially, each work reproduces versions of the primary carnivalistic act at the very core of the carnival sense of the world—the mock crowning and subsequent decrowning of the carnival king.[5]

Petronius was innovative in using a first-person narrator, Encolpius, who is also a character in the story, something not done in any example of epic or fiction known to him.[6] This narrator's education and prior experiences have not prepared him for a world dominated by arrogant social climbing, unscrupulous business dealing, the trading of sexual favors for power, extreme materialism—a mysterious social universe which both attracts and disconcerts him.[7] Fitzgerald's narrator/protagonist Nick likewise finds himself in a social world he does not fully understand, where he feels "within and without, simultaneously enchanted and repelled by the inexhaustible variety of life" (*TGG* 30).[8] Another link between the narrators regards their connection to the carnivalistic "notion of bisexuality [...] as a release from the burden of socially imposed sexual roles."[9] Encolpius' bisexuality is presented openly and exuberantly while Nick's possible erotic attraction to men is treated in a veiled manner.[10]

Most fundamentally, there are affinities between the implied ethical stances of the authors. The *Satyricon* has been read "as a depiction of a degenerate society, whose individuals are haunted by anguish" and where there is "economical, sexual and culinary [...] satiety without spiritual fulfillment."[11] Petronius has been seen as a moralist "preoccupied to the point of nausea and despair by the hopelessness of a culture corrupted by *luxuria*, a culture which turns men into the living dead, which degrades, desecrates and finally annuls, a culture without joy, without hope, [...]."[12] Although they ultimately evaluate their heroes in different ways, with Petronius offering a blanket condemnation and Fitzgerald insisting on Gatsby's essential "greatness," Fitzgerald describes the decadence, amorality, violence, and confusion of the Jazz Age, as he sees it, in terms which Petronius would understand.[13]

* * *

Even if *The Great Gatsby* is not thoroughly carnivalized, the influence of a carnivalistic masterpiece on it is evidence of its deep kinship with carnival as a sense of the world and as a form of artistic visualization. In point of fact, in Fitzgerald's literary practice, carnival forms become

> a *powerful means* for comprehending life in art, [...] a special language whose words and forms possess an extraordinary capacity for symbolic generalization, that is, for *generalization in depth*. Many essential sides of life, or more precisely its *layers* (and often the most profound), can be located, comprehended, and expressed only with the help of this language. (*PDP* 157)

Specifically, in representing Gatsby's parties and in certain other episodes, Fitzgerald conceives of time, space and value in terms of the carnival chronotope, fuses carnivalesque elements from folkloric and literary traditions such as the feast and the grotesque body with the specific features of his own time and place, and makes profoundly significant use of symbolic inversions as the defining image of climactic moments in his narrative.[14]

Chronotopically speaking, the essential characteristic of carnival is "carnival time," a temporary, atypical removal from the normal progression of biographical or historical time which flows according to its own laws and during which life is shaped according to a certain pattern of play. The natural setting is the public square and the streets adjoining it, an area where people with a range of social identities can come together and intermingle. But, "to be sure, carnival also invaded the home; in essence it was limited in time only and not in space" (*PDP* 128).

Gatsby's residence, compared to a Hotel de Ville, an elaborate roadhouse, and a World's Fair, with its enormous gardens lit up like a Christmas tree, where his guests are free to conduct themselves "according to the rules of behavior associated with amusement parks," fully qualifies as carnival space (*TGG* 34). This public arena attracts people who do not know each other or even the host: "People were not invited—they went there. They got into automobiles which bore them out to Long Island and somehow they ended up at Gatsby's door" where they hoped to find all sorts of people mixed together in a communal performance (*TGG* 34). Carnival is not set in motion by an order given by a directive figure but opens simply with some kind of signal to mark the beginning of merriment and foolery. Fitzgerald signals the start of Gatsby's parties with a stunning periphrasis for nightfall and a hint that this "time outside time" will open up a new dimension of experience where, for example, music is visually perceived and laughter is a material substance: "The lights grow brighter as the earth lurches away from the sun and now the orchestra is playing yellow cocktail music and the opera of voices pitches a key higher. Laughter is easier, minute by minute, spilled with prodigality, tipped out at a cheerful word" (*TGG* 34).

The dominant motif of carnival is transgression of conventions and prohibitions, of hierarchical boundaries and of all the rules which determine the structure and order of ordinary, that is noncarnival, life. Everyone abandons daily routines to dance and sing in the streets, consume large quantities of food and drink, enjoy a world where disorder prevails and ordinarily inappropriate behavior is not only permitted but encouraged and expected. In this new realm of existence, the participants are released from their usual alienation from each other, enter into new forms of interrelationships, and enjoy freedom "not only from external censorship but first of all from the great interior censor" (*RW* 94).[15]

At Gatsby's, up-and-coming Irish, German, Italian, Jewish, and East European immigrants rub shoulders with guests who belong to New York's social register as well as with new-money people from silent films, theater and business and there is even a yoking together of the upstanding and the disreputable. This heterogeneous crowd offers an image of some of the centrifugal forces which, during the 1920s, were transforming American society by developing new cultural forms, introducing new ethnic groups, upsetting the existing hierarchy, and shortening the distance between legal and illicit activities.

The forms of liberation offered by carnival do not remain abstract concepts but are concretely acted out in the physical experience of the festivities. The closeness of the revellers as they move through the carnival spaces has the power to make each one feel that he or she is "an indissoluble part of the collectivity, a member of the people's mass body" (*RW* 255). These spaces thus become the locus for oceanic feelings of unity with one another. Fitzgerald acutely exemplifies the visceral sense of community and the crowd's multiform nature through his sea imagery:

> The groups change more swiftly, swell with new arrivals, dissolve and form in the same breath—already there are wanderers, confident girls who weave here and there among the stouter and more stable, become for a sharp, joyous moment the center of a group and then excited with triumph glide on through the sea-change of faces and voices and color under the constantly changing light. (*TGG* 34)

Seemingly, the fragmented nature of society has been temporarily overcome, a sense of the primordial mass of pre-class society has been reestablished, and individuals have the illusion of being able to transcend their habitual roles.

Entering into a larger fellowship is also expressed by playful actions that disrupt the traditional distinction between those who produce a spectacle and those who watch it. Urged on by a sense of *communitas* as well as by the music, the alcohol, and the sheer magic of the time and place, the guests turn into performers who engage in "stunts" all over the garden, dance out alone on the canvas platform, momentarily relieve the musicians "of the burden of the banjo or the traps" or offer their heads for the formation of a singing quartet (*TGG* 39). Playacting like this permits an escape from delimiting expectations of behavior—another form of crossing a borderline—and further allows for transcendence of one's own identity and the assumption, perhaps the embodiment, of another.

In keeping with such ambivalence, costumes and masks destabilize fixed identities and help produce an atmosphere of relativity. Masked revellers either give free reign to their imagination or pretend to be what they are not by donning costumes that hide the truth about their social standing, profession, gender, and so on. Although few of Gatsby's guests "dress up,"[16] the idea of a masquerade is introduced in the list of names Nick jots down on his railroad timetable, many of which recall Bakhtin's association of the mask with "transition, metamorphoses, the violation of natural boundaries, mockery and familiar nicknames" (*RW* 40). Some guests bear the names of animals, flowers, vegetables, trees, and minerals, such as Cecil Roebuck, Clarence Endive, Henry Palmetto and the Chromes or of heroes from the past like Stonewall Jackson Abrams, Mrs. Claud Roosevelt, and Willie Voltaire. Other names allude to the principle of grotesque degradation, that is, "the lowering of all that is high, spiritual, ideal, abstract [. . .] to the sphere of earth and body in their indissoluble unity" as is the case with Claudia Hip and with Belcher, Swett and the Smirkes (*RW* 19–20). Yet other names associate the bearer with negative character traits like an excess of predatory instincts, as in the Leeches, or duplicity, as in the man reputed to be a chauffeur and a prince of something but "whom we called Duke" (*TGG* 51).

In the temporary transfer to a world of pleasure and abundance permitted by carnival, the topos of the banquet is an important element since it brings people together and opens their spirits to play and merriment. Eating and drinking are among the most significant manifestations of the grotesque body because during these actions we experience an interaction with the world that gives us an illusory triumph over our usual sense of alienation from it: "man tastes the world, introduces it into his body, [. . .] devours it without being devoured himself. The limits between man and the world are erased, to man's advantage" (*RW* 281). Moreover, the joyful consumption of food in collective feasts has the connotation of accessible happiness for all. The suppers offered by Gatsby at nightfall and at midnight contribute significantly to the lavishness and conviviality of his parties. Fitzgerald depicts them in imagery suggesting masks, jokes, illusionist transformations. Salads of "harlequin design," turkeys "bewitched to a dark gold," and, in honor of the carnival animal *par excellence*, some "pastry pigs" magically take on a life of their own so that the edibles crowd together on the buffet tables while "floating rounds of cocktails permeate the garden outside" and provoke a spontaneous surge of "chatter and laughter" (*TGG* 33, 34).

Bakhtin sees an organic bond between feasting and discourse—"bread and wine [...] disperse fear and liberate the word"—pointing to the symposium, ancient "table talks," the gay speech of medieval banquets, and even the old adage *in vino veritas* (*RW* 284–86). As drink releases Gatsby's guests from the restraints of etiquette, their language is altered to allow a familiarity not permissible at other times, and some of them even appear to adopt marketplace speech in which "there are no neutral epithets and forms; there are either polite, laudatory, flattering, cordial words, or contemptuous, debasing, abusive ones [...] the more unofficial and familiar the speech, the more often and substantially are those tones combined, the less distinct is the line dividing praise and abuse" (*RW* 420). Gatsby is invariably the subject of "romantic speculation" (*TGG* 37) and "bizarre accusations" (*TGG* 52) presented with the ironic ambivalence which turns praise into an insult and abuse into a gesture of admiration. Nick conveys these remarks in a crescendo of overheard fragments of conversation culminating in a delightfully surreal bit of dialogue about Gatsby's background, activities and even his ontological status in which mockery and exaltation are simultaneously expressed.

> "He's a bootlegger," said the young ladies, moving somewhere between his cocktails and his flowers. "One time he killed a man who had found out that he was a nephew to von Hindenburg and second cousin to the devil. Reach me a rose, honey, and pour me a last drop into that there crystal glass." (*TGG* 49)

Through contradictory definitions like this, carnival speech calls into question the values through which praise and blame are assigned and confounds the notion of truth on which their assignment is based.

Most importantly, Fitzgerald's narrative can be illuminated by the social and economic observations underlying Bakhtin's theories, especially his conviction that in the modern novel carnival "proved remarkably productive as a means for capturing in art the developing relationships under capitalism, at a time when previous forms of life, moral principles and beliefs were being turned into 'rotten cords'" (*PDP* 166). Nick comments on how lust for money permeates the atmosphere at Gatsby's parties:

> I was immediately struck by the number of young Englishmen dotted about; all well dressed, all looking a little hungry and all talking in low earnest voices to solid and prosperous Americans. I was sure that they were all selling something: bonds or insurance or automobiles. They were, at least, agonizingly aware of the easy money in the vicinity and convinced that it was theirs for a few words in the right key. (*TGG* 35)

At the time, bond-selling was becoming a common profession yet it still retained an aura of suspicion because of a perceived difficulty in distinguishing the line separating legitimate from illicit sales. Also, in that period, in order to possess an automobile, many people willingly went into debt or, as one commentator harshly put it, got involved in "the crime of installment selling [. . .] that is causing manufacturers, advertisers, merchants and consumers to go more madly after material things to the neglect of the things of the spirit."[17] Laws were passed to regulate consumer credit, converting "loan sharks [. . .] into respectable businessmen" as another commentator quipped, but this did not placate worries that purchasing without first having accumulated the necessary funds was a dangerous practice.[18]

A related indictment regards gambling which is "by nature carnivalistic" and "always a part of the image system of carnival symbols" because it brings together people from various positions in life (*mésalliances*) in an activity that in no way corresponds to the roles they ordinarily play (*à l'envers*) and because its atmosphere is one of sudden and quick changes of fate in which the lowly can reach new economic heights and the wealthy can take a step down (the turnabout).[19] Fitzgerald uses this symbol to highlight similarities between gambling and stockbroking, both aimed at getting the greatest possible return on an investment, to the extent that they become parodic images of each other:

> Da Fontano the promoter came there and Ed Legros and James B. ('Rot-gut') Ferret and the de Jongs and Ernest Lilly—they came to gamble and when Ferret wandered into the garden it meant he was cleaned out and Associated Traction would have to fluctuate profitably next day. (*TGG* 50)

Although Bakhtin makes it clear that carnival's mirthful inversions offer only a temporary alternative to official culture, he ascribes to them a deep philosophical significance. He speaks of carnival as constituting a "second life of the people" where humanity for a moment can fully realize its potential and experiment with the utopian realm of abundance, freedom, and equality (*RW* 255). In this context, "utopian" refers not to some future state of perfection but to an ideal world achieved in the here and now. The laughter that is an integral part of this utopia has emotional and cognitive value in that it "demolishes fear and piety [. . .] thus clearing the ground for an absolutely free investigation."[20] It is liberating also because it grasps phenomena not as immutably fixed but in the process of change and transition. Carnival is ephemeral but the 'unofficial truths' regarding the "gay relativity" (*RW* 11) of all things that it reveals remain in the participants' minds and hearts and, Bakhtin believes, have the potential to transform their inner relationship to the conditions of everyday life.

Aside from a common interest in flirting, gossiping, and enjoying the commodies that fill his playground, Gatsby's guests have no ties, no shared beliefs, nothing that draws them together in a meaningful community. Out of touch with the primitive magic of carnival which transforms a crowd into "the people as a whole [. . .] organized *in their own* way," (*RW* 255) these guests' external gestures express only the desperate hilarity of alienated individuals. Their absence of hope in the possibility of redefining their lives is revealed by how, even during their most festive moments, they never forget the "too obtrusive fate" which "herded [them] along a short cut from nothing to nothing" (*TGG* 84). Instead of an affirmative celebration of "the feast of becoming, change, and renewal," (*RW* 10) they are imitating models whose naive confidence they can never replicate. Most pointedly, the last minutes of the parties link back to noncarnival life to highlight its aimlessness, violence, and lack of stable relationships. If, at the start, there was music in the "blue gardens" and "men and girls came and went like moths among the whisperings and the champagne and the stars" (*TGG* 33), at the end, the gaiety degenerates into chaos as women have arguments with "men said to be their husbands" (*TGG* 42), the playfulness disappears as the departing guests create a traffic jam in the driveway, and the laughter dissipates into "the harsh, discordant din" (*TGG* 44) of a car crash.

* * *

Myrtle Wilson's party occurs in an ambience that seems to point us toward Bakhtin's description of "rococo carnivalesque" where

> the gay positive tone of laughter is preserved. But everything is reduced to "chamber" lightness and intimacy. The frankness of

the marketplace is turned into privacy, the indecency of the lower stratum is transformed into erotic frivolity, and gay relativity becomes skepticism and wantonness. And yet, in the hedonistic "boudoir" atmosphere a few sparks of the carnival fires which burn up "hell" have been preserved. (*RW* 119)[21]

Seen in this light, the party is a miniature, mock version of an eighteenth-century French *salon* culture gathering during which elegantly dressed aristocratic ladies and men would meet in a richly furnished rococo style salon to discuss an artwork or literature as well as to express their wit through storytelling and where the hostess' learning and ability to stimulate conversation were critical to the success of the event. An emblematic *maîtresse de salon* and icon of the Rococo period was Madame Pompadour. This beautiful, refined and elegant woman, trained from girlhood to believe in her superiority, rose beyond her class status and entered the ranks of the aristocracy, being pronounced the Marquise de Pompadour, the official mistress of Louis XV. She became the patroness of eminent painters, writers, philosophers and architects like Boucher, Voltaire, Montesquieu, and Lassurance. Her proud, regal figure was immortalized in many splendid portraits by painters of the stature of Boucher, La Tour, and Drouais.

For Myrtle, represented as a parodic double of Madame Pompadour, her apartment is a lavishly-appointed estate where she can assume the identity of a woman of the leisure class, high above the life she leads at the garage in the Valley of Ashes. She has decorated it in a *nouveau riche* attempt at elegance, filling it with oversized furniture upholstered in fabric depicting "scenes of ladies swinging in the gardens of Versailles," a typical subject for Rococo painters who specialized in scenes of aristocratic leisure and of love and seduction in a natural setting (*TGG* 25). Myrtle, whose face "contain[s] no facet or gleam of beauty," whose dresses "stretch [...] tight over her rather wide hips," and who "carr[y] her surplus flesh sensuously," gets her ideas about gentility from gossip magazines and has no special talents or artistic interests (*TGG* 23). Her group of guests includes Nick who "was rather literary in college" (*TGG* 7), Chester McKee who says he is in the "artistic game" (TGG 26) and would like to become a sort of official photographer of Long Island if only he could "get the entry" (*TGG* 28), Mrs. McKee, a "shrill, languid, handsome and horrible" (*TGG* 26) woman with strong opinions on everything, and Myrtle's sister Catherine whose sticky bob of red hair, complexion powdered milky-white and innumerable pottery bracelets jangling up and down her arms give her a distinctly clownish appearance. The only 'conversation pieces' available are McKee's overenlarged photograph of Myrtle's mother that "hover[s] like an ectoplasm on the wall" and an ignored copy of the 1921 bestselling novel

Simon Called Peter (*TGG* 26). Myrtle leads her guests in banal chatter about topics like getting more ice and problems with feet or in pretentious talk of unfortunate experiences at the gaming tables in Monte Carlo. Far from being refined and polite, her speech is sprinkled with mispronunciations and misusage of words and sometimes descends into the "violent and obscene" (*TGG* 29). Considering her efforts at self-fashioning, it is curious that she fails to pick up on Mrs. McKee's hint that her husband be given a commission to do her portrait—"If Chester could only get you in that pose [...]" (*TGG* 27).

Amorous intrigues in the apartment replicate, at a lower level, the action represented in Jean-Honoré Fragonard's quintessentially Rococo masterpiece, "The Swing" (1767). This painting depicts, in a lush pastoral setting with statues of cupids, a flirtatious young woman in a frilly pink dress being pulled on a swing by an older man in cleric's clothes (her husband, a servant, a bishop?) while her lover, strategically positioned on a bed of roses, looks up her skirt and she teases him by kicking off her shoe in his direction. Myrtle, whose eroticism is overt rather than playful, exchanges sexual favors with Tom and he evokes the figure of her cuckolded and perhaps impotent husband by suggesting that Chester do a photographic study of "George B. Wilson at the Gasoline Pump" (*TGG* 28). Another episode of seduction and dalliance involves the triangle made up of Nick, Mrs. McKee, and Chester whom Nick describes as "a pale feminine man" (*TGG* 26). She lets Nick accompany Chester back to their apartment and the men have a sexually-charged exchange of words in the elevator. After an ellipsis, the narration finds the two of them in the McKees' bedroom where Chester, clad in his underwear, is showing Nick his portfolio of photographs.

Myrtle intends her party as her apotheosis as royal mistress. Her path from low to high began when she encountered Tom in a "railway car [which in literature] [...] is a substitute for the *public square*, where people from various positions find themselves in familiar contact with one another. Thus there is the coming together of the *beggar prince* and the *merchant millionaire*. The carnivalistic contrast is emphasized even in their clothing" (*PDP* 174). The sight of Tom in his dress suit, patent leather shoes, and starched white shirt took her breath away, so, repeating to herself "You can't live forever, you can't live forever," she headed off with him to become his mistress (*TGG* 31).

On the day of her party, Myrtle carefully selects a new lavender-colored taxi cab with grey upholstery for her triumphant drive across New York—somewhat like the coronation parade along the city streets of a *roi-pour-rire* on the "hell." Along the way, there is the farcical scene of the acquisition of a royal gift in the form of a puppy of uncertain breed. Myrtle makes a ceremonial entrance into the apartment building "[t]hrowing a regal homecoming glance around the neighborhood" (*TGG* 25) and then sweeps into the kitchen as if "a dozen chefs awaited her orders there" (*TGG* 27). At the height of the festivities, she disappears into the bedroom to array herself in an elaborate afternoon dress of cream colored chiffon which gives out a continual rustle. How such a masquerade can confer an identity at odds with the wearer's stable sense of self and express the joy of change and reincarnation, is highlighted by Nick: "With the influence of the dress her personality had also undergone a change. The intense vitality that had been so remarkable in the garage was converted into impressive hauteur" (*TGG* 26). With carnivalesque ambivalence, her regal air mingles with grotesque exaggeration until

> [h]er laughter, her gestures, her assertions became more violently affected moment by moment and as she expanded the room grew smaller around her until she seemed to be revolving on a noisy, creaking pivot through the smoky air. (*TGG* 26–27)

Myrtle does not realize that her period of false privilege as a travesty queen is limited to the temporary and atypical moment of carnival, and that she can be punished if she steps out of line or in any other way displeases the king. Her pose is tolerated until she attempts to extend her sway beyond the permitted limits at which point she is forced into "the ceremonial of the ritual of decrowning [which] is counterposed to the ritual of crowning: regal vestments are stripped off the decrowned king, his crown is removed, the other symbols of authority are taken away, he is ridiculed and beaten" (*PDP* 125). As the evening draws to a close, Myrtle attempts to violate the sacredness of her rival by chanting her name:

> "Daisy! Daisy! Daisy!" shouted Mrs. Wilson. "I'll say it whenever I want to! Daisy! Dai—"
> Making a short deft movement Tom Buchanan broke her nose with his open hand.
> Then there were bloody towels upon the bathroom floor and women's voices scolding, and high over the confusion a long broken wail of pain. (*TGG* 41)

The party ends with the despairing figure of Myrtle on the couch, stripped of her illusions, bleeding profusely, and trying to spread a copy of *Town Tattle* over the tapestried scenes of Versailles.

* * *

As with Myrtle, in those parts of Gatsby's story governed by the carnival chronotope, "the carnivalistic act of crowning/decrowning is, of course, permeated with carnivalistic categories (with the logic of the carnival world): free and familiar contact (this is clearly manifest in decrowning), carnivalistic mésalliances (slave-king), profanation (playing with the symbols of higher authority)" (*PDP* 125). An indispensable element in Fitzgerald's representation of Gatsby is the carnival topos of the renewal of clothes and the social image. Gatsby is almost always in disguise not only for the joy of changing identities but also to hide something, to keep a secret, to deceive. After disassociating himself from his family origins and the provincial territory of his birth, he begins to fashion a new self-image modelled on the nature of the world he wishes to enter not as Jimmie Gatz but as Jay Gatsby. At eighteen, he eagerly exchanges his torn green jersey and pair of canvas pants for the blue jacket and white duck trousers given him by Dan Cody in which he looks like a millionaire's dashing son. While he courts Daisy in Louisville, he conceals his status as "a penniless young man without a past" under "the invisible cloak of his uniform" as an army officer (*TGG* 116). Only through this disguise can he overcome the socioeconomic barrier separating him from Daisy, and gain access to her world. When not actually in masquerade, he paints exaggerated verbal self-portraits. For instance, he tells Nick he is the last surviving member of a wealthy Midwestern family and that he once lived "like a young rajah in all the capitals of Europe" (*TGG* 52).

Gatsby, however, wants more than to play at what he is not. His deepest desire is a shift of position and destiny from a poor farm boy to a prince worthy of marrying "the king's daughter" (*TGG* 94). He feels this metamorphosis is at hand when he is finally reunited with Daisy. Wrapped in his golden aura, assuming the air of a monarch showing his realm to his beloved, and arrayed in his white suit, silver shirt and gold colored tie—the apparel he has chosen for his period of misrule—he escorts her through his shining, palatial home and re-values everything "according to the measure of response it drew from her well-loved eyes" (*TGG* 72). Their tour reaches its climax in his bedroom where, as surrogate emblems of a high familial lineage, he keeps photographs of Cody and of himself in a yachting outfit. Here, he opens his wardrobe and ritualistically displays his piles of custom-made imported shirts as a sign of his rank and as a tribute to her. In this emotional moment, she symbolically accepts him as her royal suitor. Having successfully drawn Daisy into his masquerade, he enjoys a taste of intense life set, as Klipspringer's song reminds us, in a very carnivalesque "*In between time*" (*TGG* 75). But already, at the height of his glory, Gatsby seems to have forebodings of his downfall and of Daisy's change of heart as if he somehow sensed that crowning and decrowning are inseparably dualistic, one invariably passing into the other. As Nick takes leave of the lovers he notices that "the expression of bewilderment had come back into Gatsby's face, as though a faint doubt had occurred to him as to the quality of his present happiness" (*TGG* 75).

Gatsby feels he is on the verge of crowning his dream on the day he encounters Daisy and Tom and they transfer from the Buchanans' mansion to the Plaza Hotel, a public setting implicitly associated with the carnival square by its very name and rendered even more appropriate by the sounds of merrymaking at a large wedding downstairs which filter into the suite where the confrontation between Tom and Gatsby takes place. Gatsby believes he has reached the moment of absolute reversal when Daisy will leave Tom and marry him. Tom, who has wearily tolerated Gatsby because he has seen him only as a clownish parvenu, finally realizes that he has become a true threat to his marriage and determines to put an end to his attempt at profanation, namely, "his presumptuous little flirtation" (*TGG* 105). What ensues is a "scene of the scandal and decrowning of the prince—the carnival king, or more accurately of the carnival bridegroom" when "the 'rotten cords' of the official and personal lie are snapped [. . .] and human souls are laid bare" (*PDP* 161, 145). Launching into verbal violence aimed at stripping away Gatsby's public image, Tom makes fun of his pink suit, ridicules his "circus wagon" (*TGG* 94) of a car, renames him "Mr. Nobody from Nowhere" (*TGG* 101), and reveals the illegitimacy of his fortune, thereby unveiling his total lack of social respectability.

For an instant during this scene of scandal, when Tom recalls tender intimacies with Daisy and she confesses that she loved him while loving Gatsby too, and Gatsby struggles to "touch what was no longer tangible [. . .] that lost voice across the room," the three of them let their masks drop and show their emotional vulnerability (*TGG* 105). The pathos of the moment is compounded by Gatsby's blindness to the truth, so evident to Nick, that Daisy "never intended doing anything at all" (*TGG* 108). The relative ease of Tom's victory reveals the fragility of the identity Gatsby has fashioned out of illusions and built on insubstantial hopes. Indeed, his painstakingly constructed persona "'Jay Gatsby' had broken up like glass against Tom's hard malice and the long secret extravaganza was played out" (*TGG* 115–16).

It is quite telling that both decrownings are followed by the ritual of dismemberment for, in carnival, the king "is abused and beaten when the time of his reign is over, just as the carnival dummy of winter or of the dying year is mocked, beaten, torn to pieces, burned, or drowned even in our time" (*RW* 197). Myrtle, "her life violently extinguished" by the car Daisy was driving, lies dead and mutilated in the road "her left breast [. . .] swinging loose like a flap," her "mouth wide open and ripped at the corners," her blood mingling with the dust (*TGG* 107). Tom escapes Wilson's wrath by directing him toward Gatsby. The next day, when Nick finds Gatsby's body floating in the pool, "his blood tracing [...] a thin red circle in the water," and sees Wilson's corpse lying in the grass, he realizes "the holocaust was complete" (*TGG* 128). With this burning of the "hell," the carnival truly comes to an end and the ruling authorities reascend the throne. The customary order has been restored and further consolidated through the kind of social control by which members of the upper classes eliminate opponents of the lower classes.

In Bakhtin's theory, the brief reign of a travesty king or queen symbolizes the relativity of human structure and order as well as a temporary victory "over supernatural awe, over the sacred, over death" (*RW* 92). The carnival monarch's divestment of power while being ridiculed, beaten, or even killed is indissolubly linked to rebirth and the possibility of renewal. The concluding episodes of Fitzgerald's novel work in ways antithetical to these premises. Myrtle's and Gatsby's carnivalesque adventures are crushed from without rather than ceding of their own accord to an appointed limit. Their tragic destinies are not charged with any kind of dialogical significance vis-à-vis Tom and Daisy, who do not allow their lives to be affected by the deaths they cause but go on living as if nothing had happened.

Notes

1. Georges Balandier, *Political Anthropology*, trans. A. M. Sheridan Smith (New York: Pantheon Books, 1970) 41.

2. Mikhail Bakhtin, *Problems of Dostoevsky's Poetics*, ed. and trans. Caryl Emerson (Minneapolis: U of Minnesota P, 1984). Cited in the text as PDP. It is worth reiterating Bakhtin's emphasis on how, during carnival, the festive crowd assigns powerful officials inferior positions while simultaneously conferring high status on individuals heretofore on the margins of society. The lowly subject who is elected to office enjoys, in an outrageous manner, the prerogatives of sovereignty for the duration of carnival, at the end of which he or she is ignominiously or savagely deposed. Nonetheless, the crowning of the mock king or queen is a potentially subversive attack on authority since it allows for "a concretely sensuous, half-real, half-play-acted form, *a new mode of interrelationship between individuals*, counterposed to the all-powerful socio-hierarchical relationships of noncarnival life" (*PDP* 123).

3. Without reference to carnival, Paul L. MacKendrick, a classicist, pointed out a number of important links in "*The Great Gatsby* and *Trimalchio*," *The Classical Journal* 45.7 (April 1950): 307–14.

4. Costas Panayotakis, *Theatrum arbitri: Theatrical Elements in the Satyrica of Petronius* (New York: E. J. Brill, 1995) 63.

5. An important analysis from a Bakhtinian perspective of carnival in the *Satyricon* is R. Bracht Branham, "A Truer Story of the Novel?" *Bakhtin and the Classics*, ed. Branham (Evanston: Northwestern UP, 2002) 175–80.

6. "Introduction" to Petronius' *Satyrica*, ed. and trans. R. Bracht Branham and Daniel Kinney (Berkeley: U of California P, 1996) xxi–xxii.

7. Mariangela Scarsi, "Il maestro 'dai piedi di vento,'" Gaio Petronio, *Satyricon*, ed. and trans. Scarsi (Florence: Giunti Gruppo Editoriale, 1996) xxxii–xxxiv.

8. F. Scott Fitzgerald, *The Great Gatsby* (New York: Charles Scribner's Sons, 1925). All quotations come from the Cambridge Edition of the Works of F. Scott Fitzgerald, ed. Matthew J. Bruccoli, 1991. Cited in the text as *TGG*.

9. Robert Stam, *Subversive Pleasures: Bakhtin, Cultural Criticism, and Film* (Baltimore: Johns Hopkins UP, 1989) 93.

10. For this aspect of Fitzgerald's characterization of Nick and its relationship to the characterization of Encolpius, see Keath Fraser, "Another Reading of *The Great Gatsby,*" *Critical Essays on F. Scott Fitzgerald's The Great Gatsby*, ed. Scott Donaldson (Boston: G. K. Hall & Company, 1984) 140–53.

11. Maria Plaza, *Laughter and Derision in Petronius' Satyrica: A Literary Study,* (Stockholm: Almqvist & Wiksell International, 2000) 46.

12. William Arrowsmith, "Luxury and Death in the *Satyricon,*" *Arion* 5.3 (1966): 304–31; 324.

13. MacKendrick 308. In contrast, William Frohock, in *Strangers to This Ground: Cultural Diversity in Contemporary American Writing* (Dallas: Dallas Southern Methodist UP, 1961) 60, asserts that "Scott Fitzgerald was no Petronius."

14. Much valid criticism has centered on parties in *The Great Gatsby* and a few critics have examined this fundamental aspect from a perspective that includes the idea of carnival. For example, in *Candles and Carnival Lights: The Catholic Sensibility of F. Scott Fitzgerald* (New York: New York UP, 1978) 111–16, written before Bakhtin's theories were available in English, Joan M. Allen discusses carnival imagery in the context of her specific interest in Fitzgerald's "Catholic sensibility"; although Christopher Ames uses Bakhtin's ideas as part of his theoretical approach in *The Life of the Party: Festive Vision in Modern Fiction* (Athens: U of Georgia P, 1991) 139–50, his reading differs from mine because it is based on the conviction that "parties, though structurally and stylistically important in *The Great Gatsby* are, finally, thematically insignificant" (41); Philip McGowan's interest in *American Carnival: Seeing and Reading American Culture* (London: Greenwood P, 2001) 68–78, is in contrasting the colorful gaudiness of Gatsby's parties with the concept of "whiteness" represented by the Buchanans.

15. Mikhail Bakhtin, *Rabelais and His World*, trans. Hélène Iswolsky (Bloomington: Indiana UP, 1984). Cited in the text as *RW*.

16. The gathering at Gatsby's in Chapter Six was originally conceived of as a costume party with the theme of the harvest dance; guests who did not arrive in costume were given bonnets or straw hats. See *Trimalchio: An Early Version of The Great Gatsby*, ed. James L. W. West (Cambridge: CUP, 2000) 80–81.

17. Roger W. Babson, *The Folly of Installment Buying* (New York: Ayer Co. Reprint ed., 1976), quoted in Michael Tratner, *Deficits and Desires: Economics and Sexuality in Twentieth-Century Literature* (Stanford: Stanford UP, 2001) 73.

18. Walter S. Hilborn, *Philosophy of the Uniform Small Loan Law* (New York: Division of Remedial Loans, Russell Sage Foundation, 1923), quoted in Tratner 73.

19. See *PDP* 171 for Bakhtin's brief remarks on gambling.

20. Mikhail Bakhtin, "Epic and Novel," *The Dialogic Imagination: Four Essays by M. M. Bakhtin*, ed. Michael Holquist, trans. Caryl Emerson and Michael Holquist (Austin: U of Texas P, 1981) 23.

21. Bakhtin notes that "in European carnivals there was almost always a special structure (usually a vehicle adorned with all possible sorts of gaudy carnival trash) called 'hell' and at the close of carnival this 'hell' was triumphantly set on fire" (*PDP* 126).

BARBARA WILL

The Great Gatsby *and The Obscene Word*

I

In a novel in which language is consistently seen to work against the demands of veracity, at least one formulation in *The Great Gatsby* rings true: Nick Carraway's pronouncement, near the start of the novel, that "Gatsby turned out all right at the end" (Fitzgerald 1999, 6). Jay Gatsby, a figure marked by failure and shadowed by death throughout most of the novel, nevertheless achieves a form of "greatness" in the final paragraphs of his story; it is at this point, in the words of Lionel Trilling, that Gatsby "comes inevitably to stand for America itself" (1963, 17). For it is in the final, lyrical paragraphs of the novel that Gatsby's fate takes on mythic dimensions, becoming an allegory for the course of the American nation and for the struggles and dreams of its citizens. This transformation occurs when the novel's narrator, Nick Carraway, finally perceives what lies beneath the "inessential" surface world of his surroundings: a vital impulse, an originary American hope. Nick sees Gatsby as the incarnation of this national impulse, this "extraordinary gift for hope," using the same term—"wonder"—to describe Gatsby's desire for Daisy Buchanan and that of the first American colonists gazing at "the fresh green breast of the new world." For Nick, Gatsby's lies, his pretensions, and his corruption are "no matter"; nor is his failure to win back Daisy; what matters is the sustaining belief in the value of striving for a "wondrous" object, not its inevitable

From *College Literature* 32, no. 4 (Fall 2005): 125–44. © 2005 by *College Literature*.

disappearance and meaninglessness. And in a significant shift in pronouns of the novel's final sentences, Nick unites Gatsby's effort with a general, if unspecified, national collective: "Gatsby believed in the green light, the orgastic future that year by year recedes before us. It eluded *us* then, but that's no matter—. . . So *we* beat on, boats against the current, borne back ceaselessly into the past" (Fitzgerald 1999, 141; my emphasis). What matters to Gatsby is what matters to "us"; Gatsby's story is "our" story; his fate and the fate of the nation are intertwined. That Gatsby "turned out all right in the end" is thus essential to the novel's vision of a transcendent and collective Americanism.

Yet this ending is in fact at odds with the characterization of Gatsby in the rest of the novel. For if Gatsby ultimately represents a glorified version of "us," then he does so only if we forget that he is for most of the novel a force of corruption: a criminal, a bootlegger, and an adulterer. As critics have often noted, the text stakes its ending on the inevitability of our forgetting everything about Gatsby that has proved troublesome about his character up to this point. What critics have generally overlooked, however, is the fact that the text also self-consciously inscribes this process of forgetting into its own narrative. Appearing to offer two discrepant views of its protagonist, *The Great Gatsby* in fact ultimately challenges its readers to question the terms through which "presence" or "visibility" can be signified.

This, to my mind, is the point of one of the most important yet least critically examined scenes in the novel: the novel's penultimate scene, the transitional scene that immediately precedes the last four paragraphs of the text. It is a scene that begins with Nick Carraway wandering idly down to Long Island Sound past Gatsby's house, killing time on the eve of his return to the mid-west: "On the last night, with my trunk packed and my car sold to the grocer, I went over and looked at that huge incoherent failure of a house once more. On the white steps an obscene word, scrawled by some boy with a piece of brick, stood out clearly in the moonlight and I erased it, drawing my shoe raspingly along the stone" (Fitzgerald 1999, 140). A fleeting, transitory scene; in the next instant, Nick is already down at the shore, "sprawled out on the sand," at which point his epiphany about Gatsby and the green light begins. Yet what this immediate sequence of events implies is that Nick's final epiphany about Gatsby is contingent for its emergence on the act that precedes this epiphany: the repression or erasure of an "obscene word." In order for Gatsby to "turn out all right at the end," to come to "stand for America itself," his link to this word must be erased. Yet by foregrounding the process of this erasure, this "forgetting," Fitzgerald also seems to be problematizing the inevitability of the text's ending: Gatsby "turn[s] out all right" only if we forget, or repress, his obscenity.

While it is easy for a reader to overlook this scene, it requires no real effort to understand why the graffiti scrawled on Gatsby's house would be an obscenity, for the link between Gatsby and the obscene has been repeatedly suggested in the text up to this point: in Nick's reference to Gatsby's "corruption"; in his opening claim that Gatsby "represented everything for which I have an unaffected scorn" (Fitzgerald 1999, 6); in his description of Gatsby's career as "Trimalchio" (88). In this penultimate scene, it is also a link that Fitzgerald frames explicitly in terms of signification, or rather, in terms of what eludes or threatens signification. For by linking Gatsby with an obscene *word*, Fitzgerald appears to be deliberately drawing attention to the etymology of "obscene": as that which is either unrepresentable or beyond the terms of the presentable ("obscene," from the Latin "obscenaeus," meaning both "against the presentable" and "unrepresentable"). Whatever the word scrawled on Gatsby's steps may be, the point is that we cannot know it; it is a word that, precisely in its obscenity, points to a signifying void. Yet as its etymology suggests, the "signifying void" of the obscene can be understood in two ways. On the one hand, the obscene is what eludes representation: it is the unrepresentable, the pre-linguistic, or the anti-linguistic, a force of disruption and implosion, of psychosexual and linguistic shattering. It is similar in process to what Julia Kristeva terms "the abject": that which "draws me toward the place where meaning collapses" (1982, 2). Yet the obscene is also what questions—and thus denaturalizes—the normative thrust of signification. The obscene works against the presentable, as Mary Caputi argues, "in its determined violation of established norms, its eagerness to proclaim from beyond the acceptable, its appeal to the uncanny" (1994, 7). Freud, speaking of "smut," defined it as an "undoing" of repression, while Bakhtin identifies "low" language ("on the stages of local fairs and at buffoon spectacles") as "parodic, and aimed sharply and polemically against the official languages of its given time" (Freud 1957, 101; Bakhtin 1981, 273). In this second sense, the obscene predominantly functions as a threat to the conventional language of narration or the normative discourses of a nation, throwing into question the status of the acceptable or the normal, of the seemingly representable and meaningful, including the political and social hierarchies that sustain "meaning."

As sections two and three of this essay will suggest, both senses of the term "obscene" summarize the life of Jay Gatsby. While Gatsby is a "mystery" for those who attend his parties, he is even more, as Nick Carraway notes, "an elusive rhythm, a fragment of lost words" (Fitzgerald 1999, 87). With his "unutterable visions" that lead to "unutterable depression" and ultimately "incoherent failure," Gatsby is constantly vanishing on the horizon of significance; and this is a problem for characters like Nick and the Buchanans, whose own sense of location in time and social space is very much dependent upon a clear distinction between truth and lies, insiders and outsiders, natives and aliens. Put another way, Gatsby is a figure who problematizes the nature of figuration itself, drawing the text toward an abject void, "toward the place where meaning collapses." But Gatsby is also a figure whose obscenity lies in the challenge he poses to "the presentable," to the natural and the normal—a particularly unsettling idea given not only the text's immediate concerns with the nature of belonging but also the historical moment in which Fitzgerald is writing, an era marked by widespread anxiety about the possible dissolution of the "natural" American in the face of an encroaching "alien menace." As we shall see, such concerns over the nature (and "naturalness") of American identity in the 1920s were shared by Fitzgerald himself, whose own politics at the time of writing *Gatsby* were directed toward immigration restriction and who remained throughout his life suspicious of those who threatened the group to which he felt he belonged, "the old American aristocracy." Given this historical context, Gatsby's indeterminacy and transgressiveness could be said to embody nothing less than the "obscene" fulfillment of Fitzgerald's own suspicions: Gatsby as the threatening figure of the alien, unassimilable to the discourse of political and social Americanism toward which the text is ultimately directed, "unutterable" within the narrative framework that seeks to represent him.

By having Nick erase "the obscene word" from the text as Gatsby's story draws to a close, however, Fitzgerald makes it possible for this story to emerge as the story of America itself. Gatsby the obscene becomes Gatsby the American. Yet while the fact of this transformation is incontestable, its terms remain troubling. Through foregrounding Nick's erasure of the obscene word from Gatsby's house, Fitzgerald deliberately emphasizes the process through which the "whitewashing" of Gatsby's reputation takes place. And as this essay will finally suggest, to emphasize this process is to reveal a central uncertainty, or void, that lies at the heart of the text's final, transcendent vision.

II

In an early draft of the novel, Nick Carraway makes an interesting observation about Gatsby: "He was provokingly elusive and what he was intrinsically 'like' I'm powerless to say."[1] Nick's crisis of linguistic disempowerment here accompanies the "provokingly elusive" nature of his subject; the problem of Gatsby's "intrinsic likeness" bears wholly on the project of signification. In a character with not enough "likeness" and no apparent "intrinsic" essence, Gatsby is nowhere and everywhere, a "vanishing presence"; and this, as Derrida reminds us, is also the nature of "*différance* . . . which prevents any word, any concept, any major enunciation from coming to summarize and to govern from the theological presence of a center the movement and textual spacing of differences" (1981, 14). If Gatsby—"the man who gives his name to this book"—is meant by Nick to "summarize" and "govern" the work of the text, the meaning and direction of its signifiers, then his "elusiveness" is also what prevents this governance from taking place. An "elusive rhythm," Gatsby could be said to embody *différance*, if embodiment can be understood as the "being-there of an absen[ce]" or the "disjointure in the very presence of the present" (1994, 6; 25). It is in his fractured and incoherent embodiment, his ever-vanishing "presence," that Gatsby throws into crisis Nick's effort to speak.

"Vanished" is indeed the predominant term in this text, as when at the end of Chapter I Nick first encounters Gatsby, only to find "he had vanished, and I was alone again in the unquiet darkness"; or when, after an awkward meeting with Tom Buchanan, Nick "turned toward Mr. Gatsby but he was no longer there" (Fitzgerald 1999, 59).[2] Gatsby "vanishes" at other key moments in the text: in his failure to appear at his own parties, in his unknowable past and shady business dealings, and in his smile, which "assured you that it had precisely the impression of you that, at your best, you hoped to convey. Precisely at that point it vanished—" (40). As this last sentence suggests, Gatsby even vanishes—literally—from the signifying system of the text itself: the dash, the graphic mark of his unrepresentability, is insistently emphasized whenever he speaks or is spoken about.[3] Although to Nick Gatsby seems at once utterly conventional, utterly knowable—being with him, he notes, was "like skimming hastily through a dozen magazines" (53)—he is also "provokingly elusive," both extending the promise of meaning or presence and "vanishing" at the moment in which that promise leans toward fulfillment. This process is apparent in a number of scenes throughout the novel. Most haunting is Nick's statement following Gatsby's confessional account of his first kiss with Daisy:

> Through all he said, even through his appalling sentimentality, I was reminded of something—an elusive rhythm, a fragment of lost words, that I had heard somewhere a long time ago. For a moment a phrase tried to take shape in my mouth and my lips parted like a dumb man's, as though there was more struggling upon them than a wisp of startled air. But they made no sound and what I had almost remembered was uncommunicable forever. (Fitzgerald 1999, 87)

Nick's effort to speak is here seen to be awakened by Gatsby's own words, with their "elusive rhythm" and nostalgic promise of a return to lost origins; yet memory is also inevitably attended by a failure of articulation ("and what I had almost remembered was uncommunicable forever"). Whoever Gatsby is, whatever he reminds one of, this "presence" ultimately lies outside the limits of the communicable. As in the earlier description of Gatsby's smile, this passage is structured around a contradictory movement (or "disjointure," to recall Derrida) in which presence and appearance pivot into absence and "vanishing" at the precise moment of seeming apprehension. Another such example is found in the party scene of chapter III, which begins with a series of gossipy suppositions about Gatsby's identity by passing partygoers: "'Somebody told me they thought he killed a man once'"; "'it's more that he was a German spy during the war'"; "'he told me once he was an Oxford man.'" With this latter claim, notes Nick, "A dim background started to take shape behind [Gatsby] but at her next remark it faded away" (40). Here, again, the promise of presence or "shape" vanishes at the moment of its emergence; suppositions lead not to truth but to indeterminacy, and who Gatsby is remains just beyond the reach of the "next remark."

Nor is Gatsby's indeterminacy within the text simply an issue of Nick's own notably distorted vision, as the comments of fellow partygoers make clear. While it is true that Nick's perceptions, especially while drunk, contribute exponentially to the idea of Gatsby's elusiveness, other observers also fail to illuminate Gatsby's character. In a crucial (and again, often overlooked) moment during the chapter III party scene, Nick and Jordan encounter a man "with enormous owl-eyed spectacles" sitting in the library of Gatsby's house, who informs them that the books on the shelves are, indeed, "real": "Absolutely real—have pages and everything. I thought they'd be a nice durable cardboard. Matter of fact they're absolutely real. . . . It's a triumph. What thoroughness! What realism! Knew when to stop too—didn't cut the pages. But what do you want? What do you expect?" (Fitzgerald 1999, 37–38). As a figure who, like Doctor T.J. Eckleberg, is linked metonymically in the text to the trope of perception, "Owl Eyes" is presented as one who pierces the façade of social life in the Eggs, exposing—as at Gatsby's funeral—the despair and loneliness that lie underneath the forced gaiety of appearances. In the library scene, Owl Eyes' ability to "expose" is both emphasized and undermined, as the fake-appearing books turn out to be real, yet semi-unreadable. The "realness" of the books signifies presence and meaning; yet their uncut pages underscore the opacity of the text-that-would-be-read. Gatsby, too, is both "really" there and absent, a figure who resists being perceived even by those with "corrected" vision, who voids the signifying process of its meaningful end. "What do you want? What do you expect?" Owl Eyes finally asks himself, Nick, Jordan, and implicitly the reader, calling into question any desire or expectation for knowledge that might attend the experience of "reading" Gatsby.

Hence those few crucial scenes where Gatsby's character promises to be revealed as meaningful and directed toward a significant end invariably prove to be "provokingly elusive." In the famous flashback scene of chapter VI, for example, Nick recalls Gatsby's past as "James Gatz of North Dakota" in order to explain Gatsby's present, portraying his youthful rejection of family and original name as a necessary precondition to his later "glory" as a wealthy, upwardly-mobile adult (Fitzgerald 1999, 76 ff.). Nick's account of Gatsby's adolescence attempts to cast him in a familiar mold: the self-made man, "spr[inging] from his Platonic conception of himself," the spiritual descendent of other hard-working national icons like Horatio Alger or Benjamin Franklin (whose famous "Plan for Self-Examination" would be invoked later in the text in Gatsby's own childhood "Schedule"). Yet the text consistently undermines these seeming "causes" of Gatsby's actions at the very moment of their "revelation." For what this chapter in fact reveals about Gatsby is not so much his identity with an American tradition of hard work and "luck and pluck" but rather his dreaminess, his entrapment in "a universe of ineffable gaudiness," his belief "that the rock of the world was founded securely on a fairy's wing." What motivates Gatsby is not the desire for material betterment ("food and bed") but the evanescent and the intangible; what satisfies him is confirmation of "the unreality of reality." Whatever is, for Gatsby, can be contradicted, "the real" is always "the unreal," and this is troubling both to the descriptive terms and to the larger narrative of American achievement within which Gatsby is meant to emerge as "great." To be sure, to tell the story of a figure trapped in the oxymoronic "unreality of reality" is to tell a modernist story, if modernity, as Jean-François Lyotard suggests, "does not occur without a shattering of belief, without a discovery of the *lack of reality* in reality—a discovery linked to the invention of other realities" (1992, 9). Consistently dreaming beyond the material, social, economic, and temporal boundaries of his surroundings, overturning and reimagining the hierarchies of power and social status that constrain him, Gatsby could be seen as a modernist figure, a deconstructive figure, a figure of *différance*, whose "motivation" is to "shatter ... belief" and hence "invent ... [new] realities." Yet *The Great Gatsby* is no *Ulysses*, capturing in the play of signifiers the movement of Gatsby's "*différance*"; however "modernist" Gatsby may be, his character can only be revealed through the moments in which he vanishes from the narrative, through oxymorons, through dashes—all of which point to an unrepresentability at the center of this textual reality.

III

In a text so haunted by indeterminacy and unrepresentability, what stands out are precisely those efforts that work against "vanishing," that attempt to affirm, make visible, and police boundaries of meaning, identity, community, sexuality, and nation. These are also efforts directed against Gatsby and his elusiveness: efforts either to make sense of Gatsby's character (as in Nick's effort to "reveal" Gatsby's formative past) or to cast him as inherently corrupt and "obscene," as outside the boundaries of sense, propriety, and order, as racially and sexually perverse. These latter efforts are centered in the character of Tom Buchanan, denizen of the isolated town of East Egg, two-timing husband of Daisy, and single-minded adherent to the nativist views of a tome called "The Rise of the Colored Empires," modeled on Lothrop Stoddard's 1920 volume *The Rising Tide of Color Against White World-Supremacy*.[4] For Buchanan, following Stoddard, "The idea is if we don't look out the white race will be—will be utterly submerged," a statement whose characteristic use of the dash emphasizes the anxiety that underwrites American nativism in the 1920s, its sense that the process of Nordic "submersion" by an ever-expanding "colored empire" may already be underway. What the dash in Tom's statement represents is what, for him, would be unspeakable—miscegenation, a process through which "whiteness" and "color" become undifferentiated, through which "race" itself, and the white race in particular, become indeterminate. For Tom, it is Jay Gatsby in particular who represents a mode of racial indeterminacy or "vanishing" that threatens to violate not only the immediate community of East Egg but also the very concept of Americanism itself.

In his recent study of nativism and American literature in the 1920s, Walter Benn Michaels argues that the threat of a disappearing white race constitutes Tom's real concern about Gatsby's union with Daisy; it is the fact that "[f]or Tom ... Gatsby (né Gatz, with his Wolfsheim [sic] 'gonnegtion') isn't quite white," that sustains his antipathy toward his rival (Michaels 1995, 25).[5] Gatsby's "off-white" status is confirmed earlier in the novel by the comment of Tom's relation-by-marriage Nick Carraway that "I would have accepted without question the information that Gatsby sprang from the swamps of Louisiana or from the lower East Side of New York" (Fitzgerald 1999, 41), a statement that associates Gatsby not with radical otherness but with creole or Jewish difference, both in the 1920s "assigned to the not-fully-white side of the racial spectrum."[6] What most disturbs Tom, and clearly troubles Nick, is not just the fact that Gatsby is a mystery but more that he signals the "vanishing" of whiteness into indeterminacy, and thus threatens the whole economic, discursive, and institutional structure of power supporting the social distinctions and hierarchies at work in *The Great Gatsby*. For Tom (and possibly Nick), whiteness and its attendant privileges—material well-being, entitlement, the feeling of being "safe and proud above the hot struggles of the poor"—is something that must be preserved, safeguarded, barricaded. Thus when Gatsby is most dangerously close to "winning" Daisy, it is not so much his social ambition that threatens Tom as the fact that his pursuit portends "intermarriage between black and white." Gatsby's "obscenity" for Tom lies in the challenge he poses to sexual and racial norms. In exposing Gatsby's link to miscegenation, Tom brings out the deeper social menace against which his own claim to whiteness stands as guardian: "Flushed with his impassioned gibberish he saw himself standing alone on the last barrier of civilization" (101).

That Gatsby is associated with a Jewish crime syndicate, moreover, only redoubles his threatening presence in the text. With his "Wolfsheim 'gonneg-tion'" Gatsby seems contaminated by more than just criminality and sexual perversity; for it is the fact of Wolfshiem's crudely stereotyped, animalistic Jewishness that most seems to "taint" Gatsby. The same "taint" is also suggested by Gatsby's layered, problematic name. "Jay Gatsby," of course, is only a WASP fiction adopted by one "James Gatz of North Dakota," yet although the text is directed toward exposing this fiction, the significance of this exposure remains obscure. While the name of "Gatz" is clearly haunted by ethnic, and specifically Jewish, overtones, "Gatz" is also a decidedly ambiguous name. Not *not* Jewish (as opposed to "Gaty," the first version of "Gatz" shown in Fitzgerald's drafts), the name "Gatz" is also not identifiably Jewish (as opposed, for example, to the more common "Katz"). Both Jews and non-Jews have the surname Gatz; moreover, the name "Gatz" sometimes appears as a germanicized alteration of a Yiddish name, "Gets."[7] That Fitzgerald knew of this etymological complexity would not be surprising; as Lottie R. Crim and Neal B. Houston have pointed out, Fitzgerald's use of names in *Gatsby* is remarkably rich and nuanced.[8] By choosing a name, "Gatz," that can generate both Jewish and gentile chains of associations, Fitzgerald seems to be emphasizing once again the way in which his protagonist is always "vanishing" into racial and hence social indeterminacy. Neither identifiably black nor identifiably Jewish, the shifting, obscure, ever-vanishing figure of James Gatz/Jay Gatsby troubles the category of "whiteness," problematizing the force of this category at a moment when such force is of crucial significance.

As Michaels suggests, the specter of a beleaguered whiteness in *The Great Gatsby* needs to be understood in light of the historical moment in which *Gatsby* was written, the early 1920s. This is a moment in which American isolationist fervor is at its peak, a moment in which fears over "the expanded power of the alien" are being openly expressed in political, intellectual, and literary forums. It is a moment marked by the social movement of nativism, with its support of the Johnson-Reed Immigration Act of 1924 and its battle cry "America for the Americans." It is also a moment in which the discourse of "Americanism"—the nativists' privileged term—is linked indubitably to the discourse of whiteness: "Americanism is actually the racial thought of the Nordic race, evolved after a thousand years of experience," writes Clinton Stoddard Burr, author of *America's*

Race Heritage (1922).[9] "The great hope of the future here in America lies in the realization that competition of the Nordic with the alien is fatal," warns nativist writer Madison Grant in his 1920 introduction to Lothrop Stoddard's *The Rising Tide of Color*, " . . . In this country we must look to such of our people—our farmers and artisans—as are still of American blood to recognize and meet this danger" (Stoddard 1920, xxxi). Charlotte Perkins Gilman, author and agitator for women's rights, simply worried in 1923, "Is America Too Hospitable?" (Higham 1973, 386, n. 25). For these and other nativists, keeping "American blood" pure—i.e., purely white—in the face of alien expansion was a predominant concern; and one that contributed its ideological part to a host of post-War social measures, from quotas to IQ tests, that were meant to establish and affirm the whiteness or "Nordicism" of the nation.

In *The Great Gatsby* (composed during 1922–24), nativist feeling is clearly exemplified by the views of Tom Buchanan, but also, though more subtly, by the discourse of Nick Carraway, with his "scorn" for the working classes, his stereotyping of immigrants, Jews, and blacks, and his claim to be "descended from the Dukes of Buccleuch"—an aristocratic lineage that, however fictional, is meant to appease any nativist fears about the non-whiteness of the Scottish. Yet while Fitzgerald presents such attempts to shore up whiteness against "alien elements" as "impassioned gibberish," external, biographical evidence suggests that the nativist ideas of Tom and Nick may not be so far from Fitzgerald's own. "Raise the bars of immigration and permit only Scandinavians, Teutons, Anglo Saxons + Celts to enter," Fitzgerald writes in an infamous 1921 letter to Edmund Wilson after a disappointing tourist trip in France and Italy: " . . . My reactions [are] all philistine, anti-socialistic, provincial + racially snobbish. I believe at last in the white man's burden" (1994, 47).[10] Some fifteen years later, in an undated letter from the 1930s to his daughter Scottie lamenting her choice of friends, Fitzgerald reiterates these views:

> Jesus, we're the few remnants of the old American aristocracy that's managed to survive in communicable form—we have the vitality left. And you choose to mix it up with the cheap lower middle class settled on Park Avenue. You know the distinction—and in most of your relations you are wise enough to forget it—but when it comes to falling for a phoney—your instincts should do a better job. All that's rude, tough (in the worst sense), crude and purse proud comes from vermin like the——'s. (Undated note to Scottie from F. Scott Fitzgerald)[11]

"Mix[ing] it up with the cheap lower middle class," Scottie fails to let her "instincts" create the necessary distinction that would preclude her "falling for a phoney." The "distinction" Fitzgerald refers to is one of class, to be sure, but even more of race—a point made clear by his emphasis on familial "vitality," which directly echoes contemporary nativist discussions of race and degeneracy. Lothrop Stoddard, for one, would differentiate between "Nordics" and "aliens" on the basis of "vitality": "there seems to be no question that the Nordic is far and away the most valuable type; standing, indeed, at the head of the whole human genus" (1920, 162). Yet Stoddard also fears that in the post-War period, "Nordic vitality" has suffered a two-fold blow: decimated by the War, which has left "the men twisted by hereditary deformity or devitalized by hereditary disease . . . at home to propagate the breed," Nordics are also victims of immigrant ambition: "the Nordic native American has been crowded out with amazing rapidity by . . . swarming, prolific aliens, and after two short generations he has in many of our urban areas become almost extinct" (181; 165). Given Fitzgerald's own failure to see action in the War, his lifelong battle with alcoholism, tuberculosis and neurasthenia, and his confession, in the 1930s, "that lack of success of physical sheer power in my life made trouble,"[12] it is somewhat ironic that he would appeal to Scottie on the grounds of their shared claim to familial "vitality." Yet "vitality" is precisely what distinguishes "the old American aristocracy"—or in Stoddard's terms, "the Nordic native American"—from "vermin," and it is the terms of this distinction that Fitzgerald means to emphasize in his letter.

Whether or not Fitzgerald means to emphasize this distinction in *The Great Gatsby* is another matter; beyond his presentation of Tom's ideas as not only hopeless but "pathetic" is the fact that Jay Gatsby is not identifiably Other—like the "modish Negroes" on the Queensboro Bridge or the Greek Michaelis—but simply "not quite white." Yet again, being "not quite" is perhaps Gatsby's most troubling aspect. Located in the liminal space between categories, the space of indeterminacy and *différance*, Gatsby consistently eludes the terms of both national and textual belonging, and it is these terms which, as Fitzgerald explains to his daughter, enable "distinctions" between self and other, white and non-white, American and un-American, to emerge with clarity. To this extent, finally, Gatsby is not only a mystery in the text, a signifier of indeterminacy and unrepresentability; he is also, quite simply, an obscene threat to the national "vitality" of which Tom Buchanan laments the loss, and which *The Great Gatsby* itself purports to celebrate in its final pages.

IV

When, near the end of his story, Gatsby dies, the event is deemed a "holocaust"—a striking term given his possible link to Jewish origins—yet this is far from the last word that the text provides about the significance of Gatsby's life and death. There is another word closer to the end of the text that seems more nearly to serve as Gatsby's epitaph: an "obscene word, scrawled by some boy with a piece of brick" on the "white steps" of Gatsby's house—a word explicitly framed as a defilement of whiteness, as a mark of impurity.[13] "Jew" or "colored" or "alien" or "Other"—any or all of these terms might appear on Gatsby's steps; but what is perhaps most significant about Nick's reference to "the obscene word" is the illegibility of this word, its location outside or beyond the presentable, its "vanished" status. For it is fitting that the sum of Gatsby's "corruption," his obscurity and indeterminacy, might be expressed by a word that literally cannot be read.[14]

I have attempted, up to this point, to trace both ways in which the figure of Gatsby might be seen as a problem for the signifying project that bears his name. Drawing the reader toward "the place where meaning collapses," Gatsby's "unutterable visions," his evanescent dreams, and his "uncommunicable" presence all point to a narrative and linguistic void that is at odds with the counter effort by Nick and others to make Gatsby into the "governing" presence in the book, into a figure of significance. Moreover, Gatsby's racial indeterminacy, his troubling "off-whiteness," and his link to ethnic criminality further obscure the significance of this figure in a context in which racial difference is seen to be defining and of crucial importance to American identity. Thus it is not surprising that as Gatsby's story draws to a close what was once "provokingly elusive" would come to be figured as "obscene."

What *is* surprising is the way in which the novel finally ends: with Gatsby's obscenity erased as speedily from the text itself as it is from the front steps of his house. After Nick's act of erasure, Gatsby's elusiveness, corruption, and "off-whiteness" are forgotten; in the next moment, a moment in which "vanished trees" appear and the "whispers" of a lost continent become intelligible, a new vision of Gatsby's significance is revealed:

> [A]s the moon rose higher the inessential houses began to melt away until gradually I became aware of the old island here that flowered once for Dutch sailors' eyes—a fresh, green breast of the new world. Its vanished trees, the trees that had made way for Gatsby's house, had once pandered in whispers to the last and greatest of all human dreams; for a transitory enchanted moment man must have held his breath in the presence of this continent, compelled into an aesthetic contemplation he neither understood nor desired, face to face for the last time in history with something commensurate to his capacity for wonder.
>
> And as I sat there, brooding on the old unknown world, I thought of Gatsby's wonder when he first picked out the green light at the end of Daisy's dock. (Fitzgerald 1999, 140–41)

In these famous concluding lines, Nick creates an explicit analogy between the gaze of the Dutch colonists as they first catch sight of the "fresh, green breast of the new world," and Gatsby's vision of the green light at the end of Daisy's dock: Gatsby and the Dutch are joined in contemplative "wonder" as they come face to face with their objects of desire; both represent in their contemplation "the last and greatest of all human dreams." This linkage reverses Gatsby's trajectory toward unrepresentability and recasts his desire in terms of a transcendent national narrative; at this moment, the problem of Gatsby's "intrinsic likeness" disappears, for what Gatsby is "intrinsically 'like'" turns out to be nothing less than "America" itself. If nationalism, as Benedict Anderson writes, "always loom[s] out of an immemorial past and . . . glide[s] into a limitless future" (Bhabha 1990, 1), then the final lines of *Gatsby* establish "America" as eternal mode of human yearning, as a quest narrative that stretches across generations from the Dutch to Gatsby, and hence from the Dutch, to Gatsby, to "us" ("It eluded us then, but that's no matter—tomorrow we will run faster, stretch out our arms farther . . ."). To be sure, this passage is also haunted by another idea of America—an "old island" that precedes the transforming gaze of the colonists and that, like Myrtle's torn and bloody breast, seems momentarily to challenge and render ironic the final, transcendent vision of "the fresh, green breast of the new world." This "old" America, this lost America, reminds us again of Kristeva's notion of the abject: that which threatens meaning, especially in its association with the irreparable loss of the mother's body. Yet abject America is quickly glossed over. What matters here, finally, is the way age, violence, and obscenity—seemingly inevitably—give way before Gatsby's and the colonist's Dream.

But what is perhaps most significant about these concluding paragraphs is their investment not only in resignifying Gatsby but in refiguring the racialist overtones that previously haunted this indeterminacy. By situating Gatsby in a chain of likeness with the "Nordic" Dutch, the text effectively asserts Gatsby's ties to whiteness and "erases" his problematically off-white status, just as it refashions his "uncommunicable" presence as nationally significant. Inasmuch as this ending articulates a triumphalist nationalist credo, it does so in terms that ring with the ideology of nativism. The very figure who represented a threat to the boundaries of linguistic and national meaning is now revealed as the inheritor and guardian of Americanist values, as the natural descendent of the "Teutons, Anglo-Saxons + Celts." Gatsby's problem of being "not quite white" is finally dismissed as so much "foul dust float[ing] in the wake of his dreams" (Fitzgerald 1999, 6).

V

Jay Gatsby, in other words, "turns out all right at the end"—as Nick Carraway had promised in the opening pages of the novel. This essay has questioned the necessity of that promise, noting the discrepancy between the novel's elegiac conclusion and the larger narrative in which Gatsby figures as troubling and suspect, as liminal and unknowable. Other critics have made similar note of Fitzgerald's desire in his conclusion to move beyond the indeterminate, skeptical, paranoid, and morally relativistic world he chronicles: Gatsby as a sign of his times and of the transcendence of his times. Jeffrey Louis Decker, for one, suggests that the resolution of the novel represents Fitzgerald's "anxious" eagerness to retain "the traditional narrative of virtuous ambitions" despite the bankruptcy of this narrative in a post-War, nativist American society: "In death Gatsby is freed from his venal partnership with immigrant gangsters and remembered within a lineage of northern European explorers," despite the fact that it is precisely Gatsby's connection to immigrant "indeterminacy" that has earlier distinguished him as a threat to Nordic ideology (1997, 78; 97).[15] Chris Fitter writes that the ending of *Gatsby* represents Fitzgerald's "misty melancholia" for a prelapsarian, precapitalist ideal that the text has, up to this point, worked hard to demystify (1998, 14). And Joyce A. Rowe succinctly captures the paradox that "Nick's epilogue . . . keeps alive the very form of that aspiration we have seen issuing in a wasteland of social and moral emptiness" (1988, 103).

As these critiques suggest, Gatsby's final transformation is far from inevitable, but rather "willed" by a Fitzgerald who, as his harshest critic Chris Fitter writes, ultimately prefers "tearful patriotic *frisson*" to any more critical or complex vision of contemporary American culture (1998, 14). Given Fitzgerald's own nativist and isolationist leanings in the 1920s, this assessment seems at least plausible: that *The Great Gatsby*, for all its demystification of American self-definition, might ultimately succumb to a "final reflex of conservative reaction" marked by an essentializing, dehistoricized vision of national belonging (19). Yet to my mind, it is also significant that Fitzgerald deliberately marks the process of this final transformation through Nick's erasure of the "obscene word" on Gatsby's front steps. By calling attention to Nick's act, Fitzgerald seems to be suggesting that the crucial turn in the text—Gatsby's apotheosis into the carrier of the American Dream—takes place by means of the same mechanism of "vanishing" that lies at the heart of his obscene indeterminacy. If the threat of Gatsby in the text lies precisely in the way in which he "vanishes" from categorization and social or racial signification, then Nick's erasure of the obscene word stages a similar process, making the obscene word "vanish" in order to cancel out the obscenity of vanishing. Gatsby is purified by this gesture, but the gesture itself reasserts the primacy of indeterminacy in the text. Put "under erasure" in the Derridean sense, Gatsby's obscenity becomes the absence that allows the text's ultimate presence to emerge: the presence of generations of Nordic American settlers, mythically united for a moment in Nick's transhistorical vision of national essence.

Ironically, the same play of absence and presence is evident in the only two other instances in the text of Fitzgerald's use of the word "obscene." The first use of the term occurs during the party at Myrtle's New York apartment, when in response to a question about her affection for her husband Myrtle lets out a "violent and obscene" answer: an answer that nevertheless remains unrepresented in the text (Fitzgerald 1999, 29). A similar but even more telling use of the term appears in a scene excised from the novel's final version, a scene in which Nick hears a comment Daisy makes to Gatsby at his party:

> "We're together here in your garden, Jay—your beautiful garden," broke out Daisy suddenly. "It doesn't seem possible, does it? I can't believe it's possible. Will you have somebody look up in the encyclopedia and see if it's really true. Look it up under G."
>
> For a moment I thought this was casual chatter—then I realized that she was trying to drown out from us, from herself, a particularly obscene conversation that four women were carrying on at a table just behind. (Fitzgerald 2000, 85)

Although Fitzgerald would delete this passage from *Gatsby*, it clearly prefigures the extant scene in the final version in which Nick erases "the obscene word" from the steps of Gatsby's house. As with the latter, Nick's reference here to "a particularly obscene conversation" is inextricably linked to the problem of Gatsby's signifying status. Daisy's effort to make sense of her present by making Gatsby legible and identifiable, by making him *signify* ("Look it up under G") is reinterpreted by Nick as an effort to repress, "to drown out from us, from herself, a particularly obscene conversation that four women were carrying on at table just behind." Gatsby "turns out all right" in this scene precisely because Nick and the reader cannot hear underneath Daisy's words the "obscene language" that has no place in this text—the language of drunken, sexually-liberated women, of criminals, of the working classes, of immigrants and blacks—all threatening, as we have seen, to the elite white social order that both Nick and the Buchanans inhabit. Daisy's act of "whitewashing," in short, represses Gatsby's link to the obscene in order to reveal him as someone socially significant and unquestionably white. Yet to drown out the obscene, in this instance or in the ultimate conclusion of *Gatsby*, is also, as Fitzgerald himself was well aware, to foreground the power of the obscene to disrupt and undo normative structures of social, national, and linguistic signification. "*We* have the vitality left," claims Fitzgerald to his daughter, but the anxious indeterminacy of his own novel seems to tell another story.

Notes

Permission to cite from the F. Scott Fitzgerald manuscript collection provided by Princeton University Library and the F. Scott Fitzgerald Literary Trust.

1. Undated note by F. Scott Fitzgerald. From the F. Scott Fitzgerald Archive, Special Collections, Princeton University Library.

2. Gatsby's vanishing during the encounter with Tom in Chapter IV precipitates one of the oddest structural shifts of the narrative, when Nick's narration suddenly gives way to the voice of Jordan Baker narrating the true story of Gatsby and Daisy's past. This is the only place in the novel in which the first-person narration is not controlled by Nick, and seems to impugn Nick's ability to keep his own subject in his sights. Jordan's momentary control over the text at the end of Chapter IV serves briefly to make Gatsby more intelligible, but her voice, no less than Nick's, fails ultimately to "correct" Nick's vision. Jordan remains "incurably dishonest" (Fitzgerald 1995, 63): a "hard, limited person" (84) with her own perceptual blindnesses, as she reveals in the end when she admits that she misread Nick's own honesty.

3. To be sure, the dash—the mark of graphic attenuation or of a "break" in dialogue or thought; the sign of signification in suspension or in the process of hemorrhaging into silence—is also the most prevalent stylistic mark in the text. "What was that word we—," Daisy asks (Fitzgerald 1999, 14), the dash performing stylistically what the question ponders. "I just meant—," George Wilson states (22), as his "voice faded off." Dashes appear throughout most of the narration and dialogue of the novel, as they do in Fitzgerald's writings in general; perhaps only Emily Dickinson, among American writers, is more liberal in her use of the dash (see Crumbley 1997). Yet in *The Great Gatsby*, it is Jay Gatsby who most often "speaks" in dashes: "It's the funniest thing, old sport," he remarks upon finally finding Daisy in his bedroom, "I can't—when I try to—" (72). "And she doesn't understand," he laments later about Daisy, "She used to be able to understand. We'd sit for hours—" (86). "'At least—' He fumbled with a series of beginnings. 'Why, I thought—why, look here, old sport'" (65). Gatsby's speech, as Nick himself notes, struggles awkwardly to mimic the "old euphemisms" of East Egg; his "old sport" and "Oxford man" represent a painstakingly studied insouciance that, according to Nick, "just missed being absurd" (40). Yet in the midst of Gatsby's effort to "certify" his social status in language, to lay claim to the terms of WASP social belonging, the repeated appearance of the dash reminds the reader of the attenuation or failure of Gatsby's effort. Like an obscene word, the dash could be said to work against "the presentable," marking textual moments of effacement, moments in which language simply fades into silence. The literal sign of his indeterminacy in the text, the dash emphasizes Gatsby's absence and presence; it is perhaps telling that Gatsby balances with a "formless grace" on the "dashboard" of his car as he greets Nick one morning (51).

4. In the text, Buchanan alludes carelessly to "'The Rise of the Coloured Empires' by this man Goddard"; according to Matthew Bruccoli, "Fitzgerald did not want to provide the correct title and author" (Fitzgerald 1995, 183). However it is interesting to speculate about Buchanan's "mistake." "Goddard" may refer to screenwriter and playwright Charles William Goddard, mentioned by Bruccoli

as a possible source for the figure of Gatsby himself (see Bruccoli 1981, 184 n.). More likely, Fitzgerald may have been indirectly citing the work of Henry Herbert Goddard, author during the teens and twenties of works on mental deficiency, "the criminal imbecile," and school training of "defective" and "gifted" children. Goddard was a contributor to the same educational series as Lewis Terman, director of the Stanford/Binet IQ tests. Goddard's views on gifted and defective behavior bear a striking resemblance to Lothrop Stoddard's schema of racial types, as well as the latter's claim that the superior "Nordic" races were being actively threatened by a defective "tide" of non-white peoples.

5. Ironically, Tom makes a similar claim about Daisy when he hesitates to include her in his category of "Nordics" ("'This idea is that we're Nordics. I am and you are and you are and—' After an infinitesimal hesitation he included Daisy with a slight nod" [Fitzgerald 1999, 14]). As Michaels points out, whiteness, for Tom, operates through a rigid system of inclusion and exclusion, one threatened by ethnic difference and femininity alike; in order for the category to sustain itself it must exclude anyone who isn't "quite" identifiable.

6. For a discussion of Jewish assimilation in the United States during the first half of the twentieth century, see Brodkin (1998, esp. 103).

7. In a biographical search, "Gatz" appears to be both a Jewish and a Gentile name. As noted, "Gatz" also appears as a germanicized form of the Yiddish "Gets." Thus the reader of *Gatsby* is faced with the possibility that Henry Gatz, father of Jay Gatsby, may already be "passing" as Gentile and is thus much more of a significant prototype for his son's own self-transformation than has previously been acknowledged.

8. The layered complexity of Gatsby's name is consistent with other names in the text that emphasize masquerade and pretense: for example, Mrs. Chrystie, who accompanies Hubert Auerbach to Gatsby's party, "whose name, more than likely, suggests the famous Christie Minstrels of the early nineteenth century. Mrs. Chrystie masquerades as a wife, and while she wears the name of her husband, she pretends to be someone she is not" (Crim and Houston 1989, 83). There is also "the prince of something whom we called Duke" at Gatsby's party (Fitzgerald 1999, 51), as well as the novel *Simon Called Peter* that Myrtle Wilson keeps in her apartment (25). Most telling, for our purposes, is the name "Meyer Wolfshiem," whose odd spelling has rarely been noticed by readers (see Michaels [1995], above), but which represents a marked variant from the German "Wolfsheim." One could argue—as does Edmund Wilson when he "corrects" the text for his 1941 edition (see Bruccoli's "Introduction," Fitzgerald 1995, liv)—that Fitzgerald, a notoriously careless speller, was simply in error in his spelling of "Wolfshiem." However, one could also see this spelling as deliberately emphasizing the same ethnic uncertainty as the name "James Gatz." "Wolfshiem" is a name that sounds and looks "foreign" (and, in this context, "Jewish"), but it does not conform to a Germanic (or German-Jewish) origin. It is a name that troubles, that confuses; a name that masks rather than reveals identity.

9. Clinton Stoddard Burr quoted in Higham (1973, 273), whose work on American nativism offers the most sustained analysis to date of the social and ideological positions adopted by intellectuals of the 1920s.

10. Fitzgerald's youthful correspondence is filled with similar sentiments. In an undated letter to Thomas Boyd, he writes, "All these 'marvellous' places like Majorca turn out to have some one enormous disadvantage—bugs, lepers, Jews, consumptives, or philistines" (F. Scott Fitzgerald Archive, Special Collections, Princeton University Library). For a discussion of how Fitzgerald's attitudes

toward ethnic and racial difference changed over the course of his life, see Margolies (1997).

11. Undated note to Scottie from F. Scott Fitzgerald Archive, Special Collections, Princeton University Library. In a letter dated 17 November 1936, Fitzgerald further explicates this typology: "Park Avenue girls are hard, aren't they? Usually the daughters of 'up-and-coming' men and, in a way, the inevitable offspring of that type" (Fitzgerald 1965, 17).

12. Undated note from F. Scott Fitzgerald Archive, Special Collections, Princeton University Library.

13. Ironically, it is a form of whiteness that illuminates this obscenity: Nick first notices the word because it "stood out clearly in the moonlight" (Fitzgerald 1995, 188). Yet while the moon may make visible Gatsby's link to "off-white" obscenity, moonlight also serves the opposite purpose several lines later when it illuminates the "essential" vision of Gatsby and the Dutch explorers that lies underneath the "inessential houses" of Long Island Sound (189). In short, the moon, like the sun and other objects in the firmament—notably, the eyes of Dr. T.J. Eckleburg—is a force of both illumination and obscurity in this text.

14. It is interesting, in this context, to consider the striking parallels between this scene in *Gatsby* and a similar scene in J.D. Salinger's *The Catcher in the Rye*, where Holden Caulfield's fantasy of going West and becoming a deaf-mute, thus rendering himself both unintelligible and uncomprehending, is shattered when he sees an obscenity scrawled on the wall of his sister Phoebe's school. Unlike *Gatsby*, *Catcher* makes this obscenity both literal and visible—"Fuck you"—as if to mock Holden's fantasy of disappearance into indeterminacy. Moreover, *Catcher* emphasizes this shattering by repeatedly restaging Holden's encounter with the obscene word (in the stairwell, in the museum) until he finally is forced to acknowledge that "if I ever die, and they stick me in a cemetery, and I have a tombstone and all, it'll say 'Holden Caulfield' on it, and then what year I was born and what year I died, and then right under that it'll say 'Fuck you'" (1951, 264). Like *Gatsby*, however, the encounter with the obscene word in *Catcher* occurs at precisely the same moment in the text, preceding the novel's final scene of redemption and reconciliation between Holden and Phoebe. To this extent, both texts seem to be emphasizing the transitional necessity of a confrontation with the obscene in their efforts to assert a final, redemptive vision.

15. Michaels makes a related point, focusing on the bond between Tom and Nick that enables this lineage ultimately to emerge: "the differences the novel works to establish between Tom and Nick . . . are in the end—to use Gatsby's phrase—'just personal.' Ironizing Tom's Nordicism, Nick nevertheless extends it" (1995, 41). In its final celebration of a "Nordicist" worldview, Michaels writes, *The Great Gatsby* is "the most obvious example" of a new literary definition of "Americanism" in the 1920s: "Americanism would now be understood as something more than and different from the American citizenship that so many aliens had so easily achieved" (47).

WORKS CITED

Bakhtin, M. M. 1981. *The Dialogic Imagination*. Trans. Caryl Emerson and Michael Holquist. Austin: University of Texas Press.

Bhabha, Homi K. 1990. "Introduction: Narrating the Nation." In *Nation and Narration*, ed. Homi K. Bhabha. New York: Routledge.

Brodkin, Karen. 1998. *How Jews Became White Folks and What That Says About Race in America*. New York: Rutgers University Press.

Bruccoli, Matthew J. 1981. *Some Sort of Epic Grandeur: The Life of F. Scott Fitzgerald*. New York: Harcourt, Brace.

Caputi, Mary. 1994. *Voluptuous Yearnings: A Feminist Theory of the Obscene*. Lanham, Maryland: Rowman & Littlefield.

Crim, Lottie R., and Neal B. Houston. 1989. "The Catalogue of Names in *The Great Gatsby*." *Re: Arts and Letters* 21:1: 77–92.

Crumbley, Paul. 1997. *Inflections of the Pen: Dash and Voice in Emily Dickinson*. Lexington: University of Kentucky Press.

Decker, Jeffrey Louis. 1997. *Made in America: Self-Styled Success from Horatio Alger to Oprah Winfrey*. Minneapolis: University of Minnesota Press.

Derrida, Jacques. 1981. *Positions*. Trans. Alan Bass. Chicago: University of Chicago Press.

———. 1994. *Specters of Marx: the State of the Debt, the Work of Mourning, and the New International*. Trans. Peggy Kamuf. New York: Routledge.

Fitter, Chris. 1998. "From the Dream to the Womb: Visionary Impulse and Political Ambivalence in *The Great Gatsby*." *Journal x* 3:1: 1–21.

Fitzgerald, F. Scott. 1965. *Letters to His Daughter*. New York: Scribner.

———. 1994. *A Life in Letters*. Ed. Matthew J. Bruccoli. New York: Touchstone.

———. 1995. *The Great Gatsby*. Ed. Matthew J. Bruccoli. 1925. Reprint. New York: Scribner.

———. 1999. *The Great Gatsby*. Ed. Matthew J. Bruccoli. 1925. Reprint. New York: Cambridge University Press.

———. 2000. *Trimalchio: An Early Version of The Great Gatsby*. Ed. James L. W. West III. Cambridge: Cambridge University Press.

Freud, Sigmund. 1957. "Jokes and the Unconscious." In *The Standard Edition of the Complete Psychological Works of Sigmund Freud*. Vol. viii, ed. James Strachey. 1905. Reprint. London: The Hogarth Press.

Higham, John. 1973. *Strangers in the Land: Patterns of American Nativism 1860–1925*. New York: Atheneum.

Kristeva, Julia. 1982. *Powers of Horror: An Essay on Abjection*. Trans. Leon S. Roudiez. New York: Columbia University Press.

Lyotard, Jean-François. 1992. *The Postmodern Explained*. Trans. Don Barry, Bernadette Maher, Julian Pefanis, Virginia Spate, and Morgan Thomas. Minneapolis: University of Minnesota Press.

Margolies, Alan. 1997. "The Maturing of F. Scott Fitzgerald." *Twentieth-Century Literature: A Scholarly and Critical Journal* 43:1 (Spring): 75–93.

Michaels, Walter Benn. 1995. *Our America: Nativism, Modernism, and Pluralism*. Durham: Duke University Press.

Rowe, Joyce A. 1988. *Equivocal Endings in Classic American Novels*. Cambridge: Cambridge University Press.

Salinger, J. D. 1951. *The Catcher in the Rye*. Boston: Little, Brown and Co.

Stoddard, Lothrop. 1920. *The Rising Tide of Color Against White World-Supremacy*. With an Introduction by Madison Grant. New York: Scribner's.

Trilling, Lionel. 1963. "F. Scott Fitzgerald." In *F. Scott Fitzgerald: A Collection of Critical Essays*, ed. Arthur Mizener. Englewood Cliffs, NJ: Prentice-Hall.

PHILIP MCGOWAN

The American Carnival of The Great Gatsby[1]

I

To argue that F. Scott Fitzgerald's long-held masterpiece *The Great Gatsby* (1925) produces in the United States of the 1920s a replication of Bakhtinian forms of carnival excess and release is an interesting, and indeed productive, deployment of Bakhtin's carnival thesis in conjunction with the multi-textured nature of Fitzgerald's novel. However, while aspects of carnivalised reality undoubtedly populate the novel, there is more going on in this text than a simple one-to-one relation between Bakhtinian carnival theory and Fitzgerald's text might suggest. The social, political and racial issues specific to 1920s America as revealed in the novel require an interpretative frame more agile and more particularised than Bakhtin's explorations of the sixteenth-century French comedies of Rabelais. Bevilacqua's argument, while tracing interesting points of comparison, overlooks the particular consequences of an American variant of carnival form that is rooted in a culture of politicised vision and display initially propagated in an interlocking set of specifically American conditions: nineteenth-century World's Fair culture; the developing commodity culture of the early twentieth century; and the production of narratives of racial and social control within America's visual, entertainment and education cultures. To read *The Great Gatsby* solely in terms of European carnival theory evacuates the particular American politics of Fitzgerald's novel, a politics specifically introduced on its opening

From *Connotations* 15, nos. 1–3 (2005/2006): 143–58. © 2005/2006 by Waxmann Verlag GmbH.

page: Nick Carraway's apparently throwaway grievance at being "unjustly accused of being a politician" (7) at college should not be forgotten in a novel that raises a series of difficult questions about political machinations, race, and social exclusion. Moreover, *The Great Gatsby* makes a number of specific as well as implicit references to American variations of carnival form that, while possibly bearing some resemblance to European variants, require specific and careful examination.

While Bevilacqua opens an array of possibilities for comparative reflection on Fitzgerald's novel, her argument can be extended beyond a reading of *The Great Gatsby* that fits the frame of European carnival as outlined by Bakhtin across his works *Rabelais and His World*, *The Dialogic Imagination* and *The Problems of Dostoevsky's Poetics*. Unlike European carnival events and festivals that can be readily situated within particular cultures in terms of yearly week-long events that may or may not coincide with dates in the Christian calendar, American carnival produces an ongoing definition of U.S. cultures through social and racial categorisation. Sited originally in the display halls of World's Fairs and the sideshow tents of freak shows and travelling carnivals, American carnival is, for the purposes of this article, presented as an interpretative and representative phenomenon: activated at both the conscious and unconscious levels, it facilitates a production of white American social control and of the alterity that it seeks to subdue. A fuller account would show the workings of this particularised and interconnected politics of American seeing, display and spectacle in a range of texts: for example Nathaniel Hawthorne's "My Kinsman, Major Molineux" (1832) or Stephen Crane's "The Monster" (1898) from the nineteenth century, or Saul Bellow's *The Victim* (1947) or Paul Auster's *Mr. Vertigo* (1994) from the twentieth.

To summarise the salient features of this form of carnival that are relevant to *The Great Gatsby*, American carnival connotes the capacity of U.S. culture to deploy methods of seeing and representation that operate along the imbricated contours of race, ethnicity and Otherness. The opportunities and potentials outlined by Bakhtin for the overturning of social order, for a temporary equalising of social status, and for 'becoming' (the social, economic, and individual development that he outlines with regard to Rabelaisian carnival) are reformulated in the United States, repackaged in its variants of carnival form, and consequently restricted to the white audience members and viewers in the nation's display arenas and entertainment zones. Whether in terms of American minstrelsy, freak shows, or World's Fairs (in particular the 1893 Columbian Exposition in Chicago, and also the 1901 New York Fair), the displayed or carnivalised identities are constricted within a mode of imagery that maintains the absolute difference between spectacle and spectator, the individual subjectivity of the deemed Other overwritten, in particular cases literally blacked out, by a cultural recourse to generalised masks and stereotyped versions of identity. The placing of the 'subversive' on display in American carnival forms from the 1850s onward produced a ready binary for reinforcing the dominance of white social ordering within the U.S. Certainly in the nineteenth and twentieth centuries, America constructed a specific carnival culture that legitimised the white cultural hegemony by displaying Otherness as both monstrous and potentially subversive of white society. America's carnival spaces function as entertainment spaces in which the (white) spectator can, for a small fee payable on admission, witness carnivalised representations of Otherness. These socially and economically sanctioned territories replicate on a larger scale the politics of carnival seeing already alive in the wider culture. As a consequence, a symbiotic relationship of reinforcing belief systems was established between the more overt carnival zones in the United States (its freak shows, its World's Fairs, its travelling carnivals) and a more covert politics of seeing by which American society was continually categorized and interpreted.

II

Turning to Fitzgerald's novel, it becomes clear how American forms of carnival developed beyond the well-defined European variants that interested Bakhtin. Gatsby's house and his parties, on first encounter, appear to offer a duplication of European carnival release, allowing the guests access to a realm where bawdy flirtations and bootleg liquor are the currencies of exchange. The "swirls and eddies" (*TGG* 47) of Gatsby's partygoers form one homogeneous mass of temporarily equated identity in a carnival realm constructed purely for purposes of spectacle. The carnival land to which they are admitted suspends the social organisations, hierarchies, and prohibitions of outside America in a zone of whites-only leisure. The differentiated identities of these people merge under the influence of alcohol and within the highly coloured carnival environment of Gatsby's mansion, a "factual imitation of some Hôtel de Ville in Normandy" (11). This imported environment of political equality and democratization has its political dimensions obscured on a number of levels: by its use as a site of carnival excess; by its placement within an American culture that carnivalises its methods of seeing and reading identity; and, by its status as a replica of an unspecified French town hall. Gatsby's mansion is simultaneously an intrinsic part of America and is disconnected from it: the replication of influences from Europe (continued in the mansion's Restoration salons and Marie Antoinette rooms) is at odds with American patterns of architecture, but is very much part of an America that juxtaposes the pastiche with the colonial, the modern with the traditional, and the replica with the original.

Gatsby's house, then, is clearly a site of representation; but it is also one of carnival replication. Displacing its previous occupant, pointedly a brewer, the bootlegging Gatsby provides, at one level, a countercultural space for carnival excess beyond the constraints of a Prohibition culture outside its gates. A straight duplication of older European carnival forms could then be argued for, but only if Gatsby's house and its entertainments exist in a realm cut off from the rest of U.S. society, or indeed are subversive of its social and cultural categorisations. However, the house, because it functions in the novel as a space of representation, is very much in tune with an American culture and landscape that deploys carnivalised methods of seeing in its organization of social space and class position.

Gatsby himself is more than the self-made hero of Nick Carraway's fiction of memory, however; he is the circus master, the creator of the carnival, the Trimalchio in control of the spectacles and entertainments on offer and upon whose financial resources this whole palace and lifestyle of illusion is based. Gatsby functions as the would-be carnivaliser of reality, a man seeking to suspend, even reverse, time in order to reclaim the object for whom his world of images is constructed. He is the driver of a "circus wagon" (127), of a car that "mirror[s] a dozen suns" (70). His is a life dedicated to the image, to spectacle, to advertisements for himself. Gatsby is both the facilitator of carnival in the text and the central image of the novel's carnival representations. The "World's Fair" (88) of his house is the ultimate incarnation of a landscape dedicated to carnival, to showing the fantasies made possible by capital wealth. Moreover, defining carnival precisely in relation to American World's Fairs culture, Fitzgerald is marking its critical difference from European carnival forms: this is not a place producing a temporary suspension of reality; rather, it is one dedicated to the ongoing illusions of progress and American materialism made possible by Gatsby's own romanticised (by himself and his party guests) if nefarious dealings.

Richard Godden importantly notes how "to see in 1925 was to see through the stencil of the commodity" (78). Indeed, the methods of American seeing in *The Great Gatsby* are also passed through the stencil or prism of American carnival, a framing device controlled by the hegemonic interests of American society. At this time corporate and economic interest groups were intimately involved in the production and maintenance of a commodity culture within the United States. The manipulation of the image, the control of what is seen, and, more importantly, *how* it is seen, is rooted in the power base of America's ruling elite. Nick functions as our representative observer at times; at others he is a liminal figure, both inside and outside, participant and observer, spectator but never the spectacle or the cause of spectacle. "I was unjustly accused of being a politician" (7); yet, he is undoubtedly a political viewer throughout the text, and his purported objective standpoint is necessarily called into question. By the close, he is tantamount to Gatsby's running mate, the supporting second narrative on Gatsby's dream ticket. As an observer, Nick functions as an ideal American viewer, attracted and repelled by the things he uncovers in the fantasy realms of the northeast coast of the United States.

Nick's house is located "on that slender riotous island which extends itself due east of New York" (10), another U.S. fantasy zone comparable to the nearby Coney Island. His house is advantaged by the views of "the water, a partial view of my neighbour's lawn, and the consoling proximity of millionaires" (11). Nick is a viewer from the outset then, a viewer in particular of the wealth of white America. Indeed, East Egg, the location of Tom and Daisy's colonial mansion, is figured by its "white palaces" (11), and white becomes the colour enduringly associated with this region and its identities. The colour coding of the text—white (Daisy), yellow (the hair colour of most of the characters), grey (the valley of ashes)—designates social and political space in the carnival realms of New York State. Both the homes in East and West Egg are sights of spectacle, Gatsby's "factual imitation" facing the "white palaces of fashionable East Egg," much as the exhibition sites of American World's Fairs, particularly Chicago in 1893, opposed the white structures connoting cultural and technological excellence and progress with the colourful and imported locations of the carnival midway. Tom's house is representative of settled colonial America, in stark contrast to Gatsby's fake palace of representation; Tom's is a house symbolizing the acceptable face of homogeneous white America, and Tom the physical force of white identity. He manipulates the (white) spectator Nick: "wedging his tense arm imperatively under mine, Tom Buchanan compelled me from the room as though he were moving a checker to another square" (17–18). In this labyrinth of continual whiteness, Tom is the unquestioned master, the controller of the white spectacles of this location; outside of this zone, his power is open to question and subversion. Nick's own self-sufficiency and power to move and to see is dominated at this stage by the physical power of Tom: "his determination to have my company bordered on violence" (30). Moreover, Tom's social and economic power is placed in unequal comparison to Nick's. Nick is not the creator or manipulator of the sights of the East that he has entered and, as with his visits to Gatsby's house, in particular with Daisy on the day of the reunion, he functions in these spaces as a tourist or visitor at an amusement park or a World's Fair.

On his first introduction to Daisy and Jordan, Nick notes that their conversation is "as cool as their white dresses and their impersonal eyes in the absence of all desire" (18). This unfathomable whiteness that Toni Morrison speaks of frames Tom's ensuing diatribe concerning race in contemporary American culture. The combination of his minimal reading, eugenecist ideology, and racist discourse, in conjunction with his economic and physical power, pinpoints Tom as the text's representative of dominant whiteness. If his house is a location of information in the text it is one akin to the eugenecist stalls for fitter families at America's town and country fairs. Eugenecist displays and, by extension, those exhibits that twinned displays of Otherness with "factual" material about them, in America's carnival spaces were able to exploit these two modes of information and entertainment, blurring the boundary between the educative and the fantastical. Tom provides space for the exhibition and consideration of such attitudes. Housed in his predominantly white and enduringly colonial mansion, Tom's need to "nibble at the edge of stale ideas" (27) is satisfied by his control of this space and the activities that take place here.

The Great Gatsby is a text that straddles *the* carnival celebration of the United States: "It was a few days before the Fourth of July" (32). This is a novel mapping the opposed states of pre- and post-Independence America, both in its annual commemoration of the defeat of the imperial forces of Britain on Independence Day, and in its opposition of carnivalised identities. If carnival is revolution (Eco et al. 3), then the Revolutionary War, and its annual commemoration, is America's main carnival event. Gatsby's house and Myrtle's apartment both contain images of pre-revolution France; these are two characters wishing to invert the realities of their lives as they are, one to gain the memory of his past in Daisy, the other the promise of a future in Tom. However, the retreats they construct speak essentially of un-American things and un-American times: images of Versailles and Marie Antoinette music rooms cut across the contemporary reality of the America in which they live. One possible reason that their dreams fail is that they wish to suspend a reality (figured in their pre-revolution home decor) that is already suspended in post-revolution America, the place where Tom, Daisy, and Nick all live. Here, such monarchical trappings have been discarded, and Gatsby and Myrtle's wishes are at odds with the new political and temporal codes of the day. Wishing to invert what has already been inverted, indeed removed, they are defeated by the realm of American politics. Moreover, the American landscape, viewed through the lens of carnival, becomes a metaphysical space: a landscape of the fantastical in which it is the essential unreality of things that captures Nick's imagination, honed as it is on the substantiality of the West. Gatsby and Myrtle are both out of their times and out of sync with the times, and they inhabit locations that predate the formation of an independent United States.

The mappings of New York in the novel alternate between a near-fantastical, wholly fantastical, or ultimately a distorted space of nightmare. It is an American territory populated by diverse carnival and carnivalised figures, and its delineations of white identity in particular highlight the social constructions inherent to this region. The gradations of whiteness in the book are manifold: Daisy and Jordan's performed white inertia; Myrtle's sister whose complexion is "powdered milky white" (36); the anemic, ghostly Wilson; Gatsby's tanned exterior; and Tom's brutal attempts at providing cohesion within his racial grouping. Nick's whiteness is unquestioned but noticeably aligned with a group at Gatsby's first party who "preserved a dignified homogeneity, and assumed to itself the function of representing the staid nobility of the country-side—East Egg condescending to West Egg, and carefully on guard against its spectroscopic gayety" (51). Nick is a trans-carnival figure, "within and without, simultaneously enchanted and repelled by the inexhaustible variety of life" (42). Spectator and participant at the same time, he gains access to both sides of America's boundaries of seeing and spectacle. His reticence and natural slow thinking, however, prevent him literally from making a spectacle of himself; he holds a reserve unknown to Gatsby and Myrtle, the two victims of America's politicized zones of seeing and being.

A narrowly Bakhtinian reading of this novel would focus on Gatsby's party and identify its apparent provision of a suspension of social hierarchies as well as of the regular calibrations of time. However, Gatsby's house and parties are not sites indicative of European carnival. As Nick notes, the correlation between Gatsby's house and a World's Fair is prevalent. This is a site of technological innovation and carnival excess: "There was a machine in the kitchen which could extract the juice of two hundred oranges in half an hour if a little button was pressed two hundred times by a butler's thumb" (45). The machinery of America's developing commodity culture is on display in this arena that shadows the multicoloured environment of the first World's Fair of the twentieth century, also staged in New York State, Buffalo's Rainbow City of 1901: there are "enough coloured lights to make a Christmas tree of Gatsby's enormous garden" (45); "the halls and salons and verandas are gaudy with primary colours" (46). Although not the white sepulchre of Chicago's 1893 Exposition, resonating in the white palace of Tom's colonial mansion, Gatsby's house is a variation on the American carnival theme. Even the food provided for the guests is entered into the spectacular realm of carnival. Conspicuous consumption is arranged as a feast of carnivalesque display: "On buffet tables, garnished with glistening hors-d'oeuvre, spiced baked hams crowded against salads of harlequin designs and pastry pigs and turkeys bewitched to a dark gold" (45).

The fluid identity of the crowd forms a brand of homogeneous whiteness in a space that matches another New York carnival location, that of Coney Island. The unrestricted entrance to all comers who "conducted themselves according to the rules of behavior associated with an amusement park" (47) figures Gatsby's house as an alternative Coney Island. It is significant that in mooting a trip away from his own carnival space, Gatsby suggests that he and Nick visit Coney Island (88). White homogeneity exists as a social construct in opposition to the spectacles of carnival on display and realized through the opposition between an observing white elite and the performing white Others at Gatsby's party. This is a land of "spectroscopic gayety," and the homogeneous whiteness to which Nick noticeably attaches himself stands at a remove from the carnival events occurring here. This is an altogether different remove to that of Gatsby; here he is the controller, the master of ceremonies, unknown to the crowd yet the central figure of the circus show. He controls a land of mutating spectacle whereas Tom dominates a land of static whiteness (for example, Daisy's immobility and inertia, the deflating of Daisy and Jordan's air-filled couch). Gatsby is the master of ceremonies in "a mansion where he dispensed starlight to casual moths" (85). As with the Coney Island theme park Luna Park for example, this is a place transformed at night, illuminated to provide an alternative carnival realm to those of American daylight.

Part observer, part journalist, part social historian, Nick records the names of the partygoers on a train schedule, "in effect July 5th, 1922" (67). This is a post-holiday timetable and a record of American identities after Independence. It signals alterations of time, the change in schedules after the date of political celebration in the American calendar. The fact that the trains begin again, possibly in a new routine after the fourth of July, indicates the return to order, or the renewal of order in the material world. The continuing suspension of this version of American 'reality' in the carnival and entertainment zones of Long Island is a marked distinction. Here, reality is the subject of deception and tricks of light. The politically coloured world of Long Island is a carnivalised one open to constant manipulation and subterfuge: Nick detects something "sinister" (71) in what Gatsby tells him of his past, having earlier been struck by "the basic insincerity" of Daisy's words leaving him "uneasy, as though the whole evening had been a trick of some sort to exact a contributary emotion from me" (24). Past and present become entities capable of manipulation in the distorting worlds of East coast carnival.

Fact and fiction in New York's arenas are seemingly interchangeable. History is a mutable concept and this underpins Gatsby's project to reclaim Daisy: "'I'm going to fix everything just the way it was before,' he said, nodding determinedly. 'She'll *see*'" (117; emphasis added). He is the carnival showman intent on manipulating time, to recreate the past in the present, to provide a space for repeating the past within the exhibition arenas of his carnival world. The ultimate carnivaliser, Gatsby dedicates his time to displays constructed solely for Daisy's vision. The past functions in his mind as another exhibit capable of repetition and redisplay in the present. To be able to do this requires a site and a sight both capable of incorporating the past and present as well as indications of an innovative future, all of which are realized in the World's Fair of his house.

However, Daisy does not see, at least not in the ways structured by Gatsby's vision. The carnival and spectacle of Gatsby's next party fail to win over this ultimate white viewer:

> She was appalled by West Egg, this unprecedented 'place' that Broadway had begotten upon a Long Island fishing village— appalled by its raw vigour that chafed under the old euphemisms and by the too obtrusive fate that herded its inhabitants along a short-cut from nothing to nothing. She saw something awful in the very simplicity she failed to understand. (114)

Her response is an unconscious questioning of the reality and substantiality of West Egg, this offshoot of Broadway located outside the city. Broadway, the ultimate incarnation of the theatrical, vaudevillian impulse within American culture, has "begotten" this dubious realm of artificiality and "simplicity," but she does not comprehend its meaning. Daisy is not an active reader of social situations and hence her inability to read the carnival excess of Gatsby's party is unsurprising. She is out of place in this multicoloured realm, at one, instead, with the white worlds of her Louisville past and the house she shares with Tom. Daisy's locations in the text are those that are predominantly white: she understands this aspect of the colour-coded register of American society. The gaudy carnival of Gatsby's party is anathema to this pure white reader. Gatsby's versions of carnival, and the creation of his carnivalised zones of entertainment and spectacle, seek something of a Bakhtinian notion of carnival as a suspension of hierarchies. Moreover, at a time of national Prohibition, the ability of Gatsby's fair to include numerous drinks and cordials possibly unknown to his younger guests, provides a flavour of this suspension of hierarchical, legal, and political realities. To the conditioned white reader from America's highest class (Tom and Daisy), such a carnival is a by-product of contemporary American entertainment culture, a miniature Broadway or Coney Island; not a suspension of reality, but an alternative one all of its own.

Boundaries and tensions, emotional, racial, and geographic, divide the carnival and social worlds of the novel. On a ride through Central Park with Jordan, Nick comments how "[w]e passed a barrier of dark trees, and then the façade of Fifty-ninth Street, a block of delicate pale light, beamed down into the park" (86). New York is a space, urban and suburban, that is mapped and marked by distinct colour boundaries. Even the grass between Gatsby's house and Nick's is registered through difference, marking a division between Gatsby's maintained carnival world and Nick's one of "normality." The racial undertones that plot the colour codings of the United States shadow the interactions of Fitzgerald's characters. Brought to a head by Tom in the hotel confrontation with Gatsby, the subversive forces threatening Tom's hegemonic and civilized whiteness are amalgamated into a generalized category of Otherness, the invisible men Tom wishes to remain out of sight:

> I suppose the latest thing is to sit back and let Mr Nobody from Nowhere make love to your wife. Well, if that's the idea you can count me out. . . . Nowadays people begin by sneering at family life and family institutions, and next they'll throw everything overboard and have intermarriage between black and white. (136)

Tom's manifesto is rooted in Republican conservative American values and stands in sharp contrast to the aspiring independence, even democratic ethos, of Gatsby's position. Conventions are in danger of being suspended or even negated by the carnival interpretations of behaviour symbolized, for Tom, by Gatsby and his dealings with Daisy. The union of black and white is what Tom must resist at all levels. In this codification, Tom is white to Gatsby's "black" Otherness or subversiveness, all of whom are written within the same political register of difference.

Daisy is an emotional and figurative currency between the two men, a valuable prize, a "silver idol" (121), over which they battle for possession. On his first re-encounter with her, Gatsby is significantly clothed "in a white flannel suit, silver shirt, and gold-coloured tie" (90–91); he dresses in a combination of whiteness and of monetary designation, silver and gold, to regain the currency of his lost love, Daisy. He leads her on a guided tour of his house that begins by entrance through an official gate: "Instead of taking the short cut along the Sound we went down the road and entered by the big postern" (97). This is the ceremonial gateway into Gatsby's space of carnival. However, she is out of place here in a World's Fair of French decor and English tailoring. This is a world of illusion to which she is unaccustomed, beyond the white American "reality" that is her home. Gatsby's house is a fantasy realm dedicated to a culture of carnival and conspicuous display and he is the son of a materialist God, the gaudy showmanship of the new century's commercial culture. As with New York's other fantasy realms, Gatsby's dreamland fills out "a satisfactory hint of the unreality of reality" (106). The contingent and material base of the culture is itself based in a visual culture of malleable spectacle, and it is to these policies of inversion and replication that Gatsby dedicates himself.

The central opposition in the text is a contrast of standards: the whiteness of the Buchanan world set in opposition to the multicoloured variety of Gatsby's. The violent and aggressive white spectator Tom, and to a lesser extent his wife, recast the world of Gatsby's second party in a new light, through the condescending lens of a higher-class whiteness. The otherwise homogeneous crowd at this party—"There were the same people, or at least the same sort of people"—is added to by a "peculiar quality of oppressiveness" (111). Noticeably, Tom seeks to blend his whiteness with that of the other anonymous partygoers: "I'd rather look at all these famous people in—in oblivion" (112). He desires to hide behind a mask of white identity, the wished-for oblivion of the white homogeneous observer wanting to be nothing but a spectator in this realm where he does not control the spectacles. His inability to do so though, together with Daisy's failure to comprehend the organized spectacles on view, leads to the termination of Gatsby's "career as Trimalchio" (119): they are incompatible white viewers within a crowd of lower social standing at this temporary amusement park. Gatsby's carnival space closes down precisely because it attempts to be both World's Fair and amusement park simultaneously. It cannot satisfy the urbane white dreams and readings of Daisy nor, as a result, can it continue to meet the more populist needs of New York's urban masses.

With the loss of Daisy and the end of his dream, Gatsby wakes to "[a] new world, material without being real, where poor ghosts, breathing dreams like air, drifted fortuitously about . . . like that ashen, fantastic figure gliding toward him through the amorphous trees" (168). Indeed, this has been the underlying situation all along: the characters move in an insistently material world in which "reality" is a questionable term open to manipulation. The formlessness of the physical world around Gatsby here matches the previously fluid, mutating world of his parties; except that now the fantasies have been turned into grotesqueries. Wilson's whiteness is that of another wrong visitor to the now-closed amusement park. The assassination of Gatsby here in this multi-coloured carnival realm provides a textual bridge with the real-life assassination of President McKinley at the 1901 Buffalo World's Fair, activating memories within the cultural subconscious of the American nation. With Gatsby's death, the fantastical has been redefined, and is continually re-categorised by the perpetual mutations of American carnival and in the inauthentic reporting of the murder in the papers: "Most of those reports were a nightmare—grotesque, circumstantial, eager, and untrue" (170). For Nick, the East becomes an area synonymous with distortion: "Even when the East excited me most [. . .] it had always for me a quality of distortion. West Egg, especially, still figures in my more fantastic dreams. I see it as a night scene by El Greco: a hundred houses, at once conventional and grotesque" (183). West Egg is the main space of distortion where reality and grotesque fantasy simultaneously commingle. Indeed, reality is a constantly uncertain commodity in this realm of controlled and manipulated spectacle. The end of Gatsby's parties signals the "huge incoherent failure" of his house (187); with the parties over, this carnival location alters its exhibition status, becoming a museum, indeed a mausoleum, of images gathering dust.

NOTE

1. Reference: Winifred Farrant Bevilacqua, "' . . . and the long secret extravaganza was played out': *The Great Gatsby* and Carnival in a Bakhtinian Perspective," *Connotations* 13.1–2 (2003/2004): 111–29.

WORKS CITED

Bakhtin, Mikhail. *The Dialogic Imagination: Four Essays by M. M. Bakhtin.* Ed. Michael Holquist. Trans. Caryl Emerson and Michael Emerson. Austin: U of Texas P, 1996.

———. *Problems of Dostoevsky's Poetics.* Ed. and trans. Caryl Emerson. Intro. Wayne C. Booth. Minneapolis: U of Minnesota P, 1984.

———. *Rabelais and His World.* Trans. Hélène Iswolsky. Bloomington: Indiana UP, 1984.

Eco, Umberto, V. V. Ivanov, and Monica Rector. *Carnival!* Ed. Thomas A. Sebeok. New York: Mouton Publishers, 1984.

Fitzgerald, F. Scott. *The Great Gatsby.* 1925. Harmondsworth: Penguin, 1974.

Godden, Richard. *Fictions of Capital: The American Novel from James to Mailer.* Cambridge: CUP, 1990.

McGowan, Philip. *American Carnival: Seeing and Reading American Culture.* Westport, Conn.: Greenwood P, 2001.

Morrison, Toni. *Playing in the Dark: Whiteness and the American Literary Imagination.* Cambridge, Mass.: Harvard UP, 1992; London: Picador, 1993.

The Trouble with Nick: Reading Gatsby Closely

Nick Carraway is a snob. He dislikes people in general and denigrates them in particular. He dodges emotional commitments. Neither his ethical code nor his behavior is exemplary: propriety rather than morality guides him. He is not entirely honest about himself and frequently misunderstands others. Do these shortcomings mean that Nick is an unreliable narrator? At times and in part, yes. But they also mean that he is the perfect narrator for *The Great Gatsby* and that Fitzgerald's greatest technical achievement in the novel was to invent this narrative voice at once "within and without" the action.

The first clue to Nick's makeup comes on the first page of the book, where he totally misunderstands his father's advice. "Whenever you feel like criticizing any one," his father had told him in his "younger and more vulnerable years," he was to remember that not everyone had enjoyed the advantages he has had. Clearly Nick's father is advising tolerance here, and it seems likely that he had detected in his son a somewhat disturbing propensity to find fault. Nick, however, interprets the remark as a judgment on others, who lack what he calls that "sense of the fundamental decencies . . . unequally parcelled out at birth" (5) and consequently misbehave. This interpretation, Nick acknowledges, is an extraordinarily judgmental one, the interpretation of a snob who admits to the charge as if to say that there are far worse things than

---

From *Fitzgerald and Hemingway: Works and Days*, pp. 98–106. © 2009 by Scott Donaldson.

157

snobbery in the world: bad manners, for example. Nick's undoubted "advantages," which include good schools, social position, family background, and even an exclusive senior society at Yale, may eventuate in an awareness of the "fundamental decencies" if one construes the phrase narrowly as conforming to conventional standards of propriety, but they hardly guarantee any moral acumen. So it is with Nick Carraway. Above all he disapproves of those who do not know how to act. That is why it takes him so long to ascertain that Jay Gatsby, a walking compendium of social gaucheries, is nonetheless worth any number of Buchanans.

Nick's misunderstanding of his father should also put us on guard against his claim that he's "inclined to reserve all judgments," especially when in the next breath he speaks of the "veteran bores" and "wild, unknown men" who have made him privy to "intimate revelations . . . usually plagiaristic and marred by obvious suppressions." Had they suppressed less, Nick might have been more interested. "Reserving judgments is a matter of infinite hope," he observes, and he is not the character in the novel possessed by infinite hope. He listens to confessions since he is "a little afraid of missing something" (5) otherwise: a vicarious sense of having drunk his cup to the lees. But he does not suspend judgment. Nick judges, and condemns, practically everyone he meets in the course of the novel.

Collectively he speaks of closing off his interest in the "abortive sorrows and short-winded elations of men" (6). Introducing individual specimens of this sorry genus, he delineates more specific physical deficiencies. Tom Buchanan has straw hair, a hard mouth, a supercilious manner, and a cruel body with which he pushes people around. There had been men at Yale who hated his guts, and if Nick is not among them, it's not because he can't see why. His wife Daisy, Nick's second cousin once removed, speaks in a thrilling voice, but she murmurs so low that people must bend toward her to hear. Her insincere remark about having "been everywhere and seen everything and done everything" (17) strikes Nick as "a trick of some sort" to exact an emotional commitment from him.

With the lower orders Nick is still less charitable. Myrtle Wilson, smoldering with vitality, carries her "excess flesh sensuously" (23) and comically takes on airs in the West 158th St. apartment Tom has secured for their rendezvous. Meyer Wolfshiem is presented as a small Jew with tiny eyes, a flat nose in whose nostrils "fine growths of hair" luxuriate, and cuff buttons made of "finest specimens of human molars" (55, 57). Sentence is passed rapidly on minor characters. Myrtle's sister Catherine—"a slender, worldly girl of thirty" with a sticky bob of red hair, rakishly painted eyebrows, and eternally jangling bracelets—is disposed of in a paragraph (26). In the catalog of those who attend Gatsby's parties, people are labeled and found wanting by name alone.

"The Dancies came, too, and S. B. Whitebait, who was well over sixty, and Maurice A. Flink, and the Hammerheads, and Beluga the tobacco importer, and Beluga's girls": something is fishy here (50).

Nick's basic contempt for mankind emerges in what he says and thinks as well as in descriptions of others. His particular way of telling the story has been variously characterized in the critical literature on *The Great Gatsby*, but surely a dominant characteristic of that voice is its irony. This sometimes leads to light-hearted bantering in conversation, as with Daisy. Is she missed in Chicago, she asks? "All the cars have the left rear wheel painted black as a mourning wreath," he answers, "and there's a persistent wail all night along the north shore" (11), a wittily casual remark that takes on resonance as the novel's motif of careless driving develops. Would Nick like to hear about the butler's nose, she inquires? "That's why I came over tonight," he responds (14). His unspoken thoughts, however, tend toward the more hostile levity of sarcasm.

In his mind Nick constantly puts others down. After listening to Tom Buchanan maunder on about impending racial struggles and the increasing (or is it declining?) heat of the sun, Nick devastates the man he has helped to cuckold when, with his eyes finally opened to the affair between Daisy and Gatsby, Tom begins to expound on the scientific proof for his "second sight" and then stops, the "immediate contingency" having "pulled him back from the edge of the theoretical abyss" (94–95). Soon after, Nick characterizes Tom's hypocritical defense of family solidarity as "impassioned gibberish" (101). Buchanan deserves such scornful treatment, but what of poor Henry Gatz, who proudly shows Nick his dead son's schedule for self-improvement, written in his copy of *Hopalong Cassidy*? "He was reluctant to close the book, reading each item aloud and then looking eagerly at me. I think he rather expected me to copy down the list for my own use," Nick sniffily observes (135). Then there is the "persistent undergraduate" who brings Jordan Baker to one of Gatsby's parties under the impression that sooner or later she will "yield him up her person" (37). When that prospect fails to develop, the undergraduate becomes engaged in "an obstetrical conversation with two chorus girls" and "implore[s]" Nick to join him (42). As Wolfshiem remarks in another sense, the undergraduate has "a wrong man" (56). Nick is not interested in making improper connections. He's not interested in making any *lasting* connections at all.

Nick Carraway carefully avoids emotional entanglements. He writes letters signed "Love, Nick" to a girl back home, but one reason he's come to New York is to avoid "being rumored into marriage" with her (19). Unable to stop thinking how "a faint mustache of perspiration" develops on her upper lip when she plays tennis (48), he finally severs the relationship. In the East he has "a short affair with a girl who lived in Jersey City and worked in the accounting department," but he lets it "blow quietly away" when her brother begins "throwing mean looks" in his direction (46). Jordan, his social peer, poses a more serious threat to his bachelor status. He is attracted to her hard, jaunty body and superior chin-in-air attitude, even though he knows she will lie to avoid responsibility and cheat to win at golf. But in the end she seems too much of a piece with Tom and Daisy, so he breaks off with her, too, before returning to the Middle West. It is not surprising that Nick has reached thirty without being married or engaged: he does not reserve judgment, he reserves himself. Prufrock-like, he contemplates his future: "a decade of loneliness, a thinning list of single men to know; a thinning briefcase of enthusiasm, thinning hair" (106).

In the light of this pattern, one regards with suspicion Nick's claim that releasing himself from a "vague understanding" with the girl back home before pursuing another with Jordan makes him "one of the few honest people" he's ever known (48). In an early draft, Fitzgerald wrote "one of the few decent people," later altering it to "honest." Apparently thinking that he had made Nick too unreliable as a narrator, in revision he also "added material which stressed Nick's belief in his own honesty and deleted passages which might undercut [his] integrity," such as offering Gatsby and Daisy the keys to his house (Parr, "Individual Responsibility," 678). Still, where honesty is concerned, it is undeniable that Nick regards telling the truth as less important than avoiding the unseemly. A case in point is his remark that Catherine had shown "a surprising amount of character" at Myrtle's inquest by falsely swearing that her sister "had been into no mischief whatever" (127), a lie designed to avert a public scandal.

Social decorum ranks high on Nick's scale of values, certainly higher than honesty, and it guides his attitude toward sexual morality. Adultery abounds in *The Great Gatsby*. It is rather the expected thing among the idle rich. As Jordan says, Daisy "ought to have something in her life" (63). Only those who contract liaisons with lovers of higher social standing (Myrtle and Gatsby), though, are punished for their sin or for their presumptuousness. What most concerns Nick about this extramarital coupling is the manner in which the affair is conducted. Daisy, he thinks, should "rush out of the house, child in arms" upon discovering Tom's infidelity. Nor can he approve of the way Tom orchestrates the affair, taking his mistress to popular restaurants to show her off and then abandoning her to chat with acquaintances. Tom further concocts the falsehood that Daisy is Catholic to explain to Myrtle why he cannot be divorced. As voyeur Nick is curious to see Tom's girl; as snob he has no desire to know her. When they do meet, Myrtle proves a veritable model of social pretentiousness. In clothes, in gestures, in conversation, Nick presents her as simply ridiculous. Not until Tom breaks her nose does she merit any sympathy whatever.

Nick himself appears rather ridiculous when, in his obsession with propriety, he twice insists on having actually been invited to Gatsby's first party, unlike most of the gate crashers. Moreover, although all around him people are conducting themselves "according to the rules of behavior associated with amusement parks" (34), he repeatedly tries to meet and thank his host, as at a formal gathering. This proves difficult, and meanwhile Jordan turns up, relieving him of the danger of addressing "cordial remarks to passers-by" (35). When be finally does encounter Gatsby late in the evening, Nick is caught off guard: he'd been expecting "a florid and corpulent person in his middle years" (40). For a long time Gatsby continues to confound Nick's expectations. Unlike almost everyone else in Nick's world, he resists classification.

It's not merely that Nick is curious about Gatsby: *everyone* is curious about him. But while others merely speculate about Gatsby's relationship with von Hindenburg or his career as a killer, Nick is exposed through two rather remarkable coincidences—moving in next door and knowing Daisy—to more intimate revelations from the figure of mystery himself. Gatsby's first preposterous account (wealthy parents from the western city of San Francisco, war hero educated at Oxford who subsequently "lived like a young rajah in all the capitals of Europe . . . collecting jewels, chiefly rubies, hunting big game, painting a little . . . and trying to forget something very sad") tends to confirm Nick in his view of his neighbor as pretentious arriviste, inventing a background to replace the one he lacks. Even though Gatsby produces the medal from Montenegro and the cricket photograph, Nick is not persuaded: "Then it was all true," he proclaims in ironic overstatement. "I saw the skins of tigers flaming in his palace on the Grand Canal; I saw him opening a chest of rubies to ease, with their crimson-lighted depths, the gnawings of his broken heart" (52–53). Nick's cynicism is further underlined in two subsequent incidents. Stopped for speeding, Gatsby flashes the policeman a white card which purchases instant immunity. "What was that?" Nick asks. "The picture of Oxford?" (54). Later, during the tour of the mansion and after the lavish display of shirts, Nick has a characteristically sardonic thought: "I was going to ask to see the rubies when the phone rang . . ." (73).

Under the circumstances Nick hardly expects *any* section of Gatsby's fabulous story to be true, yet when Gatsby modifies his tale to explain why and for how long he'd actually gone to Oxford, Nick is willing to put all the young rajah balderdash out of mind: "I had one of those renewals of complete faith in him that I'd experienced before" (101). Part of Nick wants to believe in Gatsby, just as another part holds him up for ridicule.

The snob in Nick Carraway finds Gatsby contemptible. He makes the point both on the second page of the novel ("Gatsby . . . represented everything for which I have an unaffected scorn") and on page 120 ("I disapproved of him from beginning to end"). Significantly, this second statement immediately follows Nick's "You're worth the whole damn bunch put together" speech. He can simultaneously praise Gatsby, in other words, and still disapprove of the "gorgeous pink rag of a suit" he's wearing, scorn his "old sport" affectation, disapprove of his ostentatious Hôtel de Ville and extravagant parties, scorn his shady business "gonnegtions"—above all, disapprove of his social incompetence.

Gatsby obviously lacks that "sense of the fundamental decencies" that comes with the right background. He seems to think that his awful parties are socially respectable gatherings. Yet Nick facilitates Gatsby and Daisy's affair by inviting the two of them for tea ("Don't bring Tom," he warns her), and he encourages their continuing relationship by "remaining watchfully in the garden" while they talk on the steps of his house for half an hour (66, 82). The question is why. Jordan asked him to arrange the tea, for one thing, and Nick dislikes Tom and knows of his unfaithfulness and brutality. But he would not have so willingly played the role of go-between had he not felt a curious kinship with the "elegant young roughneck" (40) in the mansion next door.

The fact is that Nick, like Gatsby, has romantic inclinations. But while Gatsby guides his life by his dream, Nick carefully separates romance from reality. What he most admires in Gatsby is the "extraordinary gift for hope," the "romantic readiness" he has found in no one else (6). Nick's first glimpse of his neighbor comes after the dinner party at the Buchanans, when he returns home to catch sight of someone on the lawn next door. He is about to call out (having concluded, in his obsessive concern with etiquette, that Jordan's mentioning Gatsby "would do for an introduction") when the solitary figure stretches "out his arms across the water" as if to reach the green light at the end of Daisy's dock. Far away though Nick is, he could swear that the man is trembling (20). Gatsby trembles elsewhere and so do Tom, Daisy, and Mr. Gatz. Nick does not, himself, tremble, but it is a physical reaction he can understand and identify with. It appeals to the side of his nature that conjures up "sumptuous and romantic apartments" concealed above Wilson's garage (!) in the valley of ashes (22), the side that imagines entering the lives of "romantic women" on Fifth Avenue, so long as "no one would ever know or disapprove." But as that last thought suggests, Nick is too proper, too emotionally cautious, to bring his fantasies about strangers to life: who would introduce them? He contents himself with vicarious experience instead. Walking alone through the theater district, Nick watches and dreams: "Forms leaned together in the taxis as they waited, and voices sang, and there was laughter from unheard jokes, and lighted cigarettes outlined unintelligible gestures inside. Imagining that I, too, was hurrying toward gayety and sharing their intimate excitement, I wished them well" (46–47). In something of the same spirit, he wishes Gatsby and Daisy well, too.

Nick imagines glamorous encounters but reads about banking after dinner in the Yale Club. Gatsby makes his fortune and sets out to capture the rest of his dream. Because of Gatsby's remarkable commitment to that dream—exactly the sort of commitment Nick declines to make—Nick can almost forgive Gatsby his presumption in courting Daisy under cover of a uniform that let "her believe he was a person from much the same strata as herself." Because of it he can very nearly pardon Gatsby's taking Daisy "one still October night," taking her "because he had no real right to touch her hand" (116). Because of it, too, he can temporarily efface from memory Gatsby's tactless offer of a chance to "pick up a nice bit of money" in return for arranging the meeting with Daisy (65). On the evidence, it's clear that Gatsby as parvenu will manage to do or say the wrong thing if given an opportunity to do so. Yet Nick finally puts aside his offended sense of propriety and decides to stick it out with Gatsby. After his death, in fact, "it grew upon me [Nick] that I was responsible, because no one else was interested—interested, I mean, with that intense personal interest to which every one has some vague right at the end" (127–28). So, for the only time in his life, Nick makes a commitment himself. And it is because this decision is so difficult for him, a man who invariably observes the social amenities and keeps his emotional distance, that it seems inevitable for the rest of us. That is why he is the right narrator for *The Great Gatsby*.

Fitzgerald enhances his accomplishment in point of view by not letting the change in Nick go beyond the bounds of credibility. Thus even while taking his "intense personal interest" in Gatsby, he behaves very much like the old Nick, trying to arrange a proper funeral with a respectable company of mourners and without sightseers. Moreover, he goes through the ritual of shaking hands with Tom *despite* finding out that Tom had directed the murderous Wilson to Gatsby's house. "I shook hands with him; it seemed silly not to, for I felt suddenly as though I were talking to a child" (140). But Tom and Daisy are not children who damage toys that can be replaced or scrawl dirty words Nick himself can erase. The Buchanans destroy *people*. Myrtle Wilson, George Wilson, and Jay Gatsby are dead because of them, and they do not even feel remorse. Even at the end, then, Nick lets the social forms obscure his moral judgment.

Nor is Nick converted into a practicing romantic by Gatsby's example. The logic of Fitzgerald's technique demands that only the narrator go inside Gatsby's head. When Nick does so in a series of reflections on Gatsby's ecstatic commitment to Daisy, he repeatedly imposes his own reserve on Gatsby's thoughts. On the day of the tea, for example, Nick notes an expression of bewilderment on Gatsby's face and decides that there "must have been moments even that afternoon when Daisy tumbled short of his dreams—not through her own fault, but because of the colossal vitality of his illusion" (75). Similarly, on the day of Gatsby's death, Nick has an idea that Gatsby didn't believe Daisy would telephone "and perhaps he no longer cared. If that was true he must have felt that he had lost the old warm world, paid a high price for living too long with a single dream" (126). Nothing that Gatsby says or does warrants either of these conclusions. Nick is unable to conceive of the depth of Gatsby's dream.

Throughout the novel Gatsby is associated with the night, and more particularly with the moon. In four of the nine chapters the action ends with Gatsby alone in the night, and twice—near the end of chapter 3, when a "wafer of a moon" shines over Gatsby's house as he gestures farewell to his guests (46) and again at the very end of chapter 7, where Nick leaves Gatsby "standing there in the moonlight—watching over nothing" (114), the moon seems to symbolize Gatsby's capacity for reverie. Hence it is deeply significant that on the last pages of the novel Nick Carraway, alone in the dark, wanders over to Gatsby's house in the moonlight, sprawls on the sand, and thinks of Gatsby's wonder when he saw the green light at the end of Daisy's dock (181–82). For a moment, perhaps, Nick felt a sense of identity with the moon person who had lived and died next door. But only for a moment, and then the rational Nick takes over to provide the novel with its coda about the Dutch sailors and the corruption of the American dream.

Nick Carraway and Jimmy Gatz come from the same part of the country, but they belong to vastly different worlds. At the Buchanans, Nick plays the naif by asking Daisy, "Can't you talk about crops or something?" But this comes from a man who is simultaneously evaluating the "corky but rather impressive claret" (14). Nick is no farmer from the country. He graduated from Yale, and so did his father. He knows about El Greco and Kant and Petronius. He has a sense of history. At college he wrote editorials, which hardly makes him "literary" (as he claims) but does suggest a breadth of knowledge and a judgmental nature. Moreover, unlike Gatsby, Nick has a place where he's known and accepted to go back to in St. Paul.

He has learned a good deal during the summer of 1922 about the power of the unrealizable dream and about the recklessness and selfishness of the very rich. Yet aside from a diminished curiosity that desires "no more riotous excursions with privileged glimpses into the human heart" (5), Nick's basic way of life seems unlikely to change. What has happened to Gatsby can hardly cure his misanthropy or open the floodgates of his emotional reserve. But if Nick is not much altered, many others have been. *The Great Gatsby* is a novel that has made a difference in the lives of many who have or will read it. One does not have to like Nick Carraway to discover something about oneself in the tale he tells.

Chronology

1896   Born Francis Scott Key Fitzgerald on September 24 in St. Paul, Minnesota, to Edward Fitzgerald and Mary McQuillan Fitzgerald.

1911   Attends the Newman School, a Catholic boarding school in Hackensack, New Jersey.

1913   Matriculates at Princeton. Works on productions for the university's amateur theatrical company, the Triangle Club.

1917   Leaves Princeton without receiving a degree. Joins the U.S. Army as a second lieutenant and goes for training at Fort Leavenworth, Kansas.

1918   Completes his first novel, *The Romantic Egotist*. Meets Zelda Sayre when transferred to Camp Sheridan, Montgomery, Alabama. In October, *The Romantic Egotist* is rejected by Scribner's.

1919   After being discharged from the Army, moves to New York and works as a copywriter for an advertising agency. In July, returns to the family home in St. Paul. Begins revising *The Romantic Egotist*. Under its new title, *This Side of Paradise*, the book is accepted by Scribner's in September.

1920   *This Side of Paradise* published in March. Marries Zelda Sayre on April 3. In September, Scribner's publishes *Flappers and Philosophers*, a collection of stories.

1921	Daughter Frances Scott Fitzgerald born on October 26.
1922	*The Beautiful and Damned* published by Scribner's in March. The short story "The Diamond as Big as the Ritz" appears in the *Smart Set* in June. *Tales of the Jazz Age*, a second story collection, published by Scribner's in September.
1925	*The Great Gatsby* published by Scribner's.
1926	A third collection of stories, *All the Sad Young Men*, published by Scribner's.
1927	Spends two months in Hollywood writing scripts for United Artists.
1930	Zelda has nervous breakdown while traveling in Europe.
1931	"Bablylon Revisited" published in *The Saturday Evening Post*.
1932	Zelda suffers from a second breakdown, after which she is committed to a psychiatric clinic in Baltimore. She is discharged in June, and her novel, *Save Me the Waltz*, is published the same year.
1934	Writes short stories in a desperate attempt to repay his debts after *Tender Is the Night* appears to disappointing sales. Suffers nervous breakdown in June.
1935	Declining physical health attributed to heavy drinking. Recuperates in Asheville, North Carolina.
1936	"The Crack-Up" essays appear in *Esquire* magazine. Zelda sent to a sanitarium in Asheville, where she remains until her death.
1937	Moves to Hollywood to work as a scriptwriter for MGM. Begins a relationship with Sheilah Graham.
1940	"Pat Hobby" stories published in *Esquire*. Dies from a heart attack on December 21.
1941	*The Last Tycoon*, an unfinished novel, published by Scribner's.
1945	*The Crack-Up*, edited by Edmund Wilson, published by New Directions.
1948	Zelda dies in a fire at the sanitarium in Asheville.

Contributors

HAROLD BLOOM is Sterling Professor of the Humanities at Yale University. Educated at Cornell and Yale universities, he is the author of more than 30 books, including *Shelley's Mythmaking* (1959), *The Visionary Company* (1961), *Blake's Apocalypse* (1963), *Yeats* (1970), *The Anxiety of Influence* (1973), *A Map of Misreading* (1975), *Kabbalah and Criticism* (1975), *Agon: Toward a Theory of Revisionism* (1982), *The American Religion* (1992), *The Western Canon* (1994), *Omens of Millennium: The Gnosis of Angels, Dreams, and Resurrection* (1996), *Shakespeare: The Invention of the Human* (1998), *How to Read and Why* (2000), *Genius: A Mosaic of One Hundred Exemplary Creative Minds* (2002), *Hamlet: Poem Unlimited* (2003), *Where Shall Wisdom Be Found?* (2004), and *Jesus and Yahweh: The Names Divine* (2005). In addition, he is the author of hundreds of articles, reviews, and editorial introductions. In 1999, Professor Bloom received the American Academy of Arts and Letters' Gold Medal for Criticism. He has also received the International Prize of Catalonia, the Alfonso Reyes Prize of Mexico, and the Hans Christian Andersen Bicentennial Prize of Denmark.

BARBARA HOCHMAN is an associate professor in the foreign literatures and linguistics department at Ben-Gurion University of the Negev. Her publications include *Getting at the Author: Reimagining Books and Reading in the Age of American Realism* and *The Art of Frank Norris, Storyteller.*

ALBERTO LENA has been an honorary research fellow at Exeter University. He authored *Benjamin Franklin and Fictive Ethnicity.*

169

RICHARD LEHAN is professor emeritus at the University of California, Los Angeles. Among his publications are *F. Scott Fitzgerald and the Craft of Fiction* and *"The Great Gatsby": The Limits of Wonder.*

JOHN HILGART has been an assistant professor in the English department at Rhodes College. He has published on American modernist aesthetics and African-American blues.

JANET GILTROW is an associate dean and professor at the University of British Columbia. She is the author of *Academic Writing: Writing and Reading Across the Disciplines* and coauthor of *Genres in the Internet: Issues in the Theory of Genre.*

DAVID STOUCK has been a professor at Simon Fraser University in British Columbia. He is the author of *Major Canadian Authors* and *Willa Cather's Imagination* and the editor of numerous books.

WINIFRED FARRANT BEVILACQUA is an associate professor at the Università degli Studi di Torino. She published *Fiction by American Women: Recent Views* and *Josephine Herbst* in the Twayne's United States Authors Series.

BARBARA WILL is an associate professor at Dartmouth College, where she teaches American literature and other subjects. She is the author of *Gertrude Stein, Modernism, and the Problem of "Genius."*

PHILIP MCGOWAN is a senior lecturer at Queen's University Belfast. He authored *American Carnival: Seeing and Reading American Culture* and he is coeditor of *After Thirty Falls: New Essays on John Berryman.*

SCOTT DONALDSON is emeritus professor at the College of William and Mary. He is the author of *Fool for Love: F. Scott Fitzgerald* and *Hemingway vs. Fitzgerald*, among other works; he also is the editor of *Critical Essays on F. Scott Fitzgerald's* The Great Gatsby.

Bibliography

Assadi, Jamal, and William Freedman, ed. *A Distant Drummer: Foreign Perspectives on F. Scott Fitzgerald*. New York: Peter Lang, 2007.

Berman, Ronald. "America in Fitzgerald." *Journal of Aesthetic Education* 36, no. 2 (Summer 2002): 38–51.

———. The Great Gatsby *and Fitzgerald's World of Ideas*. Tuscaloosa: University of Alabama Press, 1997.

———. The Great Gatsby *and Modern Times*. Urbana: University of Illinois Press, 1994.

Bloom, Harold, ed. *F. Scott Fitzgerald*. Updated ed. New York: Chelsea House Publishers, 2006.

———. *Jay Gatsby*. Philadelphia: Chelsea House Publishers, 2004.

Brauer, Stephen. "Jay Gatsby and the Prohibition Gangster as Businessman." *F. Scott Fitzgerald Review* 2 (2003): 51–71.

Bruccoli, Matthew J. *Getting It Wrong: Resetting* The Great Gatsby. Columbia, S.C.: s.n., 2005.

———, ed. *F. Scott Fitzgerald's* The Great Gatsby*: A Documentary Volume*. Detroit: Gale Group, 2000.

Cartwright, Kent. "Nick Carraway as an Unreliable Narrator." *Papers on Language & Literature* 20 (Spring 1984): 218–232.

Chambers, John B. *The Novels of F. Scott Fitzgerald*. London: Macmillan/New York: St. Martin's Press, 1989.

Christie, Stuart. "Margin and Center: Positioning F. Scott Fitzgerald." *Foreign Literature Studies/Wai Guo Wen Xue Yan Jiu* 28, no. 121 (October 2006): 22–31.

171

Claridge, Henry, ed. *F. Scott Fitzgerald: Critical Assessments*. 4 vols. Near Roberts-bridge, UK: Helm Information, 1991.

Coleman, Dan. "'A World Complete in Itself': Gatsby's Elegiac Narration." *Journal of Narrative Technique* 27, no. 2 (Spring 1997): 207–233.

Cousineau, Thomas J. *Ritual Unbound: Reading Sacrifice in Modernist Fiction*. Newark: University of Delaware Press; Cranbury, N.J.: Associated University Presses, 2004.

Decker, Jeffrey Louis. "Gatsby's Pristine Dream: The Diminishment of the Self-Made Man in the Tribal Twenties." *Novel* 28 (Fall 1994): 52–71.

de Koster, Katie, ed. *Readings on* The Great Gatsby. San Diego: Greenhaven, 1998.

Fortier, Solidelle. "Veblen and Fitzgerald: Absentee Ownership and *The Great Gatsby*." *American Studies in Scandinavia* 39, no. 1 (Spring 2007): 1–12.

Gandal, Keith. *The Gun and the Pen: Hemingway, Fitzgerald, Faulkner, and the Fiction of Mobilization*. Oxford; New York: Oxford University Press, 2008.

Giltrow, Janet, and David Stouck. "Style as Politics in *The Great Gatsby*." *Studies in the Novel* 29, no. 4 (Winter 1997): 476–490.

Goldsmith, Meredith. "White Skin, White Mask: Passing, Posing, and Performing in *The Great Gatsby*." *Modern Fiction Studies* 49, no. 3 (Fall 2003): 443–468.

Johnson, Robert, Jr. "Say It Ain't So, Jay: Fitzgerald's Use of Baseball in *The Great Gatsby*." *F. Scott Fitzgerald Review* 1 (2002): 30–44.

Kazin, Alfred, ed. *F. Scott Fitzgerald: The Man and His Work*. Cleveland: World, 1951.

Kerr, Frances. "Feeling 'Half Feminine': Modernism and the Politics of Emotion in *The Great Gatsby*." *American Literature* 68, no. 2 (1996): 405–31.

Lee, A. Robert. *Gothic to Multicultural: Idioms of Imagining in American Literary Fiction*. Amsterdam, Netherlands: Rodopi, 2009.

Lehan, Richard. *F. Scott Fitzgerald and the Craft of Fiction*. Carbondale; Southern Illinois University Press, 1966.

———. The Great Gatsby: *The Limits of Wonder*. Boston: Twayne Publishers, 1990.

Lena, Alberto. "The Seducer's Stratagems: *The Great Gatsby* and the Early Twenties." *Forum for Modern Language Studies* 34, no. 4 (October 1998): 303–313.

Lockridge, Ernest H. "F. Scott Fitzgerald's *Trompe l'Oeil* and *The Great Gatsby*'s Buried Plot." *Journal of Narrative Technique* 17 (Spring 1987): 163–183.

Lynn, David H. *The Hero's Tale: Narrators in the Early Modern Novel*. New York: St. Martin's Press, 1989.

Mallios, Peter. "Undiscovering the Country: Conrad, Fitzgerald, and Meta-National Form." *Modern Fiction Studies* 47, no. 2 (Summer 2001): 356–390.

Matterson, Stephen. The Great Gatsby *and the Critics*. London: Macmillan, 1990.

Miller, James E., Jr. *F. Scott Fitzgerald: His Art and Technique*. New York: New York University Press, 1964.

O'Meara, Lauraleigh. "Medium of Exchange: The Blue Coupé Dialogue in *The Great Gatsby*." *Papers on Language & Literature* 30 (Winter 1994): 73–87.

Pelzer, Linda C. *Student Companion to F. Scott Fitzgerald*. Westport, Conn: Greenwood Press, 2000.

Pendleton, Thomas A. *I'm Sorry About the Clock: Chronology, Composition, and Narrative Technique in* The Great Gatsby. Selinsgrove: Susquehanna University Press, 1993.

Preston, Elizabeth. "Implying Authors in *The Great Gatsby*." *Narrative* 5, no. 2 (May 1997): 143–64.

Prigozy, Ruth, ed. *The Cambridge Companion to F. Scott Fitzgerald*. Cambridge: Cambridge University Press, 2002.

Rohrkemper, John. "Becoming White: Race and Ethnicity in *The Great Gatsby*." *Midwestern Miscellany* 31 (Fall 2003): 22–31.

Rowe, Joyce A. *Equivocal Endings of Classic American Novels:* The Scarlet Letter, Adventures of Huckleberry Finn, The Ambassadors, The Great Gatsby. Cambridge [Cambridgeshire]; New York: Cambridge University Press, 1988.

Sanders, J'aimé L. "Discovering the Source of Gatsby's Greatness: Nick's Eulogy for a 'Great' Kierkegaardian Night." *F. Scott Fitzgerald Review* 3 (2004): 108–27.

Savle, Majda. "Indirect Narration: A Case Study of Conrad's *Heart of Darkness* and Fitzgerald's *The Great Gatsby*." *Acta Neophilologica* 40, nos. 1–2 (2007): 117–127, 216.

Schlacks, Deborah Davis. *American Dream Visions: Chaucer's Surprising Influence on F. Scott Fitzgerald*. New York: Peter Lang, 1994.

Seiters, Dan. *Image Patterns in the Novels of F. Scott Fitzgerald*. Ann Arbor: UMI Research Press, 1986.

Skinner, John. "The Oral and the Written: Kurtz and Gatsby Revisited." *Journal of Narrative Technique* 17 (Winter 1987): 131–140.

Tanner, Barney. *Joycean Elements in F. Scott Fitzgerald's* The Great Gatsby. Bethesda, Md.: Academica Press, 2007.

Tanner, Bernard R. *F. Scott Fitzgerald's Odyssey: A Reader's Guide to the Gospels in* The Great Gatsby. Lanham, Md.: University Press of America, 2003.

Weinstein, Arnold. "Fiction as Greatness: The Case of *Gatsby*." *Novel* 19 (Fall 1985): 22–38.

White, Patti. *Gatsby's Party: The System and the List in Contemporary Narrative*. West Lafayette, Ind.: Purdue University Press, 1992.

Acknowledgments

Barbara Hochman, "Disembodied Voices and Narrating Bodies in *The Great Gatsby.*" From *Style* 28, no. 1 (Spring 1994): 95–118. Copyright © 1994 by *Style.*

Alberto Lena, "Deceitful Traces of Power: An Analysis of the Decadence of Tom Buchanan in *The Great Gatsby.*" From *Canadian Review of American Studies* 28, no. 1 (1998): 19–41. Copyright © 1998 by the Graduate Centre for the Study of Drama, University of Toronto. Reprinted by permission of Canadian Association for American Studies, www.utpjournals.com

Richard Lehan, "*The Great Gatsby*—The Text as Construct: Narrative Knots and Narrative Unfolding." From *F. Scott Fitzgerald: New Perspectives,* edited by Jackson R. Bryer, Alan Margolies, and Ruth Prigozy. Copyright © 2000 by the University of Georgia Press.

John Hilgart, "*The Great Gatsby*'s Aesthetics of Non-Identity." From *Arizona Quarterly* 59, no. 1 (Spring 2003): 87–116. Copyright © 2003 by the Arizona Board of Regents.

Janet Giltrow and David Stouck, "Pastoral Mode and Language in *The Great Gatsby.*" From *F. Scott Fitzgerald in the Twenty-first Century,* edited by Jackson R. Bryer, Ruth Prigozy, and Milton R. Stern. Copyright © 2003 by the University of Alabama Press.

Winifred Farrant Bevilacqua, "'. . . and the long secret extravaganza was played out': *The Great Gatsby* and Carnival in a Bakhtinian Perspective." From

Connotations 13, nos. 1–2 (2003/2004): 111–29. Copyright © 2005 by Waxmann Verlag GmbH.

Barbara Will, "*The Great Gatsby* and The Obscene Word." From *College Literature* 32, no. 4 (Fall 2005): 125–44. Copyright © 2005 by *College Literature.*

Philip McGowan, "The American Carnival of *The Great Gatsby.*" From *Connotations* 15, nos. 1–3 (2005/2006): 143–58. Copyright © 2005/2006 by Waxmann Verlag GmbH.

Scott Donaldson, "The Trouble with Nick: Reading *Gatsby* Closely." From *Fitzgerald and Hemingway: Works and Days.* Copyright © 2009 Scott Donaldson, Columbia University Press. Reprinted with permission of the publisher.

Index

177